Art as Performance

November 2003

To Paul,

David D~

New Directions in Aesthetics

Series editors: Dominic McIver Lopes, University of British Columbia, and Berys Gaut, University of St Andrews

Blackwell's New Directions in Aesthetics series highlights ambitious single- and multiple-author books that confront the most intriguing and pressing problems in aesthetics and the philosophy of art today. Each book is written in a way that advances understanding of the subject at hand and is accessible to upper-undergraduate and graduate students.

Art as Performance

DAVID DAVIES

Blackwell
Publishing

© 2004 by David Davies

350 Main Street, Malden, MA 02148-5020, USA
108 Cowley Road, Oxford OX4 1JF, UK
550 Swanston Street, Carlton, Victoria 3053, Australia

The right of David Davies to be identified as the Author of this Work has been
asserted in accordance with the UK Copyright, Designs, and Patents Act 1988.

First published 2004 by Blackwell Publishing Ltd

Library of Congress Cataloging-in-Publication Data

Davies, David, 1949–
    Art as performance / David Davies.
        p. cm.
Includes bibliographical references and index.
    ISBN 1-4051-1666-8 (alk. paper)   ISBN 1-4051-1667-6 (pbk. : alk. paper)
    1. Aesthetics.   2. Art—Philosophy.   I. Title.

    BH39.D38 2004
    111′.85—dc21

                                                                    2003011349

A catalogue record for this title is available from the British Library.

Set in 10/12.5pt Galliard
by SNP Best-set Typesetter Ltd., Hong Kong
Printed and bound in the United Kingdom
by MPG Books Ltd, Bodmin, Cornwall

For further information on
Blackwell Publishing, visit our website:
http://www.blackwellpublishing.com

To the memory of my father

Contents

Preface

Vermeer's canvas *The Art of Painting*, reproduced in part on the cover of this book, shows an artist in the process of depicting the muse of history. It seems natural to characterize what is going on here as follows. We have an artwork (the painted canvas resulting from Vermeer's labors) that represents the manner in which artworks are brought into being. What the picture represents – a generative performance on the part of an artist – is distinct from the work that the depicted artist is creating, that work being the product of his performance. Analogously, we might assume, the performance whereby Vermeer produced his canvas is quite distinct from the work *The Art of Painting*, which is the product of *his* performance. Our interest in a work, so conceived, may perhaps take account of features of the generative performance, which may have conferred appreciable properties upon the work. Artworks, it may be said, are, in this respect, no different from non-artistic artifacts such as bridges and vases. In particular, we may expect a work to possess certain interesting representational and expressive properties in virtue of the context in which it was created and the resources available to the artist for such generative purposes. This is presumably why it matters that the canvas exhibited as *The Art of Painting* is from the brush of the seventeenth-century Dutch painter Vermeer, rather than from the brush of the notorious twentieth-century "copyist" van Meegeren.

But there is an irony here, if we take seriously the claims of contemporary writers such as Philip Steadman (2001). For, according to the latter, Vermeer did not generate the canvas of *The Art of Painting* by executing a performance of the sort depicted in the painting. Rather, he employed a very sophisticated kind of camera obscura that would have been positioned at the far end of the room in which the represented subjects were arrayed. This device would have produced an optical image which guided Vermeer's manipulations of the physical medium of oil paint in marking the canvas so as to result in the object displayed in the Kunsthistorisches Museum, Vienna. If Steadman's hypothesis is accepted, certain pertinent facts about the provenance of the canvas seem to bear upon our appreciation of the work not, as suggested above, by affecting the meaningful properties ascribable in virtue of the arrangement of pigment, but by changing our conception of what was achieved in generating such an arrangement of pigment having such meaningful properties.

Philosophical orthodoxy in the ontology of art attempts to take such examples in its stride. Works, it is claimed, are the decontextualized or contextualized products of the generative acts of their creators. Facts about how Vermeer produced the canvas titled *The Art of Painting* – facts that are not manifest even to the cultured eye – are either irrelevant to the appreciation of the work (if works are decontextualized products) or bear on appreciation through grounding relational properties of the work (if works are contextualized products). It is a principal contention of this book, however, that we can properly accommodate the bearing of such facts upon appreciation only by embarking upon a more radical rethinking of what artworks are and what their appreciation involves. Artworks in the different arts, I argue, must be conceived not as the products (decontextualized or contextualized) of generative performances, but as the performances themselves. Vermeer's *Art of Painting*, then, represents not a possible performance productive of a work, but a moment in the unfolding of a possible work – although, if Steadman is right, the representing work, qua performance, differs importantly from the work represented.

My thesis is, to put it mildly, heterodox, and my dialectical strategy reflects an awareness that the reader will be persuaded to accept my conclusions only if the benefits of embracing such a view are considerable and the costs slight. In the first three chapters, I lay the groundwork for my arguments. I set out a number of challenges that artistic practice presents to our intuitions about the nature of art and of artistic appreciation, and critically marshall a number of considerations to be found in the recent literature that militate against conceiving of artworks as decontextualized entities. This allows me to identify what I take to be the principal alternative to the position I wish to defend – a "contextualism" that views artworks as the contextualized products of the creative acts of their producers. In the remaining chapters of the book, I present a cumulative argument against contextualism and for the alternative conception of artworks as generative performances. The latter conception, I argue, is better equipped than contextualism to account for a number of things: the role that context of creation plays in artistic appreciation, our modal intuitions about works, the modes of artistic value, and the complexity and diversity of modern art. In arguing for these conclusions, I offer detailed proposals as to how the performances that are artworks are to be construed, how they are to be distinguished from structurally similar performances that are not artworks, how the performance theory is to be reconciled with our ordinary discourse about art, and how performances of a more conventional kind enter into the identity and appreciation of artworks if the latter are themselves conceived as performances. The aim is to show how thinking of art as performance allows us to develop a broader conception of the being and the being appreciated of artworks, providing a framework for resolving many central questions in the philosophy of the arts.

In writing this book, I have drawn upon and developed ideas and arguments that have appeared in the following publications: "Artwork, Action, and Process," *Acta Analytica* 20 (1998), 131–53; "Artistic Intentions and the Ontology of Art," *British Journal of Aesthetics* 39 (April 1999), 148–62; "Aesthetic Empiricism and the Philosophy of Art." *Synthesis Philosophica* 15 (2000), 49–64; "Medium," in J. Levinson, ed., *Oxford Handbook of Aesthetics* (Oxford: Oxford University Press, 2003), 181–91; "Against 'Enlightened Empiricism,'" forthcoming in Matthew Kieran, ed., *Contemporary Debates in Aesthetics* (Oxford: Blackwell).

The working out of this project has itself involved an extended performance, whose final product no longer bears the visible marks of many earlier attempts to work out its central themes. In the process of manipulating the conceptual medium to arrive at this result, I have benefited from the input of many people. I would like to thank those students in my graduate and undergraduate classes in the philosophy of art at McGill University over the last half-dozen years who have acted as critical sounding-boards for many of the ideas developed in this book. I would also like to thank all who have offered constructive criticism of my ideas over the last decade, and even earlier, either in informal conversations or in more formal discussions at conferences and departmental colloquia. While I cannot hope to list everyone whose contributions have helped to form this book, I would like to extend my appreciation to the following: Jesus Aguilar, Karen Bardsley, John Dilworth, Frankie Egan, Berys Gaut, Sherri Irvin, Peter Lamarque, Jerry Levinson, Eric Lewis, Paisley Livingston, Dom Lopes, Iain Macdonald, Jim McGilvray, Carl Matheson, Bob Matthews, Nenad Miscevic, Philip Percival, and Bob Stecker. I would like to extend special thanks to Guy Rohrbaugh for his very perceptive and constructive critical reading of the entire manuscript, which helped me to make certain ideas more accessible to readers. I would also like to thank Jeff Dean for his editorial advice and his tolerance of my occasional authorial anxieties, and Fiona Sewell for her assistance in preparing this book for publication. The initial research which enabled me to generate this manuscript out of my more long-standing interests in the ontology of art was generously supported by a grant from the SSHRC of Canada, whose assistance I gratefully acknowledge. Finally, I would like to record a debt of gratitude to my doctoral supervisor, the late Robert Butts, not only for his unfailing support of my professional activities but also for encouraging me to return to my philosophical roots in aesthetics.

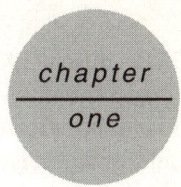

Introduction

1.1 Challenges to Aesthetic Empiricism

All these years, along with countless kindred souls, I am certain, I had made my way into the galleries of Lower Madison and Lower Soho and the Art Gildo Midway of Fifty-seventh Street, and into the museums, into the Modern, the Whitney, and the Guggenheim, the Bastard Bauhaus, the New Brutalist, and the Fountainhead Baroque, into the lowliest storefront churches and grandest Robber Baronial temples of Modernism. All these years I, like so many others, had stood in front of a thousand, two-thousand, God-knows-how-many-thousand Pollocks, de Koonings, Newmans, Nolands, Rothkos, Rauschenbergs, Judds, Johnses, Olitskis, Louises, Stills, Franz Klines, Frankenthalers, Kellys, and Frank Stellas, now squinting, now popping the eye sockets open, now drawing back, now moving closer – waiting, waiting, forever waiting for . . . it . . . for *it* to come into focus, namely, the visual reward (for so much effort) which must be there, which everyone (*tout le monde*) knew to be there – waiting for something to radiate directly from the paintings on these invariably white walls, in this room, in this moment, into my own optic chiasma. All these years, in short, I had assumed that in art, if nowhere else, seeing is believing. Well, how very shortsighted! Now at last . . . I could see. I had gotten it backward all along. Not "seeing is believing" . . . but "believing is seeing," for *Modern Art has become completely literary: the paintings and other works exist only to illustrate the text.* (Wolfe 1976: 6; stress in the original)

These words, taken from Tom Wolfe's witty and provocative polemic against late modernism in the visual arts, may strike a responsive chord in many readers who have experienced similar frustration in their attempts to appreciate the most celebrated visual artworks of the last half-century.[1] As is apparent from the closing sentence of the quoted passage, Wolfe's central contention is that there is a radical discontinuity in visual art following the emergence of Abstract Expressionism in the late 1940s. The discontinuity relates to the role that art *theory* plays in both the generation and the appreciation of works. The activities of late modern painters, Wolfe maintains, are driven by the proclamations of art theorists such as Clement Greenberg and Harold Rosenberg, and their products serve as "illustrations" of those theories. Thus one cannot make sense of the paintings unless one knows the relevant theories. It is the internal logic of art theory, rather than the proper concerns of artistic practice, that explains the "reductionist" tendencies in late modern painting, beginning with anti-representationalism and culminating in what Lucy Lippard termed "the dematerialisation of the art object."[2]

Wolfe reinterprets the history of late modern visual art in terms of those factors that purportedly enabled theory to attain its hegemony in the visual arts. "Success" in the fine arts, he maintains, is a matter of being taken up by that small group of patrons and curators who make up "le monde." The roots of American late modernism are to be found in the efforts of those who, seeking to establish New York as the centre of activity in the visual arts, invested both in artworks taken to be *avant-garde* and in galleries that promoted such works. Late modernism begins when the "culturati" encounter the work of painters like Jackson Pollock and try to appropriate it with the aid of intellectual critics like Greenberg. In the story told by Wolfe, the development of late modern art is a function of the sociological structure of the artworld, on the one hand, and the driving force of art theory, itself to be explained in terms of sociological variables, on the other.

Wolfe's account of late modernist art is unabashedly *externalist*, appealing to the same sorts of sociological variables as the externalist histories of science offered by proponents of the "strong programme."[3] His account might therefore be challenged by an *internalist* history which

---

1 Were Wolfe to be penning his critique today, he would surely exclude very little that has happened in the visual arts subsequent to his original polemic from his criticisms. Indeed, it is entertaining to imagine how Wolfe would deal with the contributions of Charles Saatchi to the development of the new "BritArt" of artists such as Damien Hirst, Tracey Emin, Gary Hume, and Jake and Dinos Chapman! See, for example, Nicci Gerrard's preview (1999) of the exhibition *Neurotic Realism: Part I* staged at the Saatchi Gallery in early 1999.

2 See Wolfe 1976: 97ff, and Lippard 1973.

3 For a philosophical defense of the "strong programme," see Bloor 1981; Bloor and Barnes 1982. For internalist and externalist histories of science, see, for example, Laudan 1977.

represents the very same historical episodes as expressions of a desire, on the part of artists, to realize the proper values of the practice in which they are engaged. In contrast to externalist histories that focus on the institutional structure of science and the extra-scientific concerns of scientists, internalist histories of science represent developments in science as the result of rational deliberation on the part of agents whose goals are truth or empirical adequacy. Analogously, internalist histories of visual art represent developments in art as the result of the pursuit by artists of whatever are taken to be the proper goals of painting – for example, the manipulation of media in novel ways in the interest of producing objects of "intentional visual interest."[4]

Consider, for example, the origins of Jackson Pollock's distinctive style of painting, and his relationship to the art critic Clement Greenberg. Wolfe tells the following story:

> Peggy Guggenheim picked Pollock. He was a nameless down-and-out boho Cubist. She was the niece of Solomon (Guggenheim Museum) Guggenheim and the center of the most chic Uptown art circle in New York in the 1940's, a circle featuring famous Modern artists from Europe (including her husband Max Ernst) who were fleeing from the war, Uptown intellectuals such as Alfred Barr and James Johnson Sweeney of the Museum of Modern Art, and young boho proteges such as two members of Pollock's cénacle, Baziotes and Robert Motherwell. In a single year, 1943, Peggy Guggenheim met Pollock through Baziotes and Motherwell, gave him a monthly stipend, got him moving in the direction of Surrealist "automatic writing" (she loved Surrealism), set him up on Fifty-Seventh Street . . . with his first show – in the most chic Modernist salon in the history of New York, her own Art of This Century Gallery, . . . got Sweeney to write the catalogue introduction . . . and Barr inducted one of the paintings, *The She Wolf*, into the Museum of Modern Art's Permanent Collection – and Motherwell wrote a rave for the *Partisan Review* . . .
>
>   But Greenberg did something more than discover Pollock or establish him. He used Pollock's certified success to put over Flatness as *the* theory . . . of the entire new wave of the Tenth Street cénacle des cénacles. (Wolfe 1976: 52–6)

In Wolfe's story, it is Peggy Guggenheim's personal tastes in painting that account for Pollock's artistic direction, the members of her circle who account for his becoming established as a painter of importance, and Greenberg who provides a theory in terms of which that importance can

---

4 See Baxandall 1985: ch. II for this characterization of the goal of painting.

be communicated – a theory that the hapless Pollock is then committed to illustrating through his paintings (Wolfe 1976: 63ff).

Compare this with the account of Pollock's development in a representative internalist history, Edward Lucie-Smith's *Late Modern* (1976: 32–6). Lucie-Smith begins with Pollock's training as a painter under Thomas Benton, and then talks of his falling under the influence of Diego Rivera, which "may have helped to develop Pollock's sense of scale." He refers briefly to Pollock's flirtation with Surrealism and his being under contract to Peggy Guggenheim, before stating that "by 1947, Pollock had broken through to the style for which he is now best known: free, informal abstraction, based on a technique of dripping and smearing paint on the canvas." After citing at some length Pollock's own description of his method of painting, where he claims to be indebted to some of the methods used by Navajo painters, Lucie-Smith quotes, in comparison, André Breton's instructions on the production of a Surrealist text, remarking how the passivity prescribed by Breton is a large component in the sort of "gestural" or "action" painting practiced by Pollock. Lucie-Smith then proceeds to discuss Pollock's distinctive treatment of pictorial space, something that links him to Cézanne rather than to surrealism. Finally, Lucie-Smith notes that Pollock's impact, first in America and then in Europe, depended upon his participation in an artistic community whose founding figure was the painter Hans Hofmann. In the internalist history told by Lucie-Smith, what drives the development of late modern art is not "theory" but, rather, problems that arise within a tradition of painting concerning the ways in which established and novel media can be worked so as to realize certain plastic values. Artists explore the aesthetic potentialities of different media and, in so doing, draw upon resources available to them in both their own and other artistic traditions. The variables to which we appeal in telling this story about late modern art are continuous with the ones to which we would appeal in furnishing an account of the development of traditional painting. There is no striking discontinuity of the sort assumed by Wolfe.

Greenberg himself offers a more sophisticated internalist defence of the historical continuity of the visual arts in his article "After Abstract Expressionism" (1962). Like Lucie-Smith, he stresses how painters learn from, are influenced by, and react to what is done by other painters and by their earlier selves, and how the manipulation of the medium is the principal focus of the artist's attention. More interestingly, however, Greenberg also avails himself of conceptual machinery employed by one of the most famous historians of traditional painting, Heinrich Wölfflin. In his *Principles of Art History* (1950), Wölfflin argues that we can explain the development of painting from the High Renaissance to the Baroque, and from Neoclassicism to Impressionism, in terms of certain binary oppositions. These define a space of possibilities within which alternative styles of painting work themselves out. The best known of these oppositions is between "linear" and "painterly" styles, which differ in their manner of articulating pictorial space, their mode of representation, and the cognitive capacities of the spectator to which they principally appeal. Greenberg argues that Post-Impressionist painting can be seen as a further working out of the oppositions between the linear and painterly styles. Abstract Expressionist painting demonstrates, against the "linear" style of the synthetic Cubism of Picasso and Braque, that purely abstract art can be painterly. The color-field painting of Newman, Rothko, and Still represents a new kind of synthesis of the two ur-styles: it furthers the goals of painterliness – openness and color – by utilizing linear means.[5]

Internalist stratagems of this sort may serve to counter Wolfe's charge of historical discontinuity, and suggest that the development of late modern art can be seen as a function of the same sorts of internalist variables to which many historians of modernist and pre-modernist art appeal. But this is not, or at least not obviously, to answer what I take to be Wolfe's more serious charge against late modernism – namely, that there is discontinuity at the level of *appreciation*. This is the more serious charge because, as may be apparent from the passage cited at the beginning of this chapter, it carries the implication that late modernist art *fails as art* in the sense that it fails to yield the sorts of values properly sought in our engagement with works of visual art. Wolfe is able to trade here upon the uncertainty experienced by many "traditional" viewers as to what is required if one is to appreciate much contemporary art. The spectator who feels quite competent when placed before a painting by Rembrandt, Cézanne, or Picasso, or when admiring a sculpture by Rodin or Henry Moore, may experience considerable unease when she confronts, within the confines of the same gallery, a "Readymade" by Duchamp, a minimalist canvas by Stella, the documentation for a conceptual piece by Robert Barry or a performance piece by Vito Acconci, a pile of fabric exhibited by Robert Morris, or an "installation" scheduled to be

---

5 It is also worth noting, in light of Wolfe's claims about the role of theory in the reductionist tendencies of late modern art, that Greenberg takes such "self-criticism" to arise entirely from problems that present themselves to painters in their artistic practice: "The aim of the self-criticism, which is entirely empirical and not at all an affair of theory, is to determine the irreducible working essence of art and the separate arts. Under the testing of modernism more and more of the conventions of the art of painting have shown themselves to be dispensable, unessential" (Greenberg 1962: 30).

disassembled at the end of the exhibition. The auditor who feels equally at home listening to Bach, Bartok, or Berg may have difficulty knowing quite what to do with the aleatoric works of John Cage or the free improvisations of Anthony Braxton. The suggestion that one can only "get" such works if one is in possession of an appropriate "theory," or, more radically, that the objects before one function essentially as *illustrations* of such a theory, is thus appealing to many "traditional" spectators. It explains the difficulties they experience in respect of late modern visual and non-visual art, and does so by reference to another fact about late modernism of which they are aware, namely, the prevalence of art theory, and of "movements" connected to such theory, in the contemporary artworld.

Wolfe's claim about the role of theory in the appreciation of late modern art entails a "discontinuity" thesis concerning appreciation only when conjoined with a particular view about what is involved in the appreciation of "traditional" works. Such a view is explicit in the opening quotation from Wolfe and provides the deeper and more serious basis for his polemic against late modernism. This view, furthermore, is deeply ingrained in our ordinary ways of thinking about art, and seems to be entailed by central features of our appreciative and critical practice. What I shall term the "common-sense theory" of art and of art appreciation, to which Wolfe openly subscribes in the quoted passage, can be represented in terms of the following claims:

1 Instances of works are the kinds of things we encounter in galleries, concert-halls, libraries, theaters, and cinemas. The works themselves are the kinds of things that hang on the walls of galleries, are performed in concert-halls or theaters, can be read in books, or are projected on screens. Paintings, for example, are the entities that hang on the "invariably pure white walls" of the temples of late modernism listed by Wolfe.
2 To properly appreciate a work, it is both necessary and sufficient that one have a direct experiential encounter with an instance of the work. Such an encounter is *necessary* because there are appreciable properties bearing on the distinctive value of a work that are graspable only in such an experience – it is not enough to read another person's *description* of a work or another person's critical judgment, for example. And such an encounter is *sufficient* in that any properties of a work not accessible in an experiential encounter with one of its instances have no bearing on a work's artistic value, and no bearing on its artistic appreciation.

3 The consummation of such a direct experiential encounter with an instance of a work – say a painting – is the "reward" of which Wolfe speaks, an intrinsically valuable experience elicited by the work. It is in virtue of the experiences elicited in receivers who engage in such encounters with instances of works – who scrutinize canvases, listen to performances of string quartets, watch performances of plays, read volumes of poetry, for example – that art is valued. The experiences in question are taken to be valuable and not generally available in other ways.

4 Artworks differ from other things in that their instances possess, or are intended to possess, properties, accessible to receivers who engage in such direct experiential encounters, capable of eliciting such experiences. Given standard ways of talking about such things, we may characterize these experiences as "aesthetic," and maintain that those things we value as artworks are artifacts distinguished by the "aesthetic" properties conferred upon them by their creators.

It should be apparent that the common-sense theory embodies some broadly "empiricist" views about artistic appreciation and artistic value. Works are given for appreciation in an experiential encounter with a perceptible entity – a canvas on a gallery wall, or the sequence of sounds produced by an orchestra – and artistic value is essentially a matter of the kind of experience elicited in us through such an experiential encounter. Empiricism concerning artistic appreciation will be more or less pure according to the role assigned, in the appreciation of works, to knowledge that is not derivable from, but must be brought to, such an experiential encounter. Empiricism concerning artistic value will be compromised to the extent that one acknowledges values properly attributable to artworks in their appreciation that are not consequent upon qualitative features of the elicited experiences. It is worth noting that the common-sense theory contains, in germ, a comprehensive philosophy of art. The four defining theses offer, respectively, an ontology of art, an epistemology of art, an axiology of art, and a definition of "artwork."

The common-sense theory will strike some readers as obviously right, at least in essentials. It has certainly had, and continues to have, philosophical advocates, some of whom have endeavored to make it sound a little less "common-sense" by couching it in impressively esoteric terms. Clive Bell (1914), for example, talked of a sui generis "aesthetic emotion" elicited in receivers who enjoy unmediated perceptual access to the objects that hang on the walls of galleries. Artworks, as the eliciters of the aesthetic emotion, are distinguished by their possession of "significant form." The "aesthetic emotion," for Bell, has a value not to be found in ordinary emotional experience. Monroe Beardsley (1983) offered a less revisionary version of this sort of view, making the intention to elicit aesthetic experience, rather than the realization of that intention, a requirement for arthood. The common-sense theory of artistic value is either simply assumed or explicitly defended by many contemporary authors.[6] While some philosophical elaborations of the common-sense view focus on the formal properties of artworks, this is not an essential element in the view. To the extent that representational and expressive properties can be given in the sort of experiential engagement with an instance of a work that is central to common-sense epistemology of art, such properties can bear upon the appreciation of works, and the experiences elicited through the recognition of such properties can bear upon a work's artistic value.

The common-sense theory fits well with what seems to be going on in the appreciation of traditional and "early modern" works in the various arts. When one considers much contemporary art, however, it runs into trouble. Of course, one may *try* to apply the same techniques, in appreciating Duchamp's *Fountain*, as one applies in appreciating the sculptures of Rodin and Henry Moore, admiring the gleaming and sinuous surfaces of the former as of the latter. One may, in the manner Wolfe describes, perform ocular gymnastics before late modern canvases by Newman, Pollock, and Louis. But in the case of many late modern works, it is difficult to imagine *how* the appreciation of such works could satisfy the requirements set forth in the common-sense theory. What is it that one is intended to *aesthetically* appreciate in large monochrome canvases painted in industrial shades, for example, or in apparently randomly assembled piles of felt, or in stacks of Brillo boxes, or in the sorts of "conceptual" pieces created by Robert Barry? Wolfe's contention is that the common-sense theory *cannot* accommodate late modern art. The mediatory role of art theory in our engagement with later modern works finds no parallel in the appreciation of traditional works as characterized by the common-sense theory. Thus, even if one can offer an internalist response to the discontinuity thesis concerning the historical development of late modern art, one seems committed to a fundamental discontinuity in the epistemology of art.

---

6   For example, Roman Bonzon (2003) adopts, without further argument, what he terms "the familiar idea" that to take literary works as having value as art is to take them as valuable in virtue of the value of a certain kind of experience they are uniquely able to afford. He cites, in support, Budd 1995: 4–11, and Kieran 2001: 215–17.

It is worth noting that the sorts of things exhibited as late modern art-works pose a number of distinct challenges to the common-sense view of art. Some late modern works most obviously challenge common-sense axiology ("CSA," let us say), some also challenge common-sense epistemology ("CSE"), and some seem to be irreconcilable even with common-sense ontology ("CSO"), thereby calling into question the entire common-sense framework. A work like *Fountain*, for example, seems to present us with an art-object (satisfying CSO) possessed of manifest properties whose contemplation might elicit a "visual reward" of the sort stipulated in CSE. But, while the art-object is open to appreciation in this way, to so appreciate it is, according to many critics, to miss the point of the work, and to miss whatever value it can be said to have as an artwork – thereby violating CSA. This, by the way, allows us to refine our formulation of Wolfe's discontinuity thesis concerning artistic appreciation. The claim is presumably not that we *cannot* find suitably "aesthetic" properties in at least some late modern works – the works of Pollock and some works by de Kooning are obvious examples – but that this is not what is required for *proper* appreciation of these works. Proper appreciation is possible only if one has knowledge of the relevant "theory."[7]

In the case of certain other late modern works, while there is still indisputably something satisfying the CSO conception of a work – an "art-object" exhibited in a gallery – the entity in question seems to lack the sorts of manifest properties that could serve to elicit the sorts of experiences on the basis of which the work could be valued. Some American "junk sculpture" and Robert Morris's piles of felt may fall into this category, as might Ron Mueck's somewhat grotesque shrunken "corpses."[8]

Pieces that fall into a third category of late modern "works" pose the most direct challenge to the common-sense theory in that there is nothing that serves as an "art-object" in the CSO sense, therefore no art-object that can satisfy CSE and CSA. In the case of many of the pieces catalogued by Lucy Lippard in her invaluable *Six Years: The*

7 Consider, also, "Pop Art" and the Sol LeWitt piece in the Canadian National Gallery in Ottawa discussed in section 9.4 below.
8 Care is necessary, however, in that much of the work in the Italian "minimalist" tradition represented by the Arte Povera movement, superficially similar to American minimalist works, is more easily accommodated by the common-sense theory. The "art-objects" seem not only to be appreciable as "aesthetic objects," in spite of the unusual media employed (freshly ground coffee and worn bean sacks, for example, in the pieces of Jannis Kounellis) but to have value as artworks precisely in virtue of being so appreciable.

Dematerialisation of the Art Object 1966–1972 (1973), there are indeed objects open to inspection, but these objects seem to serve as *documentation* for an event that has occurred, rather than as "art-objects" of the sort required by CSO.[9,10] In the case of the purer "conceptual" pieces by artists like Robert Barry, there appears to be only a verbal *description* of a piece which itself neither is nor can be physically instantiated.[11] In such cases, none of the component theses of the common-sense theory seem able to get a grip on what is going on. To the extent that one *tries* to make sense of such works in terms of the common-sense theory, one is likely to finish up agreeing with Wolfe that art theory has taken over from art, or, as he picturesquely puts it, that, in conceptual art, "art made its final flight, climbing higher and higher in an ever decreasing turning spiral until . . . it disappeared up its own fundamental aperture . . . and came out the other side as Art Theory" (1976: 109).

Subscribers to the common-sense view are not without resources with which to defend late modern art against Wolfe's charges. One option is to argue that, while theory does indeed play a mediatory role, it plays that role in the generation of experiences of the sort celebrated by common-sense axiology. Indeed, Wolfe himself considers this sort of approach, talking of receivers who tried "to *internalize* the theories to the point where they could *feel* a tingle or two at *the very moment* they looked at an abstract painting" (66). While this might make some sense in the case of Abstract Expressionist works, however, where knowledge of the theory may affect what the spectator sees in the painting, it seems implausible for many late modernist works.[12]

Another response echoes the claims of those who seek to account for "aesthetic experience" in general in terms of an "aesthetic attitude" that

9   This is not always the case. The performance pieces of Vito Acconci, for example, are sometimes documented by still photographs and sometimes by videos. In the latter case, and in the case of some of the photographed performances, "aesthetic" properties of the documenting images *do* seem to play a vital role in the overall functioning of the work, albeit a role that is heavily mediated by non-manifest aspects of the works. See the discussion in chapter 9 below, on the place of performance in the arts, for further reflections on the differences between these kinds of cases.

10   Examples, here, would include Vito Acconci's "performances" pieces, including his "body art," James Collins' "Introduction Pieces," and John Latham's witty *Art and Culture*. See Lippard 1973: for Acconci, 117, 231, 232; for Collins, 177; for Latham, 14–16.

11   The best-known piece by Barry is his *All the things I know but of which I am not at the moment thinking – 1:36 P.M.; 15 June 1969, New York*. See Binkley 1976 for philosophical meditations on the significance of Barry's piece.

12   For a critical examination of this sort of defence of common-sense *axiology*, see the discussion of "enlightened empiricism" in chapter 10.

can be adopted to any object whatever. It might be claimed that even the most radical late modern pieces can yield up Wolfe's "visual reward" if we just learn to overcome our prejudices and look at the objects in a disinterested way. Greenberg himself subscribed to such a view in his account of Duchamp's Readymades. Some have viewed the latter as celebrating a discontinuity between traditional and modern art. Joseph Kosuth, for example, claims that the Readymades "changed the nature of art from a question of morphology to a question of function . . . All art (after Duchamp) is conceptual (in nature) because art exists only conceptually."[13] Others, such as Beardsley, subscribing to the letter of the common-sense view of appreciation, have simply denied that the Readymades are artworks at all: they are, rather, an unconventional mode of art *criticism*, commenting on the way in which the art institutions operate (1983: 25). Greenberg, however, maintains that

> art like Duchamp's has shown, as nothing before has, how wide open the category of even formalised aesthetic experience can be . . . Since [Duchamp's Readymades] it has become clearer too, that anything that can be experienced at all can be experienced aesthetically; and that anything that can be experienced aesthetically can also be experienced as art. In short, art and the aesthetic don't just overlap, they coincide. (1976: 93; 1971: 129)

There is, however, another option open to us if we wish to resist Wolfe's discontinuity thesis concerning artistic appreciation and the implied devaluing of much late modernist art. Rather than try to reconcile late modernism with the common-sense view of art – perhaps by offering more philosophically sophisticated variations on the latter's defining theses – we may challenge the common-sense view of appreciation. In so doing, as we shall see, we imperil the entire edifice of common-sense philosophy of art. For, given the plausible methodological principle to be enunciated in the following section, to challenge common-sense epistemology of art is to call into question common-sense ontology of art, the common-sense definition of art, and common-sense axiology. For the present, we may illustrate how such a defence of continuity in the epistemology of art might proceed by citing yet another interpretation of the significance of Duchamp's Readymades.[14]

13 Joseph Kosuth, "Art after Philosophy I and II," p. 80. Cited in de Duve 1996: 300.
14 Such interpretations provide a trustworthy barometer of the philosophical leanings of commentators on the arts! One is reminded of George Dickie's remark that "as works of art, Duchamp's readymades may not be worth much, but as examples of art they are very valuable for art theory" (1974: 34). It is noteworthy, however, that, as we have already seen,

A number of commentators have maintained that Duchamp is properly viewed as challenging the common-sense understanding of what makes something an artwork and of what the appreciation of artworks involves, rather than as establishing a radical discontinuity in respect of artistic appreciation, or as broadening the range of things that can be appreciated "aesthetically." For some, the lesson to be drawn from Duchamp is that arthood is an essentially institutional matter. George Dickie reads Duchamp's "invaluable example for art theory" as demonstrating that arthood is a status definable in terms of, and conferred by one acting on behalf of, that particular set of social practices that he terms "the Artworld."[15] More forthrightly, Joseph Beuys asserts that Duchamp "entered this object into the museum and noticed that its transportation from one place to another made it into art" (1985: 7, trans. de Duve 1996: 285).

More interesting, in the present context at least, is Richard Wollheim's contention (1968: 395) that Duchamp revealed something important about the nature of artistic making. Wollheim claims that "minimal" works from Duchamp onward "force us to reconsider what it is to *make* a work of art." Such making, which usually involves the manipulation of a material of some kind, also involves decisions as to which manipulations should take place and when the process of manipulation should stop. Minimalist artists, who "work" (in the decisional sense) with pre-fashioned materials, focus upon and celebrate the decisional element in the "work" of making art, and make us aware of this element in more traditional pieces. Timothy Binkley makes an analogous point, arguing that artists in the tradition stemming from Duchamp bring to our attention that artworks, traditional and modern, are the products of acts of "piece-specification" which draw upon certain conventions for the "intensional" individuation of pieces.[16] Both Wollheim and Binkley suggest that what we should learn from late modern art is that art-making only contingently involves the bringing into being of entities capable

art theorists have displayed enormous ingenuity in cutting Duchamp's enigmatic works to fit the cloth of their theories. For a very illuminating account of the historical circumstances surrounding the Readymades, see de Duve 1996.

15   Dickie 1971, 1974. Dickie's views are discussed in chapter 10 below. On the other hand, Stephen Davies, who also sees Duchamp's work as illuminating the essentially institutional nature of art, subscribes to a form of "discontinuity" thesis. He claims that what Duchamp did in exhibiting *Fountain* was *change* the institutionalized conventions for the conferral of art-status. See his 1991: 84ff.

16   Binkley 1976. We shall return to Binkley's claims, and clarify this terminology, in chapter 3.

of eliciting "aesthetic" experiences in receivers who perceptually engage with them.

While the readings of Duchamp surveyed in the preceding paragraph do not directly address the discontinuity thesis concerning appreciation, they do undermine it indirectly by challenging the other component theses of the common-sense view that help to sustain it. If arthood is not essentially a matter of possessing, or being intended to possess, "aesthetic" properties – if, in other words, the common-sense definition of art fails – then it is not clear why experiences elicited by manifest properties of the entities produced by artists must be central either to the appreciation of artworks or to the values ascribable to such works. Furthermore, if what is interesting or valuable in Duchamp's works is the manner in which they comment upon the art-making process itself, then this challenges the common-sense axiology of art. Indeed, it is precisely because the interest of Duchamp's works can be thought to lie in their commentary on art that Beardsley denies that the Readymades are artworks. Furthermore, if it be acknowledged that actual or intended possession of manifest pro-perties capable of eliciting a particular kind of valuable experience is *not* the key to arthood, and that artistic value can be quite independent of the qualities of such experience, then even if there *is* the sort of discon-tinuity in appreciation claimed by Wolfe, this no longer stands as an obvious indictment of late modern art. We may begin to appreciate the complex interrelations that exist between the component theses of the common-sense view of art, and we shall address these interrelationships at a more theoretical level in the following section.

I have thus far dwelled at some length on the difficulty one has in taking seriously, as art worthy of interest, many of the "contemporary" pieces exhibited in both American and European galleries, if one shares with Wolfe a general sympathy toward the common-sense view of art. I have also suggested that one might argue for the continuity of traditional and late modern fine art by contending that the common-sense view misrepresents what is going on in traditional art. To provide some pre-liminary motivation for this contention, which will be defended at length in the following two chapters, it is worth noting that the common-sense view faces problems in accounting for certain prominent features of our comportment toward more traditional pieces. Such problems arise when we consider how our beliefs about the history of making of an object bear upon the appreciation of, and the ascription of artistic value to, the work we take to be in some sense embodied in that object. Of particular inter-est are cases where an object is passed off as having a history of making different from its actual history of making, and where this deception is later discovered – "forgeries" on at least one definition of this term. Sometimes we have two objects which it is very difficult to tell apart, each of which is put forward as "the original." In other, more interesting, cases, we have a single object which is presented as being by an artist of some note, when it has actually been fabricated by a different individual at a later date with the intention of deceiving spectators. The most notorious examples of the latter kind are the purported "Vermeers" painted by van Meegeren in the first half of the twentieth century.

Both kinds of forgeries present the defender of the common-sense view with the following puzzle. If artworks are entities distinguished by their manifest properties which are intended to elicit valuable experiences in receivers, and if the value of a work is a direct function of the experiences it does elicit in appropriate receivers, how can it matter from the point of view of either arthood or artistic value whether the object before me is the original or a copy (if they are perceptually indistinguishable), or whether the object before me was painted by Vermeer in the seventeenth century or van Meegeren in the twentieth? Philosophical defenders of the common-sense view, with admirable consistency, have responded that, *to the extent that our concerns are purely artistic rather than economic, social, or historical,* such things *do not* matter. Thus Clive Bell, not explicitly addressing the question of forgeries, affirms that "to those who have and hold a sense of the significance of form what does it matter whether the forms that move them were created in Paris the day before yesterday or in Babylon fifty centuries ago?" (1914: 37).

We find a more sophisticated defense of this response to the problem of forgeries in a paper by Alfred Lessing (1995). Lessing's argument invokes some assumptions that will have a familiar ring. Artistic appreciation, he maintains, is concerned with the aesthetic properties of a work, those properties capable of eliciting aesthetic experience in suitably attentive receivers. Furthermore, it is distinctive of aesthetic experience that it is "wholly autonomous" in the following sense: "It does not and cannot take account of any entity or fact which is not aesthetically perceivable in the work of art itself" (20). To the suggestion that the *originality* of what is done in a painting bears legitimately on the artistic value of a work, and that originality always depend upon an object's history of making, Lessing responds that we value originality as a quality in *artists* rather than in paintings, and that originality is valued in artists only to the extent that it permits the generation of novel objects capable of eliciting aesthetic experience. We praise as "original" those artists who produce "aesthetically valuable or beautiful works of art; that is, works which are to become the object of an aesthetic experience"

(20). Given the autonomous nature of aesthetic experience, facts about the provenance of an object not given in a perceptual encounter with it can have no bearing on its aesthetic value. As Lessing forcefully puts this point:

> The fact that a work of art is a forgery is an item of information about it on a level with such information as the age of the artist when he created it, the political situation in the time and place of its creation, the price it originally fetched, the kind of materials used in it, the stylistic influences discernible in it, the psychological state of the artist, his purpose in painting it, and so on. All such information belongs to areas of interest peripheral at best to the work of art as aesthetic object, areas such as biography, history of art, sociology and psychology. (11)

Thus, so Lessing maintains, our treatment of forgeries, whether forgeries of existing works or of styles, cannot be justified on aesthetic grounds. When we discover that *The Disciples at Emmaeus* was painted by van Meegeren in the first half of the twentieth century, rather than by Vermeer in the seventeenth, a properly aesthetic experience of the painting will be unaffected by such extrinsic considerations. Similarly, when we discover that, of two indistinguishable canvases, one is the original and the other a later forgery, nothing changes aesthetically. Forgeries are *morally* or *legally* flawed because the act of forgery involves deception, usually with an eye to financial gain: but there is no *aesthetic* flaw in a forgery, and thus nothing that bears upon the proper concerns of artistic appreciation.

A second feature of our treatment of traditional artworks that calls for an explanation from the common-sense theorist can also be illustrated by reference to the works of Vermeer. There has been much recent discussion about the methods used by Vermeer in the generation of his canvasses. In the catalogue of a large Vermeer retrospective exhibition held in the early 1990s (National Gallery of Art, Washington 1995), much was made of an ingenious technique, using string, pins, and chalk. This technique supposedly enabled Vermeer not only to render the tiled floors in the foregrounds of his interiors in exact accordance with the demands of geometrical perspective, but also to determine the disposition of all other surfaces in the picture plane with respect to the vanishing point. Since then, however, there has been increased speculation about Vermeer's use of the camera obscura,[17] and debate about this issue was one of the focuses

17   See in particular Steadman 2001.

of critical attention at the 2001 exhibition of paintings by Vermeer and the Delft school at the National Gallery of London. A common-sense theorist like Lessing will relegate all such concerns to fields of scholarship exterior to our properly artistic interest in the works of Vermeer. Indeed, he explicitly does this in the passage cited above. But, as we shall see in chapter 3, the issue over Vermeer's use of the camera obscura is just an extreme example of a much more general phenomenon. Our interest, when standing in front of a canvas, is not only in the perceptible properties of that canvas but also in how those properties result from the agency of a maker. Sometimes there is visible evidence of such agency for the informed eye to detect (if we permit the "informed" eye to get into the picture!). This is one of the reasons why viewers of Impressionist paintings tend to engage in a "two-step" movement, stepping back to appreciate the overall effect of the painting and then forward to determine how a particular way of distributing paint on the still visible canvas is able to produce such effects. But, if this is a legitimate part of our appreciative interest in paintings, why should it become illegitimate when the evidence about the history of making is not immediately given in this way?

1.2 Methodological Interlude: The "Pragmatic Constraint" on the Ontology of Art

I have dwelt on Wolfe's critique of late modernism for a number of reasons. First, it highlights a central claim in this chapter – that the common-sense view renders it difficult for receivers to make sense of much that has gone on in late modern art – and motivates us to engage in a radical critique of the common-sense view, to see if we can establish secure conceptual foundations for the sort of alternative picture of the arts and of artistic appreciation implicit in much recent literature that attempts to take late modernism on board. Second, it introduces a number of themes that will be developed in what follows – in particular, the relevance of artistic making to the appreciation of artworks, and the possibility of finding continuity where Wolfe posits discontinuity in both the history and the epistemology of art.

But third, and of most significance in the present context, it has allowed us to present, albeit in simplified form, the sort of debate we can expect to ensue when the merits of a view of art like the common-sense one are under consideration. While we have thus far characterized this debate almost exclusively by reference to the visual arts, traditional and modern, a similar point could be made for any other art form that has gone through a late modernist phase. Consider, for example, Beardsley's attempts to give an account of dance in accordance with what is broadly speaking the common-sense theory. He proposes that "artwork" be defined as follows: "An artwork is *either* an arrangement of conditions intended to be capable of affording an experience with marked aesthetic character *or* (incidentally) an arrangement belonging to a class or type of arrangements that is typically intended to have this capacity" (1982b: 299).

The elements that make up a dance, according to Beardsley (1982a), are certain bodily motions which, in virtue of satisfying specific "generating conditions," count as what he terms "movings" and "posings." The "generating conditions" here require that the bodily motions possess certain "expressive" qualities which we refer to the volition of the agent. It is in virtue of what he terms "an overflow or superfluity of expressiveness" that bodily movements and pauses qualify as movings and posings, and that the ensemble of such movements and pauses counts as dance, in the artistic sense. This proposal has been challenged by Noel Carroll and Sally Banes (1982), however, on the grounds that, inter alia, it cannot accommodate certain celebrated contemporary pieces classified as dance. They cite, in particular, Yvonne Rainer's *Room Service*, where the whole point is that movements are *not* carried out in an "intensified" way, but, rather, that viewers are made aware of the perceptible qualities of ordinary movement. It is in virtue of the context in which the movements are performed, rather than any independently identifiable "regional qualities" of the movements themselves, that we have dance.

Whether we focus on dance, theater, film, literature, music, or the visual arts, we can formulate a common-sense view of what counts as a work in that art, what is involved in appreciation, and what constitutes artistic value, and can then find entities that pass as works in the late modernist tradition in that art, yet that seem to present problems for such a view. This, however, raises a number of methodological questions. What bearing do such appeals to artistic practice have upon the assessment of a theory of art? To what extent can the sorts of examples I have discussed be brought against the common-sense view without begging some questions? And, more particularly, how are the different elements within any comprehensive theory of art to be established relative to one another?

In the succeeding chapters, I shall assume that "artistic practice," properly construed, must serve as the touchstone for our philosophical theorizing about art, and that, as a result, the default assumption must be that those things treated as artworks in our artistic practice are indeed artworks. To the extent that talk about our "artistic practice" is talk about the ways in which we treat and characterize the things we term "artworks" in our critical and appreciative engagements with the arts, claims about the ontological status of artworks are importantly constrained by those features of our creative, critical, appreciative, and individuative practice in the arts that would withstand rational scrutiny. Ontology of art is in this way answerable to epistemology of art. According to what I shall term the "pragmatic constraint" on the ontology of art,

> Artworks must be entities that can bear the sorts of properties rightly ascribed to what are termed "works" in our reflective critical and appreciative practice; that are individuated in the way such "works" are or would be individuated, and that have the modal properties that are reasonably ascribed to "works," in that practice.

A number of considerations can be offered in support of the pragmatic constraint as a methodological principle guiding philosophical inquiry. In the first place, it has explicitly or implicitly regulated much of the most significant work on the ontology of art in the analytic tradition over the past forty odd years. Jerrold Levinson, for example, explicitly endorses something very like this constraint in arguing for a thesis concerning the ontological status of musical works. Such works, he claims, "must be specific enough to bear the aesthetic and artistic attributes we importantly ascribe to them. We have to conceive them so that they are what such attributions are *of*" (1990a: 241). In other words, the work of art, as a subject of inquiry in the philosophy of art, is the unit of criticism and appreciation – the entity of which we predicate the properties we ascribe in criticism and appreciation – and the individuation of works must reflect this fact. Gregory Currie, in a similar vein, begins his *An Ontology of Art* by committing himself to the methodological principle that ontologies of art must fit with "the ways in which works are to be judged and appreciated." We can elucidate the term "work of art" only in the context of "an overall aesthetic theory which describes and analyses the sorts of relations that hold between us as critics and observers, and the works themselves" (1989: 11–12). In particular, works are to be assigned to a particular ontological category only if it can accommodate the sorts of features of works that an examination of critical practice reveals to be relevant to their proper appreciation *as* works of art. Robert Stecker, addressing the issue of definition rather than ontology in his book *Artworks*, argues that a definition of "artwork" must be assessed in terms of the sense it makes of our overall artistic practice, while acknowledging that features of that practice are themselves open to critical assessment (1997: 26). Stephen Davies, also in a work on defining "artwork," offers an explicit defense of something like the pragmatic constraint (1991: 74). Implicit endorsements of the pragmatic constraint can be found in Wollheim's *Art and its Objects* (1980) – where competing ontological proposals are held accountable to our artistic practice – and in Danto's *Transfiguration of the Commonplace* (1981). To cite just one more example, Timothy Binkley defends his use of certain conceptual pieces, in an argument against the project of defining art, on the grounds that such pieces

> are made (created, realized, or whatever) by people considered artists, they are treated by critics as art, they are talked about in books and journals having to do with art, they are exhibited in or otherwise connected with art galleries, and so on . . . The same critics who write about Picasso and Manet write about Duchamp and Barry. The same journals that publish articles about Abstract Expressionism publish articles about Conceptualism. The same people who made Pollock's drips and splashes objects of derision scoff at Barry's acts of specification. (1976: 95)

Of course, the fact that a methodological principle is widely adhered to does not make it correct. We need to address possible objections to the "pragmatic principle," and also provide some positive arguments for accepting it, if our reliance on it in the rest of this book is to be justified. Perhaps the most obvious objection to treating artistic practice as the arbiter in the ontology of art is that practice neither can nor should play such a role. It *cannot*, because our actual artistic practice, incorporating the critical and appreciative judgments we actually make about works, is almost certainly internally inconsistent, reflecting the various incompatible quasi-theoretical or explicitly theoretical assumptions of individual receivers and critics. Given the different paradigms operative in art criticism, the actual practice of critics is surely an unlikely source of a consistent set of shared assumptions to which ontology of art must be accountable.[18] And it *should not* because features of our actual critical practice may be mistaken, and their critical evaluation must be one of the tasks of the philosophy of art.

Certainly, those philosophers who have appealed to artistic practice in arbitrating ontological matters have on occasion seemed to be uncritical in their attitude to that practice – one might read the passage cited

18 Nicholas Wolterstorff makes this point in his 1991.

from Binkley in that way, and the manner in which Currie employs his methodological principle has led at least some commentators to read him in a similar fashion. But the formulation of the pragmatic constraint offered above evades such an objection by making ontology of art accountable not to the norms implicit or explicit in our actual artistic practice but to those norms governing that practice that would survive "rational reflection." The claim, then, is that a theoretical account of our commerce with artworks stands in an essentially normative, and not merely descriptive, relationship to the norms that operate in actual critical practice and the judgments in accordance with those norms that we actually make. A proposed ontology of art must cohere with a theoretical representation of the norms that *should* govern the judgments that critics make concerning works. Of course, any such theoretical representation is to be assessed against its implications for our actual practice, and is open to criticism if it entails revisions in that practice that we would be unwilling, after rational reflection, to undertake. A defense of any such theoretical representation of "right artistic practice," or of any unwillingness to revise our actual practice in the light of such a representation, will necessarily appeal, implicitly or explicitly, to conceptions of the goals of our critical practice, the values sought in such practice, and the values offered by the works that such practice takes as its objects. It is in the context of such debates, where we weigh the merits of alternative theoretical reconstructions of our actual practice and its objects, that ontological proposals find themselves accountable to artistic practice.[19]

However, in meeting the first objection against the pragmatic constraint in this way, it might appear that we have made the constraint vulnerable to a different kind of criticism. For surely our "rational reflection" on the judgments made in actual critical and appreciative practice will turn, among other things, upon whether those judgments rightly ascribe properties to works. And, in order to assess this, we must be at least tacitly appealing to a conception of the kinds of things that works *are*. Doesn't the rational assessment of the norms reflected in our actual critical and appreciative practice thereby *presuppose* an ontology of art, in which case it cannot be the neutral arbiter against which proposed ontologies are to be measured? Certainly, we must grant that all elements in a

---

19   This conception of a theoretical representation of our artistic practice to which our ontological theories are accountable is of course deeply indebted to the Rawlsian notion of "reflective equilibrium," and to the Goodmanian idea that a practice is justified through a "codification." See Rawls 1971: ch. 1, sec. 9, and Goodman 1955: 65–8.

philosophical account of art must be assessed and indeed comprehended in terms of their place in the sort of "overall aesthetic theory" to which Currie refers in the passage quoted above. But the construction of such an overall theory must begin somewhere, and there are compelling reasons to think that the starting place must be artistic practice broadly conceived.

In the first place, our philosophical interest in "art" and in "artworks" is grounded precisely in such practice. It is because certain features of that practice puzzle us, or because the entities that enter into that practice fascinate us, that we are driven to philosophical reflection about art in the first place. To offer an "ontology of art" not subject to the pragmatic constraint would be to change the subject, rather than answer the questions that motivate philosophical aesthetics. Put bluntly, there is no alternative but to start from critical reflection on our actual artistic practice because the very notions of "art" and "artwork" are parasitic upon that practice – artworks just are the things that play a particular kind of role in a particular kind of practice.[20]

This point is controversial to the extent that there are clear examples of "theories of art" that seem quite prepared to maintain, in violation of the pragmatic constraint, that most of what we call "art" is actually not art at all. Tolstoy (1960), for example, having defined "art" in terms of the communication of felt emotions, proceeds to dismiss, as non-art, most of the accepted works of "high art" of his time. More generally, one might try to divorce arthood from the things that play a particular role in what we would classify as "artistic practice" by proposing some independent ground or "origin" of such practice, and then arguing that much of our actual practice has fallen away from this ground or origin. Either in philosophical anthropology or in systematic metaphysics, one might claim to find such an "origin" of art against which our practice could be measured and found generally wanting.[21] Theories such as Tolstoy's are best viewed as persuasive "definitions" whose function is to bring to our attention certain artistic *values* which are thought to have been accorded insufficient weight in our artistic discourse.[22] As for proposed ontologies of art that seek a ground quite independent of our artistic practice, I

20 An analogy might be drawn with the Kuhnian maxim (1970) that philosophy of science without history of science is empty – that we cannot proceed in our attempts to understand what science *is* without holding ourselves accountable in some sense to what scientists *do*.
21 One might read a work like Heidegger's "The Origin of the Work of Art"(1971) in this way, although it would be unfair to claim that such writings in the broadly "continental" tradition operate without concern for the pragmatic constraint.
22 This is the view taken of such proposed "definitions" by Weitz in his 1956.

acknowledge the possible interest and depth of such studies, but question their status as theories of *art*.

Second, the process of rationally reflecting upon our artistic practice in the interests of clarifying the ontological status of the artwork does not, as the objector suggests, presuppose anything like a developed ontology of art. If we take Goodmanian "codification" or the Rawlsian quest for "reflective equilibrium" as our model, we must measure our actual practice against a set of principles offered as a model of right practice, and assess our willingness to revise either our practice or the principles in the face of incompatibilities between the two. In making such assessments, we rely heavily on our intuitions as to what is or is not acceptable to us. But, in reflecting upon our artistic practice in this way, the intuitions that are strongest will be those that relate to practical aspects of that practice itself – judgments made, ways in which entities are treated, etc. – rather than intuitions about what works *are*, ontologically speaking. I hope I speak for the reader in suggesting that, to the extent that I have pre-theoretical intuitions about the latter, they are grounded in my intuitions about the former. If, as suggested above, our artistic practice must provide us with our starting point if we are to make headway in the ontology of art, then it is our reflective intuitions about what is or is not acceptable in that practice that allow us to move beyond this starting point.

Third, in rationally reflecting upon our artistic practice – the ways we talk about and treat the things that enter into that practice, and the ways in which we bring such things into existence – our primary interest should lie in uncovering the broader structural features of that practice, rather than in arriving at definitive answers with respect to particular judgments. We need to ask what kinds of properties of things are the focus of our appreciative attention to works, and – what may amount to the same question – what kinds of properties of things enter into our assessments of artistic value. As I shall argue in chapter 3, what is required, as a basis for progress in the ontology of art, is a clearer conception of the structure of the focus of our appreciative attention to a work. This again requires rational reflection from within our critical and appreciative practices, rather than the measuring of our critical judgments against an ontological theory.

The pragmatic constraint enables us to bring an account of our critical and appreciative practice to bear upon theses in the ontology of art by means of arguments having the following schematic form – let me call any argument of this kind an "epistemological argument" in the ontology of art:

1 an epistemological premiss. Rational reflection upon our critical and appreciative practice confirms that certain sorts of properties, actual or modal, are rightly ascribed to what are termed "works" in that practice, or that our practice rightly individuates what are termed "works" in a certain way.

2 a methodological premiss – the pragmatic constraint. Artworks must be conceived ontologically in such a way as to accord with those features of our critical and appreciative practice upheld on rational reflection.

3 an ontological conclusion. Either (negative) artworks cannot be identified with X's, or (positive) artworks can or should be identified with Y's.

The pragmatic constraint, as befits its methodological status, is neutral between competing views in the ontology of art, holding only that such views are accountable to what we take to be right practice. The ontological conclusions licensed by the pragmatic constraint will therefore depend upon the epistemological premisses with which it is conjoined, that is, on what we take to be involved in the right appreciation of a work. If, for example, we hold that the only properties that bear on artistic appreciation and artistic value are those that a receiver can determine in a direct engagement with a manifest work, then the natural ontological conclusion to draw, given the pragmatic constraint, is that the work is some kind of perceptible structure given in an encounter with a concrete embodiment of the work, or perhaps a physical object in the case of arts such as painting and sculpture. Alternatively, if one believes that the only constraints on right appreciation of a work come from the *consumer* rather than the producer, so that an interpretive appreciation of a work is acceptable or right just in case it represents the work in a way that is interesting or relevant to the receiver, then facts about a work's actual history of making will again have no privileged role to play in appreciation of that work, and thus no consequent bearing on the individuation and identity of works.

Our focus in the following chapters, however, will be on applications of the epistemological argument whose epistemological premisses maintain that facts about an object's or structure's history of making *do* play a crucial role in the interpretive appreciation and artistic evaluation of works. Those who argue in this way seek to undermine the common-sense conception of the ontological status of the artwork by first undermining common-sense epistemology of art. In the next chapter we will look in more detail at the case that has been made against common-sense epistemology, and thus for the first premiss in an epistemological argument against common-sense ontology. Only after offering a deeper diagnosis of the failings of common-sense epistemology in chapter 3 will we turn to matters ontological, in asking what kind of ontological conclusion can be drawn once we plug the resulting epistemological premiss into the epistemological argument.

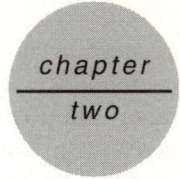

Aesthetic Empiricism and the Philosophy of Art

2.1 Aesthetic Empiricism

In chapter 1, I sketched what I termed the common-sense view of art, which, so I maintained, underlies the sort of critique of late modernism developed by Wolfe. One of the central components of the common-sense view is a proto-epistemology of art, according to which an appropriate direct experiential encounter with an instance of a work is both necessary and sufficient for the proper appreciation of that work. The desired consummation of such an encounter with a painting is the "visual reward" of which Wolfe speaks, an intrinsically valuable experience elicited by the work. I also suggested that there is a strongly empiricist flavor to this view of appreciation, a flavor which will be more or less pronounced depending upon the kinds of resources we have to bring to our encounter with an instance of a work in order to properly appreciate that work. In this chapter, I shall critically examine more refined versions of the common-sense epistemology. In so doing, my ulterior interest is in the possibility of developing an "epistemological argument" of the sort sketched at the end of the previous chapter against common-sense ontology of art.

"Aesthetic empiricism" is the term coined by Gregory Currie for epistemologies of art that minimize the role, in artistic appreciation, of resources not available in or derivable from an immediate experiential encounter with an instance of a work. The aesthetic empiricist advances a substantive thesis concerning the kinds of properties that bear upon the proper appreciation of a work of art, and that, in consequence, "can be cited as reasons for an aesthetic judgment (a judgment as to the quality of the work)" (Currie 1989: 19). Currie terms these the "aesthetic properties" of a work. However, as we shall see, the aesthetic empiricist's central claim is that a work's "aesthetic properties" (in the foregoing sense) are aesthetic properties in a more traditional sense – properties given in an "immediate" perceptual encounter with an object that elicit qualitatively distinctive kinds of experience. I shall therefore employ the term "artistic properties" to refer to aesthetic properties in Currie's sense. For analogous reasons, I shall characterize judgments as to the quality of works, qua objects of artistic appreciation, as *artistic* judgments (where Currie talks of "aesthetic judgments"), and the value ascribed in such judgments as *artistic* value (where Currie talks of "aesthetic value"). Artistic value is one kind of value ascribable to artworks – economic value being a second, and art-historical value being perhaps a third. As we shall see, whether there is a principled distinction between artistic value (in my sense) and art-historical value is one of the main questions posed by aesthetic empiricism. Characterizing things in these terms allows us to set out more perspicuously a central issue to be addressed in this chapter, namely, whether artistic properties, in my sense, can be identified with aesthetic properties as traditionally conceived. I defer until chapter 10 the closely related question whether artistic *value* can be identified with a mode of aesthetic value.

Epistemology in general is concerned with the nature of knowledge and the conditions under which it is possible. By extension, epistemology of art is concerned with the nature of artistic appreciation and understanding and the conditions under which *it* is possible. In appreciating an artwork, we appreciate something that exists through a generative act on the part of one or more individuals. Even in the case of "environmental art" or exhibited pieces of driftwood, where the object that confronts us in a gallery has not been designed or shaped by human agency, there is an artwork to appreciate only in virtue of such an act. A central question in the epistemology of art is the relationship between the generative act that brings a work into existence and the receptive act that is a proper appreciation of that work. In what ways does the former act constrain the latter? More specifically, how should we construe the product of the generative act in so far as that product enters into the proper appreciation of the work? Let me introduce the term "focus of appreciation" to denote the product of the generative act so construed. The focus of appreciation, then, is that which, as the *outcome* or *product* of a generative performance on the part of one or more individuals, is *relevant to the appreciation* of the artwork brought into existence through that performance.

Aesthetic empiricism in its purest form is the thesis that the focus of appreciation is what we may term the "manifest work" – an entity that

comprises only properties available to a receiver in an immediate perceptual encounter with an object or event that realizes the work. Only these
properties of the product of the artist's generative act are relevant to the
appreciation of his or her work. In particular, the process whereby the
manifest work came to have the properties it has can bear upon the appreciation of the work only to the extent that the nature of that process is
itself manifest to receivers of the work. For the purposes of appreciation,
the "pure" empiricist maintains, artworks are properly regarded as
"sensuous surfaces," or as "aesthetic objects." To oppose "pure" aesthetic
empiricism, then, is to argue that at least some features not determinable
from inspection of the manifest work bear crucially upon artistic appreciation. The arguments to be considered in this chapter hold, more strongly,
that it is necessary to take account of many different aspects of the performance generative of a manifest work in order to properly appreciate an
artwork.

This thesis is perhaps most explicitly elaborated by Denis Dutton in his
paper "Artistic Crimes" (1979). In attempting to show that our treatment of forgeries is grounded in legitimate artistic considerations, Dutton
argues that artworks, as the products of intentional agency, testify to the
achievements of their creators: "As performances, works of art represent
the ways in which artists solve problems, overcome obstacles, make do
with available materials" (24). To appreciate something as an artwork
always requires that we ask, "What has been done, what has been
achieved?" To discover that a painting is a forgery is to discover that it
represents a different performance, and a different achievement, from the
one we had previously taken it to represent. This quite rightly leads us to
re-evaluate the painting as an artwork.

Others have broadly concurred with this view. As we shall see below,
Currie, like Dutton, has argued that our critical and appreciative attention to artworks focuses upon the kind of *achievement* creditable to the
artist. Richard Wollheim (1980: 185ff) has defended the thesis that the
understanding and appreciation of an artwork is a matter of *"retrieval,"*
of striving to reconstruct the creative process terminating in the product
of the artist's activity. Michael Baxandall (1985) has argued that the
appreciation of a painted canvas – an object of intentional visual interest
– as a particular *artwork* involves grasping it as "something with a history
of making by a painter and a reality of reception by beholders" (7), a
product of directed agency whereby problems are resolved by drawing
upon resources available to the artist in the general pursuit of aesthetic or
artistic ends realized (or attempted) in the art-object. And Arthur Danto
(1964) has maintained that to see and appreciate something as art is to

locate it in a tradition of artistic making and of thinking about art: only when placed in the context of an "artworld" so conceived can constitutive properties of the work be rightly ascertained, and the work be open to appreciation in its particularity.

To challenge aesthetic empiricism, however, it is not sufficient to offer a non-empiricist conception of artistic appreciation. The non-empiricist conception must also be supported by arguments that are robust in the face of possible empiricist counters. I shall critically examine two kinds of anti-empiricist strategies, one indirect and the other direct. Indirect strategies try to undermine empiricist claims about a work's artistic properties by appealing to possible differences in the artistic values of works not explicable in empiricist terms. I shall argue that such strategies are inconclusive. Direct strategies, on the other hand, point to properties not explicable in empiricist terms that must be accepted as properly artistic given the role such properties play in our critical and appreciative discourse about artworks. I shall endorse a direct anti-empiricist strategy but argue that it needs to be provided with firmer conceptual foundations. In chapter 3, such foundations will be offered.

2.2 Indirect Arguments Against Aesthetic Empiricism

Currie's critical discussion of aesthetic empiricism provides us with a clear example of what I am terming indirect anti-empiricist strategies. He considers both basic and more nuanced forms of empiricism, and offers in each case examples intended to establish that there are genuine artistic differences not capturable in empiricist terms. As we have seen, aesthetic empiricism, in its purest form, is the thesis that the artistic properties of an artwork are given to a receiver in an immediate perceptual encounter with the work – they are, in this sense, its "manifest" properties. In the case of a painting, for example, the pure aesthetic empiricist holds that the artistic properties of a work can be detected by "merely looking" at it. If we assume that what can be seen by merely looking at a painting are *patterns of colors* – what Currie terms "pictorial properties" – then the empiricist maintains that all judgments concerning the artistic value of a painting are accountable to its pictorial properties alone. ("Artistic properties," it will be recalled, are those that can be cited in support of claims about the artistic value of works.) Those properties of a work that are *not* manifest are irrelevant to its proper appreciation, which rightly disregards "the history of a work, the influences upon it, its influence on other works, its place in the development of pictorial style, the aims and intentions of the artist who painted it."[1] Similarly, the artistic properties of a musical work are those properties that might be discerned by "merely listening" to performances of that work.[2] A strict extension of aesthetic empiricism to the literary arts seems implausible, given that the appreciation of literary works requires an understanding of the words visually or aurally presented to the receiver.[3] However, a broadly empiricist account of the appreciation of literary works might take their artistic properties to be those locatable in a *text* taken independently of history of writing and authorial intention.

Even if modified to accommodate literary works, though, this pure form of empiricism[4] is open to at least two crippling objections. First, the distinction between "manifest" and "non-manifest," or "directly perceivable" and "indirectly perceivable," properties is notoriously difficult to draw in a principled way.[5] At the very least, it seems necessary to specify *to whom* the artistic properties of a work are "manifest."[6] What would be manifest to the untrained observer clearly differs considerably from what would be manifest to an observer possessed of various perceptual and cognitive skills that can be brought to bear upon a work. If we take a work's artistic properties to be those that would be manifest to a skilled observer, we must ask what *knowledge* the latter must bring to her encounter with the work. More generally, we need to know which kinds of skills are relevant to being the sort of skilled observer to whom a work's artistic properties are manifest. Second, as aesthetic empiricists have acknowledged,[7] it is not clear that all, most, or even any of the artistic properties of works

1 Currie 1989: 18. This implication of aesthetic empiricism is forcefully expressed by Bell 1992: 126, and Lessing 1995: 11, quoted in chapter 1.
2 See, for example, Beardsley 1958: 31–2.
3 To think of a literary work as a "sensuous surface" is to conceive it as a form of "poésie pure." This view is criticized by Wollheim in section 25 of his 1980. An alternative strategy, suggested by recent work in linguistics, would be to maintain that competent speakers of a language *directly perceive* the explicit meanings of utterances and inscriptions in that language, without having to engage in a process of interpretation based on mere shapes or sounds given as inputs.
4 In the remainder of this chapter, I shall use the terms "aesthetic empiricism" and "empiricism" interchangeably, on the understanding that the former is the only species of empiricism under consideration.
5 See, for example, Wollheim 1980: 44ff.
6 See Wollheim's discussion of the view he terms "criticism as scrutiny" in his 1980: 185–204.
7 See, for example, Sibley 1959, 1965.

satisfy the pure empiricism characterized above. For what we normally cite in justifying our judgments of artistic value on a painting are *not* in any obvious sense manifest properties of the design – its being a particular arrangement of pigment on canvas – but, rather, more traditional "aesthetic" qualities such as balance, symmetry, grace, and expressiveness.

According to what may be termed *sophisticated* pure aesthetic empiricism, the artistic properties of a painting are indeed *distinct from* its manifest pictorial properties, but the two kinds of properties are intimately related in that the former *supervene on* the latter.[8] Thus only if two paintings differ in their pictorial properties can they differ in their artistic properties. The same applies, mutatis mutandis, in the other arts. The import of sophisticated pure empiricism depends upon how we understand the posited relation of supervenience. As Currie argues, the supervenience claim is theoretically interesting only if it supports at least some counterfactuals – that is to say, if it commits us to claims about the artistic properties an entity would have if it were to have different pictorial properties. If all that is claimed is supervenience in the actual world, for example, this would be trivially satisfied for paintings if there were, as a matter of fact, *no* pairs of objects sharing relevant manifest pictorial properties. Thus the supervenience relation must hold either within a relevant class of possible worlds or across such worlds.[9]

Given an appropriate characterization of the kind of supervenience at issue, however, the sophisticated pure empiricist can meet the objections against her naive counterpart while still insisting that differences in the origins of manifest works cannot affect their artistic properties unless these differences are expressed at the level of manifest properties. She can maintain, in response to the second objection, that one can determine the artistic properties of a work – say, a painting – by "merely looking" at a suitable realization of the work's pictorial properties as long as one possesses the necessary *discriminatory abilities* or *taste*. As long as different artistic judgments on a work with a given set of manifest properties can be explained in terms of possession, or lack, of taste, the *first* challenge to the pure empiricist can also be met without smuggling in reference to an

8　Properties of type-A are said to "supervene on" properties of type-B just in case there can be no difference in type-A properties without a difference in type-B properties. "TypeA/type B" supervenience is therefore compatible with a difference in type-B properties in the absence of a difference in type-A properties. In such a case, type-A properties may be said to admit of *different realizations* by type-B properties. A standard example of supervenience is the relation between mental-state properties and brain-state properties, on so-called "token-identity" theories of the mental.

9　For a discussion of these issues, see Currie 1989: 22–7.

"ideal receiver" whose knowledge – perhaps of aspects of provenance – would undermine the fundamental empiricist requirement that artistic properties be distinct from properties non-manifestly dependent on a history of origin.

Even in its sophisticated version, however, pure empiricism of this sort is open to an objection advanced by Kendall Walton (1970). Walton maintains that the artistic value of a work is not uniquely determined by its pictorial properties, or, more generally, its manifest properties, but also depends upon the *kind* of work it is, where this may *not* be manifest. Artworks, according to Walton, are assessed relative to their categorization as works of a particular kind. For a work to belong to an artistic category, it must possess certain features that are *standard* or required, and it must not possess certain features that are *contra-standard*. For example, being two-dimensional and having a picture-plane are standard, and having moving parts is contra-standard, for works belonging to the category "painting." In addition, there are kinds of features that are *variable* for works belonging to a category. The artistic properties and the artistic value of a work depend not merely upon its manifest properties, but also upon which category it belongs to, and whether its manifest properties are standard or variable relative to that category. Two objects with identical manifest properties might possess different artistic properties and warrant very different judgments of artistic value if assigned to different artistic categories.

Walton offers the following example. We are to imagine a culture with a category of artworks called *guernicas*. What is standard for a guernica is that a work, when viewed at right-angles to its frame, should have the pictorial (or perhaps design) properties of Picasso's painting of that name. What is variable is the *topology* of the work, guernicas being understood to be three-dimensional entities whose artistic value depends crucially upon their topological features. Picasso's work, or an object possessing the manifest properties of Picasso's work, while highly valued as a painting, would presumably be quite uninteresting as a guernica. Or, if it *were* an interesting work qua guernica, this would rest upon entirely different considerations from the ones that ground the interest and value of Picasso's work as a painting. For example, it might be regarded as a striking example of minimalism in the art of guernicas! Walton concludes that aesthetic empiricism must be *moderate* rather than pure: artistic properties supervene on manifest properties and category of art, but no other aspects of the history of making of a work – no "supra-categoreal" aspects, we might say – bear upon its artistic value.

To challenge moderate empiricism, we require examples of works that differ in artistic properties while sharing both manifest properties and artistic category. In responding to Walton, Currie initially proposes the following sorts of examples. We imagine that Picasso's oeuvre still includes a work having the pictorial properties of *Les Demoiselles d'Avignon*, but that this work is painted much later. In such a case, Currie argues, we would not ascribe to the work the same artistic value as we ascribe to the actual painting, for the value we ascribe to the latter reflects, in part, our recognition that "with this work Picasso was struggling to bring forth a new conception of representational painting" (1989: 35). Thus, it seems, we have a profound difference in artistic value, but sameness in both pictorial properties and artistic category. A second example might be the painting of *The Disciples at Emmaeus* by van Meegeren, discussed in chapter 1. If we grant that the provenance of this painting affects its artistic value, without this effect being explicable in terms of either manifest pictorial properties or category of art, we must reject the moderate empiricist's supervenience claims.

However, as Currie acknowledges, Walton can respond that the differences in ascribed value in such examples are not differences in artistic value, in our sense, but differences in *art-historical* value. Such value, it will be claimed, is ascribable to a work in virtue of its place in the historical development of an art form, and may testify to the achievement of the work's creator, but has no more bearing on the proper appreciation of a work qua work, and on a work's artistic value, than does economic value. Thus we cannot conclude that, in our examples, there is a difference in artistic properties, and the empiricist can continue to hold that a work's artistic properties are independent of the artist's achievement.

Currie therefore offers an amended example, which is intended to counter this response. We are to imagine a culture – the Martians, as Currie describes them – whose members share our aesthetic interests and sensibilities but who possess vastly superior abilities of the sort relevant to the generation of art-objects: "What for us would be a work of consummate skill and subtle expression would be for them something unremarkable if it were the product of an average five-year-old Martian" (36). We assume, further, that the Martians share our categories of art. We suppose, then, that a Martian child generates an entity *G2* that is perceptually indistinguishable from Picasso's *Guernica*, and that the Martians ascribe very little value to *G2*, whereas we hold *Guernica* to be a very valuable work.

The moderate empiricist must hold that there is no artistic difference between the two works, since ex hypothesi they share both pictorial properties and artistic category. The moderate empiricist must therefore hold, so Currie argues, that either we or the Martians are wrong in our evaluative judgments. But, he further maintains, there is no principled reason to give priority to one of these judgments, for they are supported by parallel considerations. We must therefore conclude that there *is* an artistic difference between the two works, grounding the different evaluations, and moderate empiricism must be rejected:

> We have shown that attributions of [artistic] properties depend not only on the work's appearance and its artistic category, but on facts about the prevailing levels of skills and abilities in the community where it was produced. And this shows that [artistic] judgments are, in part, judgments about the artist's achievements in producing the work. (1989: 38–9)

Currie further reasons that artistic judgments require not only knowledge of a work's manifest properties and its artistic category, but also detailed knowledge of features of its provenance over and above those that bear upon categorization (supra-categoreal features of provenance, as we have termed them):

> For there is no telling what someone has achieved unless we can assess the influences upon his work, the extent to which he borrowed ideas from others and worked within an established framework; the extent to which he went beyond existing ideas and frameworks. We need to understand the limitations that were imposed upon him or which he may have imposed upon himself, so we need to understand the technical means at his disposal, the conventions he chose to adhere to and the conventions he chose to ignore. (39)

Indeed, Currie makes an even bolder claim, maintaining that *all* artistic judgments about works presuppose a knowledge of provenance of this sort:

> The [artistic] judgments we make are *essentially* bound up with presuppositions about what constitutes an accomplished performance by the artist. Not even the most innocent seeming aesthetic response ("this is a beautiful picture") is purely aesthetic . . . They are possible only against a background of assumptions (no doubt often vague and scarcely conscious) about what constitutes an achievement in the way of combining lines and colours. And these assumptions depend in their turn upon complex assumptions about what is remarkable and what merely ordinary concerning skill and general artistic ability within a community. (40–1)

I have quoted Currie at length for a couple of reasons. First, the claim that all ascriptions of artistic properties to works rest upon assumptions concerning supra-categoreal features of provenance represents the most direct and radical challenge to any form of aesthetic empiricism. Second, however, as I shall now argue, this claim in no way follows from the considerations adduced by Currie, although it may be defensible on other grounds.

We may reconstruct Currie's argument against moderate empiricism as follows – for convenience I shall use *G1* to refer to Picasso's work:

P1   By hypothesis, we ascribe a higher artistic value (AV) to *G1* than the Martians ascribe to *G2*.

P2   Since (by definition) artistic properties (APs) are the properties that can be cited in support of a judgment of AV, then, if there is a genuine difference in AV between *G1* and *G2*, there must be a genuine difference in APs also.

P3   There is no basis for selectively dismissing either our or the Martians' judgments of AV on the respective works.

P4   So, from P1 and P3, there is a genuine difference in AV between *G1* and *G2*.

P5   So, from P2 and P4, there is a genuine difference in APs between *G1* and *G2*.

P6   But, by hypothesis, *G1* and *G2* share all pictorial properties and belong to the same category of art.

P7   So, from P6 and the definition of supervenience, *G1* and *G2* share all APs that supervene on pictorial properties and category of art.

P8   But, for moderate empiricism, *all* APs so supervene.

P9   So, for moderate empiricism, there can be no genuine difference in APs between *G1* and *G2*.

C1   So, from P5 and P9, moderate empiricism must be false.

C2   Further, any difference in APs between *G1* and *G2* must derive from what was *achieved* in each case.

This argument against moderate empiricism is open to two objections, however, one directed at P1 and the other (more serious) at P2. First, we need to clarify the nature of the supposition, in P1, that *G1* and *G2* are ascribed different artistic values. Recall that the initial "counter-examples" to moderate empiricism – a relocation within Picasso's oeuvre of the work having the pictorial properties of *Les Demoiselles d'Avignon*, and the re-evaluation of *The Disciples at Emmaeus* upon learning that it was by van Meegeren rather than Vermeer – were acknowledged to be inconclusive. As we saw, the empiricist can respond that the differences in value pertain not to *artistic* value but only to art-historical value. Since Currie has offered no general argument against the empiricist's appeal to the latter distinction, the basis for the difference in ascribed artistic value in P1 cannot be anything that the empiricist would regard as bearing only on the art-historical value of the two canvases. Thus we must discount any value accruing to Picasso's work in virtue of its contribution to his oeuvre or to a broader tradition of painting.

However, as we have seen, Currie grounds the difference in ascribed artistic value in P1 not in art-historical properties of this sort, but in the fact that the Martians possess "artistic abilities vastly greater than ours." The difference in ascribed artistic value stipulated in P1 is supposed to be grounded, then, in different valuations of what is achieved in generating a work with certain manifest properties. While *the same* abilities are exercised in generating *G1* and *G2*, we take this to be a remarkable achievement, and value the work accordingly, whereas the Martians take this to be, quite literally, child's play, and do not value the work.

To the extent that the abilities in question are a matter of facility in the practical manipulation of a medium for aesthetic effect, however, the moderate empiricist might respond that *this* sort of achievement is quite irrelevant to the proper appreciation of artworks.[10] It is instructive, here, to consider how empiricists tend to view the bearing of the exercise of skills, in general, on the artistic value of works. As noted in chapter 1, there has been much recent debate about whether painters like Vermeer made use of optical devices such as the camera obscura in achieving their representational effects. Empiricists tend to treat such matters as *art-historical*, and as having no bearing on the artistic value of the resulting paintings. If, as Alfred Lessing maintains, knowledge of the medium used by a painter is irrelevant to artistic judgment on the work, then surely knowledge of how the painter manipulated that medium is also irrelevant. Even if we take the abilities in question to involve the exercise of intellectual or imaginative powers, it is far from clear that the aesthetic

10 Such a view would accord with the sentiments of conceptual artists such as Sol LeWitt who locate all of the artistic value of works in the *conception*, and view the practical manipulation of a physical medium as a matter of "perfunctory execution," to be delegated to practitioners of mere craft. See further chapters 8 and 9 below. A more sophisticated defense of such a view is found in the writings of "Ideal" theorists such as Croce and Collingwood (see Wollheim 1980: 36ff, for a critical summary of the "Ideal" theory, but see also Ridley unpublished for a reading of Collingwood according to which he is not open to Wollheim's objection). Of course, the empiricist differs radically from both LeWitt and Ideal theorists in another respect. They take the manifest properties of an art-object to be at best evidence as to a work, whereas the empiricist takes artistic value to relate *only* to such manifest properties.

empiricist must grant the difference in ascribed *artistic* value assumed in P1. For it is difficult to see how we could take account of such exercises on the part of an artist without locating them in a broader context of agency involving artistic intentions realized or unrealized in the work. However, the aesthetic empiricist denies that the reconstruction of artistic intentions has any part to play in artistic judgment.

Of course, the sorts of empiricist stratagems adduced here might be challenged on the grounds that they utterly distort our practices of appreciating and critically responding to artworks, and greatly impoverish works by excluding from the realm of artistic value many of the qualities for which works are most highly valued. But *this* response to the aesthetic empiricist can be made as soon as the latter appeals to the distinction between artistic and art-historical value. If we allow this distinction to stand for the sake of argument, we cannot unproblematically appeal, as Currie does, to differences in artistic value in setting up a counter-empiricist argument.

Suppose, however, that Currie's "Martian child" example *can* be redescribed so that the difference in ascribed value is a difference in *artistic* value, a difference pertaining to what all parties would acknowledge to be artistic properties of the two works. Even in this case, it doesn't follow, from the fact that we and the Martians ascribe different artistic *value* to the two works, that attributions of specific artistic properties are "essentially" bound up with judgments about what the artist has achieved – the latter being what Currie has to show if he is to counter the moderate empiricist's supervenience thesis and her attempt to drive a wedge between artistic and art-historical properties. Currie assumes that, given different judgments as to the artistic *value* of two works, there must be a corresponding difference in the artistic *values* (or value-relevant artistic properties) realized in the works (this assumption is expressed in P2 of my reconstruction of Currie's argument). But this doesn't follow. *One* explanation for the difference in ascribed artistic value is indeed that there is some artistic property, whose specific bearing on a work's artistic value is generally acknowledged, which *G1* possesses but *G2* lacks. A competing explanation, however, is that there is no difference in artistic properties, but only a difference in the *weight accorded* to different artistic properties in arriving at an overall evaluation of a work. In this case, while we might look to more general cultural and historical differences – perhaps different conceptions of achievement – to explain the differences in weighting, the moderate empiricist's conception of artistic properties would be unchallenged. Such properties would supervene upon manifest properties and artistic category alone.

To take a historical example, consider the significance accorded to pictorial symmetry in late Renaissance and Baroque art. The symmetry of a pictorial design can plausibly be taken to supervene upon the manifest properties of a painting, and both Renaissance and Baroque paintings belong to the same category of art in Walton's sense. If we follow Wölfflin's influential account (1950) of the differences between the "linear" style of the late Renaissance and the "painterly" style of the Baroque period, however, pictorial symmetry, having been a *positive* artistic property for painting in the linear style, acquired a *negative* value in the painterly style, because it militated against the attainment of the sort of pictorial openness sought within that style. Thus, if we take a typical pictorial design generated by a late Renaissance painter and consider how the artistic value of that design might have differed if it had been generated by a Baroque painter, we have an example parallel to Currie's, where we have a difference in ascribed artistic value yet no difference in pictorial properties and category of art. But this surely *doesn't* show that the works differ in artistic properties, or, indeed, that symmetry, as an artistic property, depends upon judgments concerning what the painter achieved. Rather, the difference in ascribed artistic value is grounded in the different *weighting* given to the artistic properties that are common to the design in its actual and hypothetical incarnations.[11] Thus, even if we grant P1, Currie's argument fails to undermine the moderate empiricist's "supervenience" thesis because P2 is false.

This has implications not just for Currie's anti-empiricist argument, but for any purported counter-example to moderate empiricism having the same basic structure. Even if the moderate empiricist grants that artistic value can differ where category and manifest properties are the same, she can maintain that artistic properties supervene upon a work's manifest properties and category of art, as long as she is willing to concede that *artistic value* doesn't so supervene. Rather, she can maintain, artistic value supervenes on artistic properties and the contextually determined weighting given to those properties. This is not a trivial concession, although it might seem so in the context of Currie's example, where the context is given by the range of human capacities. However, as the symmetry example demonstrates, the context may be historically and culturally

11 Note that Currie cannot meet this objection by appealing to the assumption that the Martians share our aesthetic interests and sensibilities. For if this assumption is construed in such a way that it rules out any difference in the weighting of artistic properties in the evaluation of works, Currie's argument begs the question against the moderate empiricist by simply stipulating a situation in which there is disagreement over artistic value while pictorial and categoreal properties are identical.

specific, and only one who possesses appropriate historical and cultural knowledge can properly assess the artistic value of the work. Thus the sorts of considerations raised by Currie may challenge some forms of empiricist *axiology*. But it is important to note that his argument establishes neither of the substantive conclusions that he wishes to draw. It neither disproves the moderate empiricist's supervenience claim concerning artistic properties, nor establishes the more general claim that all artistic judgments are essentially tied to judgments about what an artist has achieved.

2.3 Direct Arguments Against Aesthetic Empiricism

Our examination of Currie's anti-empiricist arguments suggests that, if we wish to establish that artistic properties depend, or may depend, upon supra-categoreal features of provenance – features of which the receiver must be aware in order to properly appreciate the work – we must proceed more directly. The "indirect" argument from differences in ascribed artistic value fails for two reasons. First, overall artistic value is a function of ascribed artistic properties only given a weighting of those properties, and, second, the empiricist can reject the sorts of hypothetical cases canvassed above on the grounds that they involve differences in art-historical value rather than differences in artistic value. We can overcome the second difficulty only if we can avail ourselves either of a principled distinction between artistic and art-historical properties, or of an independent argument against the very possibility of drawing such a distinction. But, if we have such resources, it is not apparent why we need the indirect strategy. The conclusion we should draw, then, is that the argument against empiricism must focus on purported artistic *properties* ascribed to works in our critical and appreciative practice, rather than on the overall evaluations of works predicated upon the ascriptions of such properties. The task is to show that the properties in question are properly "artistic," and therefore relevant to the artistic value of works.

Two kinds of more direct arguments against empiricism suggest themselves. First, as noted above, the most decisive counter to moderate empiricism would be a demonstration that all ascriptions of properties to artworks bearing on the artistic value of those works presuppose assumptions about supra-categoreal features of provenance. We might render such talk about "presupposed assumptions" more precise by reformulating the counter-empiricist thesis in the following manner: all ascriptions of artistic properties to artworks are in principle defeasible in light of supra-categoreal facts about a work's provenance. If this thesis is true, moderate empiricism must be false, for no artistic property will supervene on manifest properties and category of art alone. For reasons that will become clear shortly, I shall term this the "strong" formulation of the counter-empiricist thesis.

Currie, as we saw, seems committed to the counter-empiricist thesis in this strong form, but we did not find arguments sufficient to establish such a claim. Another writer who seems to endorse the strong counter-empiricist thesis is Michael Baxandall, in some tantalizing remarks in the introduction to his *Patterns of Intention* (1985). He claims that, in our attempts to understand and appreciate a visual artwork, our engagement with the work is always mediated by a verbal description which specifies how we think of the picture after looking at it attentively. The language in terms of which we conceive the object of appreciation is characteristically not a language that catalogues the pictorial properties of the painting – the distribution of pigment on canvas. It is, rather, a language that relates those properties to our affective responses, and, most significantly, to an action or process taken to be generative of an object capable of eliciting such responses: "Awareness that the picture's having an effect on us is the product of human action seems to lie deep in our thinking and talking about pictures" (6). The language we use in describing the art-object speaks to the interests that lead us to look at pictures in the first place: "Implicitly, we treat [a picture] as something with a history of making by a painter and a reality of reception by beholders" (7). This also applies to our talk about such paradigmatically "aesthetic" properties as the "firm design" of a picture. When we talk in this way, we are not merely registering a quality of the arrangement of pigment on canvas, but "speculating about the quality of the process that led to its being an object of a kind to make the impression on [us] that it does" (7).

I shall develop this line of reasoning further in the following chapter. For the moment, I shall only note that, even if one could defend the strong counter-empiricist thesis on such grounds, the thesis is much stronger than is required if our sole concern is to defeat moderate empiricism. The latter is committed to the claim that *all* artistic properties supervene on manifest properties and category of art, and is therefore open to refutation if it can be demonstrated that at least some indisputably artistic properties of artworks fail to so supervene. To counter the claims of the moderate empiricist, we need only find indisputably artistic properties that are possessed at least in part in virtue of a work's having a particular history of making, and defeasible if such a history of making turns out to be lacking. It is not necessary to maintain that *all* artistic properties are provenance-dependent in this way. We may term the claim that at least some genuine artistic properties are provenance-dependent the weak counter-empiricist thesis.

If an argument for the weak counter-empiricist thesis is to succeed where the indirect argument against empiricism failed, it must provide a principled reason to think that the provenance-dependent properties to which it appeals are genuinely "artistic." The strategy of choice, in the recent literature, is to identify a range of properties whose centrality to our discourse about works and to our sense of the value of those works precludes their being excluded from the realm of the properly artistic. If we accept the pragmatic constraint as a more general constraint on theorizing about the arts, then our rational reflection on our actual practice cannot yield a notion of artistic properties radically at odds with central values that we attribute to works of art in our critical and appreciative discourse about them. The argument for the weak counter-empiricist thesis characteristically hypothesizes entities that share all those manifest and categoreal properties upon which the empiricist's artistic properties supervene, but that differ in a wide range of properties of kinds that are central to our discourse about art. The difference in properties is taken to depend upon a difference in non-manifest features of those entities – in particular, their different histories of making and the cultural-historical contexts in which those histories unfolded.

An oft-cited model for all such arguments is Jorge Luis Borges' story "Pierre Menard, Author of the *Quixote*,"[12] where the linguistic structure-type exemplified in copies of *Don Quixote* is separately instantiated by Cervantes and by a (fictional) nineteenth-century French symbolist writer Pierre Menard. Here we have two distinct tokenings of the same linguistic structure-type – the same "text" – in very different contexts, such that, so it is claimed, we would treat the two generative performances as eventuating in very different artistic achievements. Borges very wittily compares the two "works" by ascribing different and even incompatible properties to them in virtue of the very same textual features. What, in Cervantes' text, is "a mere rhetorical praise of history" is, in the work of a contemporary of William James like Menard, "brazenly pragmatic." The works differ crucially in style, the "archaic" and "affected" style of Menard's *Quixote* contrasting with the easy style of Cervantes. Menard's work is "more subtle" than Cervantes' in its manner of representing the

12   Reprinted in English in his 1970: 62–71.

historical episodes selected for the narrative, contrasting favorably with Menard's contemporaries and, in so doing, pointing to "a new conception of the historical novel." Provenance, it is claimed, affects the artistic properties possessed, and not merely the value accorded to the work in virtue of properties acontextually determined.

One finds a similar range of appreciable properties in examples which Jerrold Levinson (1980) brings against "structuralist" conceptions of the musical artwork which identify a musical work with a decontextualized sound-structure. Levinson's argument against structuralism is "epistemological" in the sense defined at the end of the previous chapter. His examples are offered as illustrative of the sorts of properties ascribed to musical works in our critical and appreciative discourse. Two of these examples relate to the expressive or affective properties ascribed to musical works. Which such properties a listener ascribes to a musical passage is partly a function of the musico-historical context in which she locates the piece which contains it. A passage that we find exciting in the eighteenth-century symphonies of Stamitz, for example, would be amusing or absurd if located in the work of a twentieth-century composer. A musical structure relocated in musico-historical space might sound bizarre or anguished, although it lacks such properties when placed in its actual musico-historical location. Other properties ascribed to musical works in Levinson's examples are more obviously dependent upon a history of making: the *originality* of the "elfin delicacy and feel for tone colour" in a work of Mendelssohn, the property of being *influenced* by Liszt ascribable to a work by Brahms, and the references to the work of other contemporary composers in pieces by Bartok. While the empiricist may object that some of the latter properties are merely "art-historical," it would surely greatly impoverish our critical and appreciative discourse about musical works to exclude all of these kinds of properties as irrelevant to the artistic appreciation of works. Once we have admitted some of these properties as properly artistic, however, it is difficult for the empiricist to find principled reasons to exclude the others, given that all are functions of the same sorts of musico-historical variables and of the actual history of making of the work.

As a further example, we might consider Arthur Danto's reasoning in *The Transfiguration of the Commonplace* (1981). Danto focuses on works like Duchamp's Readymades and Warhol's *Brillo Boxes*, where the art-object seems to be indistinguishable, in its manifest properties, from "real things" which are not classified as artworks. He maintains that what distinguishes such works from the "real things" with which they share manifest properties is that, in virtue of the activity of the artist, they possess properties that relate them to other artworks and to a tradition of artistic making. To create an artwork is to bring into being something that possesses such non-manifest properties, properties that are essential to its being the particular work that it is.

Danto offers a hypothetical example (1981: 1–3) where we have eight perceptually indistinguishable painted rectangles, six of which are works and two of which are "mere things." The works, he maintains, differ from one another in many significant respects in virtue of the ways in which their creators conferred upon them non-manifest properties through acting with reference to a developing artistic tradition as it existed at the time of generation of the works. As he describes them, the six works belong to very different genres – "historical painting, psychological portraiture, landscape, geometrical abstraction, religious art, and still-life." The provenance-dependent properties that he cites include expressive, formal, and representational properties ascribable to the works embodied in the different (but indistinguishable) canvases, as well as the sorts of more obviously historically grounded properties offered by Levinson. Generalizing from this kind of thought-experiment, Danto claims that to appreciate something *as art* always requires that it be located in relation to an "artworld" if we are to grasp its distinctive non-exhibited properties as well as its manifest properties. Empiricism, in excluding such non-manifest properties from the realm of artistic properties, thereby fails to capture a fundamental feature of what it is to appreciate something *as an artwork.*

2.4 Drawing Ontological Conclusions from the Counter-Empiricist Arguments

As we noted above, if all one wishes to do is undermine moderate aesthetic empiricism, one need only defend the weak counter-empiricist thesis. But many of the authors who argue against aesthetic empiricism – Currie, Levinson, and Danto, for example – have a larger agenda. For such authors, the attack on aesthetic empiricism is intended to furnish the epistemological premise for an "epistemological argument" in the sense defined at the end of chapter 1. Indeed, the authors in question wish to develop both negative and positive epistemological arguments, the former targeting among other things the ontological views that fit most naturally with the common-sense theory of art, and the latter shoring up the alternative ontology of art that each author wishes to defend. The question to be addressed in this section is whether the weak counter-empiricist thesis, defended in the manner outlined above, can cut such ontological ice. I shall identify a number of problems with the negative arguments offered by Currie and Levinson. It is worth stressing, however, that even if the weak counter-empiricist considerations sketched in the preceding section *were* sufficient to undermine common-sense ontology of art, we will need a more systematic account of the kinds of artistic properties ascribable to works in our critical and appreciative practice if we are to offer a positive epistemological argument for an alternative ontology of art. It will be the task of the next chapter to develop such a systematic account of what I shall term the "structure of the focus of appreciation," preparatory to addressing ontological issues in the following chapters.

Given the pragmatic constraint, aesthetic empiricism entails that works may be identified only with entities that bear, or are capable of bearing, artistic properties in the empiricist sense. A natural ontological concomitant of aesthetic empiricism is some form of "structuralism," which Currie characterizes as the thesis that "the work itself is a certain pattern of lines and colours, structures of sounds, or sequences of words" (1989: 47) – the "pattern" or structure given to the receiver in her experiential engagement with an instance of the work. While the relevant structure may, as a matter of fact, be embodied in only one physical object, as seems to be the case with many if not all paintings and non-cast sculptures, this is in no way an essential property of the *work*, for the structuralist. In principle, all works – not just those in the musical and literary arts – are capable of being multiply realized in different physical objects or events, and no works are properly identified with the physical objects or events that realize them on particular occasions. Structuralism, as a view in the ontology of art, shares with aesthetic empiricism a disregard for the historical origins of either the structures identified with works or the realizations of those structures.

It is worth asking whether anyone has ever held such a view. There is no doubt that certain philosophers have espoused structuralism as a thesis about the ontological status of works in *particular* arts. Goodman, for example, identifies literary artworks with linguistic structures, "texts" (Goodman 1976: 207–11; Goodman and Elgin 1988: ch. 3), and Wollheim, among others, seems to share this view (1980: 4–10, 74–83). Peter Kivy (1983) embraces a structuralist view of musical works, identifying them with sound structures prescribed by scores. But, we may note, Goodman identifies a *musical* work not with a structure but with a class of performances that *comply* with a musical score (1976: 210). And Goodman (1976: 210) and Wollheim (1980: 1–4) resist any identification of *visual* artworks with structures or patterns. Both take works of visual art to be physical objects. We may therefore distinguish between "global" and "local" forms of ontological structuralism. In its local form, structuralism is a thesis about the ontological status of works in one or more particular arts, whereas in its global form it is intended to apply to all the arts.[13]

There is a further question that any proponent of global or local structuralism needs to address. We have distanced questions of ontology from questions of definition, so there is no suggestion that a structuralist is *defining* an artwork as a type of structure. Obviously, even if we narrow our attention to particular artistic media, no one would seriously suggest that being a linguistic structure-type is necessary and sufficient for being a literary artwork. The previous sentence is an instance of a linguistic structure-type but is not an instance of an artwork. There is, however, a separate issue concerning structures of the sort that *are* artworks, on a structuralist view. The structuralist maintains that a literary or musical work is a structure-*type*. It is implausible that works in general be identified with particular *instances* or *tokens* of structure-types, for such tokens can usually come into and go out of existence without affecting the existence of the work. A literary work survives the destruction of individual copies of its text, even the copy originally generated by the author, as long as knowledge of the structure-type instantiated by those copies is preserved. But structure-types might be thought to exist prior to, and independent of, the existence of particular tokens of those types. They exist, it might be said, in virtue of the structural possibilities permitted by the symbol system to which they belong. The structuralist may wish to resist the conclusion that works pre-exist the activities of the artist to whom they are rightly ascribed, however. In this case, it might be argued that works are not structure-types, but instantiated structure-types. More might be said about the sorts of refinements open to the structuralist.[14]

---

13   It is worth noting, however, that Goodman may be committed to the thesis that musical artworks are *individuated* in a manner co-extensive with musical structure-types, and perhaps to the thesis that the individuation of those works that are not themselves identified with structures is co-extensive with a structuralist individuation of those works. This is significant because, as we shall see, the sorts of arguments that have been presented against structuralism challenge the manner in which works are *individuated* by the structuralist.

14   This issue is central to recent debates over Levinson's "creatability" requirement on artworks, and his charge that structuralism fails to meet this requirement. See the discussion in his 1980. For a critical response to Levinson, and a defense of the view that no types or kinds are creatable, see Dodd, 2000. These issues are further examined in chapter 8 below.

However, given our present concerns, I shall ignore such matters unless they bear upon the viability of structuralism in the face of the objections to be presented below.

Currie acknowledges (1989: 47ff) that one cannot argue directly from the (purported) failings of an empiricist view of artistic appreciation to the inadequacy of a structuralist ontology of art, even if one thinks that structuralism is the ontological view that fits most naturally with aesthetic empiricism. What the anti-empiricist arguments supposedly demonstrate is that supra-categoreal features of provenance play an ineliminable role in determining a work's artistic properties. The pragmatic constraint requires that works be the kinds of entities that can possess artistic properties determined in such a manner. Given the anti-empiricist arguments, the structuralist can satisfy the constraint only if he can demonstrate that works, if identified with "structures" of the relevant sort, can possess artistic properties that *fail* to supervene on those structures. It seems that the structuralist can meet this challenge in the following manner. Works, for the structuralist, are simply "patterns" or "structures" of the relevant sort. Given that a work W is identical to a given structure-type S, any appropriate (in some way that would need to spelled out) instantiation of S – in the actual world or in another possible world – is an instance of W. But, the structuralist may argue, works, as structures, possess some of their artistic properties essentially – namely, those properties that supervene on manifest properties of their instantiations and category of art – and other such properties contingently – those that depend on supra-categoreal features of provenance that may differ from one instantiation to another. A work's essential properties are, intuitively, those which something must possess in a counterfactual situation if it is to be an instance of that particular work, while its contingent properties are ones which something could lack in such a situation yet still be an instance of that work. Artistic properties that depend upon supra-categoreal features of the provenance of the work in the actual world, while contingent, are genuine properties of the work that are relevant to its appreciation, for it is the *actual* instantiation(s) of a structure that is the object of criticism and appreciation. But, because such properties are merely contingently possessed by the work, this is compatible with a structuralist conception of the work.[15]

---

15   This distinction between necessary and contingent properties of a work, which bears upon the identity of works both within and across possible worlds, should not be confused with the distinction between correct and incorrect realizations of a work in a given world. One might hold, for example, that a set of constraints on right performance of a musical

Currie claims that any such attempt to uphold structuralism while acknowledging the failings of aesthetic empiricism falls victim to an argument presented by Levinson (Levinson 1980: 68ff). As interpreted by Currie, Levinson's argument runs as follows. The same artistic structure-type might be tokened more than once within a given world. In such circumstances, a difference in the appreciable properties consequent upon the distinct tokenings may require that we treat the separate tokenings of the structure-type as *instances of different works*, rather than as *different instances of the same work*, as structuralism requires us to say. Levinson offers a number of hypothetical examples in support of this claim. In one of these examples, we are to imagine that, in a given world, a work identical in musical structure to a piece by Brahms is generated independently by Beethoven. Differences in the provenance of the two tokenings of the same musical structure-type lead us to ascribe different artistic properties to the products of the activities of Brahms and Beethoven. For example, we would describe the Beethoven piece as "visionary," but would not so characterize the structure-type as tokened by Brahms. Even more obviously, while the Brahms piece might be described as "strongly Liszt-influenced," the ascription of any such property to the Beethoven piece would be anachronistic. Currie maintains that it is not open to the structuralist to respond that the properties in question are ascribable not to *works* but only to the generational activity of the composer. For, he argues, such a response would violate the pragmatic constraint, being "contrary to the practice of informed criticism in the arts, which emphasizes features of works such as originality of thematic invention or of orchestration. Critics clearly regard an understanding of such features as important for an understanding of the work itself" (1989: 51).

Rather, Currie maintains, we have to acknowledge that we have different works that *share* their artistic structure:

> If we agree that properties like *being visionary* and *being influenced by the work of Liszt* are properties of the work, rather than merely properties of the compositional activity of the composer, . . . then we have a case which is undoubtedly a case of the composition of distinct works. One and the same work cannot be both visionary and non-visionary in the same world, for nothing can have a property and the negation of that property within a world. (1989: 52–3)

work is a necessary property of that work, while allowing for performances of that work that are incorrect in that they fail to satisfy all of those constraints. See chapter 9 for further discussion of the issue of correctness of realization of a work in the performance arts.

More formally, Levinson's anti-structuralist argument, as expounded by Currie, runs as follows:

1 The structuralist, who identifies a work with a structure-type S, must say that two (appropriate) tokenings of S are two instances of the same work.

2 The structuralist, we are assuming, accepts the weak counter-empiricist thesis, according to which at least some of a work's artistic properties depend upon the art-historical context (AHC) in which an object or structure is generated.

3 Consider a property P that is so dependent.

4 Consider two AHCs, AHC1 and AHC2, such that S as tokened in AHC1 possesses P while S as tokened in AHC2 lacks P, where both tokenings are "appropriate."

5 Let W1 be the work that results from the tokening of S in AHC1.

6 Let W2 be the work that results from the tokening of S in AHC2.

7 Leibniz's law of the "indiscernibility of identicals" requires that, if A = B, then A and B have all of their properties in common.

8 Since, by (4), W1 and W2 differ in at least one of their artistic properties, then, by Leibniz's law, not (W1 = W2).

9 So, given (1) and (8), structuralism must be false.

As presented by Currie, however, Levinson's argument is open to the following objection (Wolterstorff 1991). The supposedly problematic provenance-grounded properties ascribable to works – *being Liszt-influenced, being archaic*, etc. – can be viewed as properties that a work, qua structure-type, possesses *relative to a given act of discovering or generating that structure*. In this case, a given work identified with the linguistic or musical structure-type separately instantiated on different occasions in a world will possess provenance-grounded properties of the form *being-archaic-as-generated-by-Menard* or *being-Liszt-influenced-as-generated-by-Brahms*. That a work possessing such properties does not possess the properties *being-archaic-as-generated-by-Cervantes* or *being-Liszt-influenced-as-generated-by-Beethoven*, respectively, presents no problems for the structuralist, for there is nothing contradictory in such a state of affairs.

That Levinson's anti-structuralist argument is open to such a response stems, at least in part, from a failure by Currie to bring out a central feature of that argument. The basic premise of Levinson's argument[16] is that works "must be specific enough to bear the aesthetic and artistic

---

16 Levinson's argument is developed in his 1980. A summary of the argument can be found in his 1990a: 241.

attributes we importantly ascribe to them. We have to conceive them so that they are what such attributions are *of*" (1990a: 241). The need to preserve the *specificity* of our aesthetic and artistic ascriptions is central to this argument. Levinson claims that structuralism cannot accommodate the sorts of *determinate* aesthetic and artistic properties ascribed to (musical or literary) works in our critical and appreciative practice. Consider, again, Borges' story "Pierre Menard, Author of the *Quixote*." As we have seen, Borges' narrator maintains that we take "being archaic" and "being shamelessly pragmatic" to be properties of the text *Don Quixote* as generated by Menard, while incompatible properties are true of the text as generated by Cervantes. Crucially, we ascribe such determinate properties to *works*. We don't ascribe to works "relational" properties such as "being-archaic-*as-generated-by-Menard*." While Wolterstorff describes a possible critical and appreciative practice, it is not *our* practice, so Levinson would maintain. But, if works are structure-types, then, as Wolterstorff maintains, it could only be the latter "relativized" properties that are rightly ascribed to the work. If Levinson correctly describes our practice, then the structuralist who grants the case against aesthetic empiricism cannot both accept the pragmatic constraint *and* adopt Wolterstorff's strategy to counter the prospect of multiple instantiations of an artistic structure in a world.

It might be objected, however, that, there is something odd about appealing to the pragmatic constraint in arguing against the structuralist in this way. For the examples of "ascriptive practice" to which appeal is being made are generally *hypothetical* rather than actual. We do not have actual examples like the Cervantes/Menard or Brahms/Beethoven cases where the *same structure-type* is tokened in a creative manner (that is, not merely transcribed) on separate occasions. Thus we have to appeal to *what we would say* or *what we would do* in such hypothetical situations. We can point to features of our actual ascriptive practice in support of such counterfactual judgments, of course. For example, critics do seem to debate the comparative merits of interpretations that ascribe incompatible provenance-related properties to a work, and our ascriptions of provenance-grounded properties to a work are not overtly relativized to a generation of a structure. However, this might be explained by the very fact that the artistic structures with which we deal in our critical and appreciative practice are *not* multiply instantiated, so that there is no need to overtly relativize the provenance-grounded properties to a particular act of generation.

Of course, as noted in our discussion of the pragmatic constraint in chapter 1, it involves a necessary appeal to our intuitions about non-actual cases because it requires that we adopt a normative stance toward our actual artistic practice. It is only after being "codified" that our practice stands as a constraint on the ontology of art. But it might still be maintained that we lack clear and shared intuitions about the kinds of hypothetical cases upon which Levinson and Currie rely. One of the merits of the anti-empiricist and anti-structuralist strategy to be pursued in the following chapter is that it may assuage any such lingering doubts about the sorts of arguments considered thus far.

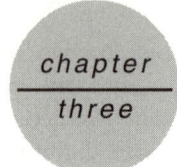

chapter

three

The Fine Structure
of the Focus
# of Appreciation

3.1 The Structure of the Focus of Appreciation

In this chapter, I want to look more closely at the role that provenance plays in the epistemology of art. The goal is to clarify why an adequate account of what is involved in the proper appreciation of artworks must take account of specific aspects of generative artistic performances. In the previous chapter, I introduced the term "focus of appreciation" to characterize that which, as the product of a generative performance on the part of one or more individuals, is relevant to the appreciation of the artwork brought into existence through that performance. I shall argue that reflection upon our critical and appreciative discourse about works reveals a "fine structure" to the focus of appreciation. This "fine structure" can be analyzed in terms of relationships that obtain between three inter-definable elements, to be identified in the remainder of this section. The analysis of the fine structure of the focus of appreciation furnishes us with a more systematic and conclusive response to aesthetic empiricism, for it brings out how inextricably properties that enter into the focuses of appreciation of works are bound up with histories of making. In the final section of this chapter, I shall begin to explore the implications of this analysis for the ontology of art.

3.1.1 The articulation of artistic statements

In the Prado in Madrid hangs a large monochorome canvas labelled *Guernica*. The canvas, we are informed, was painted by Picasso in 1937. It can be seen to represent a number of intertwined and overlapping figures, some human and some animal. There is a screaming woman, a number of other figures either dead or in the process of dying, a terrified-looking horse impaled on a javelin, a bull with an ambiguous expression, and an electric lightbulb. Such facts about the representational content of the painting are accessible to any receiver who is able to classify pictures of this type as woman-pictures, horse-pictures, etc., on the basis of their observable features.[1] Viewers familiar with twentieth-century European history will probably also take the image to be a representation of the destruction of the Basque town of Guernica by the Luftwaffe in April 1937. Such viewers may further take the painting to express revulsion at this event, and perhaps to express other attitudes, depending upon the significance ascribed to the "symbolic" elements in the painting – in particular the bull, which seems to be assigned a number of symbolic roles in Picasso's paintings, the horse, and the lightbulb.

The product of Picasso's generative activity is clearly something to which viewers can and do ascribe these sorts of representational and expressive properties. Some such properties seem to be ascribable without reference to the canvas's history of making, whereas others are only ascribable if one assumes such a history. For the moment we need not rule on whether the empiricist is right in holding that only the first kind of property bears upon the appreciation of the work *Guernica*. What can be agreed is that, in our attempts to critically appropriate and appreciate works of visual art such as *Guernica*, we take at least some of the representational and expressive properties of the object produced by the artist to bear upon the appreciation of the work. In other words, such properties enter into the focus of appreciation for such a work.

Take, as another example, the canvas by Piero della Francesca that bears the label *The Baptism of Christ*. As with the physical product of Picasso's labours, what a receiver takes the painting to represent will depend upon what knowledge she brings to her engagement with the canvas. A viewer who is ignorant of the history of making of Piero's canvas and of the significance of the title of the picture will see it as a representation of a number of figures present at some kind of ceremony on the banks of a stream. A viewer who is familiar with the New Testament will be able to give a somewhat richer description of the events portrayed, identifying one central figure as John the Baptist and the other as Christ. What will also be apparent to most receivers is that Piero has produced an image which exhibits a striking visual symmetry and geometrical order. In his

1 See Goodman 1976: 27ff for this way of thinking about representational content, and for the distinction between such content and what a picture may be taken to denote.

illuminating discussion of the picture, Michael Baxandall (1985: ch. 4) illustrates this fact through a diagram of the picture which indicates, for example, that the head of the dove flying over Christ's head, and Christ's hands which are pressed together in supplication against his chest, lie on a vertical line that is at right angles to the foot of the picture and is in the precise centre of the painting. These geometrical properties of the image, which are characteristic both of Piero's work and of more general concerns with mathematical proportion in the paintings of his culture, are clearly appreciable properties of the product of Piero's activity, no less than the representational properties. They are, further, geometrical properties of the image qua representation: it is in virtue of the representational content of the picture that such geometrical relations obtain. And indeed, as Baxandall argues, they bear upon our reading of the representational content of the picture. Most obviously, they lead us to relate certain of the represented elements in meaningful ways – the dove and the clasped hands, for example. But they also enter crucially into our attempts to explain puzzling features of the represented scene. We explain these features, so Baxandall claims, by taking account of Piero's idiom as a painter, the pictorial tradition in representing the baptism of Christ, and requirements stemming from the nature of Piero's commission, to paint an altarpiece on a relatively large vertical panel (1985: 121ff).

As in the case of the painting by Picasso, empiricists may resist the idea that those representational properties that clearly depend upon a painting's history of making and are not independently discernible in the pictorial array are, properly speaking, artistic properties. But these two examples taken from our appreciative engagement with paintings are intended to make a more general point which seems undeniable, namely, that our appreciative interest in the product of an artist's activity is most naturally thought of as an interest in the "meaningful" or formal properties of the object or structure issuing from that activity. In much of our discourse about works, our interest is in what the product of the artist's activity can be taken to represent or express, or the formal properties that it can be taken to exemplify or make manifest.

It will be helpful here to appropriate terminology introduced by Timothy Binkley in a couple of insightful papers (1976, 1977). Binkley maintains that works in the visual arts are the results of acts of "piece-specification." In performing such an act, an artist "articulates [an] artistic statement" (1977: 266). Traditionally, according to Binkley, this involves articulation in a medium, which permits the generation and identification of a set of perceptible properties intended for aesthetic appreciation. In manipulating a medium, an artist is able to isolate those "aesthetic" properties which are taken by the receiver to be partially constitutive of the piece produced. Obviously, Binkley's talk of "artistic statements" is not to be taken in a literal "propositional" sense, given that his primary concern is with non-literary art forms, and that, even in the case of literary art forms, it is rarely a positive feature of a work that it "makes a statement" in the propositional sense. Rather, the idea is that the artist produces an object or structure having certain meaningful or formally interesting perceptible properties which belong to what I am terming the focus of our appreciative attention to the work. As the above examples demonstrate, the "artistic statement" articulated in a work standardly includes what would normally be described as representational, expressive, and formal properties of the object or structure generated by the artist.

To think of such properties as elements in an "artistic statement" articulated in the work is appropriate because such properties are "meanings," broadly construed, conferred upon the product of her activities through the artist's generational activity. By doing what she does, the artist produces something to which we may legitimately ascribe certain representational and expressive "meanings," and certain manifest formal values. To bring out this relationship between the product of the artist's activity in the fullness of its properties and the artistic statement articulated through that product, Binkley talks, perhaps somewhat opaquely, about the "intensional individuation" of the pieces specified by the artist. The idea here is that a piece is to be thought of as comprising a set of meanings or values conferred upon some object or structure through the artist's activity. It seems, then, that we can imagine a situation in which that very object or structure "houses" a different piece in virtue of the fact that the activity generative of it, occurring in a different context, confers upon it a different set of meanings or values.[2] On this basis, Binkley argues[3] that the process whereby artworks are created – "piece-specification" – cannot be thought of as a kind of status-conferral, since the thing that has a status

2   Whether this "possibility" is really coherent will depend in part upon the sorts of "meanings" or "values" that can enter into the artistic appreciation of the products of an artist's generative activity, of course. For the aesthetic empiricist, since all that matters is what can be found in an instance of the work in abstraction from any knowledge of supra-categoreal aspects of provenance, the "possibility" is not actually a coherent one unless it can be cashed out purely in terms of differences in artistic category.

3   His target, here, is George Dickie's "Institutional Theory" of Art (see Dickie 1974), according to which arthood is a status conferred on an entity by someone acting on behalf of "the artworld." See chapter 10 below for further discussion of Dickie's view and Binkley's criticisms of it.

conferred upon it is an object or entity in the fullness of its properties. Status-conferral is *extensional,* in the sense that, if the sentence "John has status S" is true, the sentence remains true if we replace the word "John" with any other expression that refers to the very same individual (or, more technically, that has the same extension) – for example, "my best friend," if John is the individual who fits that description. Piece-specification is *intensional,* because what are specified as pieces are not objects or structures per se, but sets of meanings or values conferred upon objects or structures through the very act of piece-specification. A similar point is made by Levinson. To recall one of his examples, a piece composed by Beethoven having the same pure sound-structure as Brahms' Piano Sonata op. 2 would have a visionary quality that Brahms' piece lacks. Levinson maintains that one should reject what he terms the "extensionalism" to which one is committed if one identifies musical works with pure sound-structures, and embrace instead the view that "musical works [are] intensionally individuated by their more fine-grained aesthetic meanings and artistic significances" (1990a: 249).

3.1.2 "Two-foldness" and articulation in a medium

I shall return to Binkley's account shortly. First, however, we need to take note of another more general structural feature of the focus of appreciation. Consider the following observations by Kenneth Clark, from his book *Looking at Pictures.* Clark is remarking upon certain features of Turner's painting *Snowstorm* "The swathes of snow and water swing about in a wholly unpredictable manner, and their impetus is deflected by contrary movements of spray and mysterious striations of light" (1960: 143). Here, fairly clearly, we are discussing aspects of the "artistic statement" articulated by Turner – certain representational properties ascribable to the painted object. But our appreciative interest in the artwork is not merely in what it *represents,* but also in something else. In earlier attempts to represent the power of nature, such as his *Shipwreck,* Turner relied on design and composition. But

> when I look back across the gallery, with Turner's dark, early sea-pieces in mind, I no longer think about its design, but about its colour; and I see that the dramatic effect of light is not achieved by contrast of tone (as it is in the *Shipwreck*) but by a most subtle alternation of colour. As a result, oil paint achieves a new consistency, an iridescence, which is more like that of some living thing . . . than a painted simulacrum. The surface of a late Turner is made up of gradations so fine and flecks of colour so inexplicable

that we are reminded, whatever the subject, of flowers and sunset skies. (1960: 146)

The interest here is not in the artistic statement articulated per se, but in the *manner* in which that artistic statement has been articulated in the medium of oil paint. This interest exemplifies a thesis of Wollheim's concerning what it is to be interested in an artwork as a representation. Our interest in an artistic representation involves what he terms "seeing-in" (Wollheim 1980: 213ff). To see A in B is to be aware not just of something A-like in B, but also of *how* A is rendered by means of properties of B. In the case of Turner's painting, it is to be interested in how Turner has applied oil paint to canvas in a particular way in order to realize certain representational values in the painting, and thereby to articulate a particular artistic statement. Such an interest is furthered by attending to details of the painted canvas not merely as a means to determine precisely what is thereby articulated, but also to appreciatively reflect upon the way in which the articulation has been achieved. To think of artistic representation as a matter of seeing-in is, for Wollheim, to accept what he terms the "two-foldness" of our legitimate interest in artistic representation. Our interest is two-fold in that it always involves an interest not just in what is represented by B but also in the means whereby B represents A, where neither mode of interest is simply a means to further our interest in the other.

We may generalize from Wollheim's account of representation to our broader appreciative interest in something as a product of generative artistic activity. Such interest is always in an artistic statement *as articulated* in a medium. To interest oneself solely in what a work articulates is to fail to take a properly artistic interest in the work. This is why, for example, university courses on the "Art of the Film" spend so much time educating students on the ways in which the film medium can be used to realize various representational, expressive, and formal ends. That the proper artistic appreciation of an artwork involves a two-fold interest in the product of the artist's generative activity also helps to clarify the somewhat puzzling idea, frequently endorsed but rarely elucidated, that, in appreciating and evaluating artworks, we take the products of artistic activity to have "intrinsic value," or to be valuable "for their own sakes." This is usually contrasted with the merely "instrumental" value that other things are taken to have. If our interest in artworks were only an interest in the contents of their articulated artistic statements, then products of artistic activity would serve merely as instruments whereby those statements are transmitted, in principle expendable once the statements have been identified or if there proves to be another way of articulating the same statements. But, because our interest is always at least in part an interest in the *manner* of articulation, close and repeated attention to the product of the artist's activity is always a necessary part of the appreciation of works, and their value is never merely instrumental in the ways just described. I shall return to some of these points in chapter 10.

3.1.3 *"Artistic medium" and "vehicular medium"*

I have formulated the thesis of two-foldness in terms of the need to include, in the focus of appreciation, not merely an articulated artistic statement but also the manner in which that statement is articulated in a medium. But the notion of a "medium" needs to be further refined, or, rather, disambiguated. Consider, again, the passage from Clark on the painting by Turner. Note how Clark moves from (a) talk about an articulated artistic meaning – the representational and expressive properties of Turner's painting, and especially the representation of light – to (b) talk about the articulation of such meaning using "contrast of tone" and "alternation of colour," to (c) talk about oil paint, the paint-flecked surface of the canvas, and color understood as a physical property of the paint-covered canvas. Talk of the "medium" employed in the arts is sometimes talk of what, at least in the Turner example, is a kind of physical stuff – oil paint and canvas – and sometimes talk of ways of manipulating a kind of physical stuff in order to achieve certain ends. Joseph Margolis (1980) has attempted to capture this in terms of a distinction between what he terms the "physical medium" and the "artistic medium" of a work. In the case of paintings, for example, the physical medium consists of pigments (oils, tempera, watercolors . . .) applied to a surface (wood, canvas, glass . . .), while the artistic medium is "a purposeful system of brushstrokes." Similarly, in talking about dance, the physical medium of bodily movements is to be distinguished from the artistic medium of articulated steps. As we saw in chapter 1, Beardsley (1982a) makes a similar point in arguing for a distinction between the physical medium of bodily movements and pauses, on the one hand, and the "movings" and "posings" that are elements in the artistic medium of dance, on the other.

Margolis insists that, while the artistic medium may be physically embodied, we must think of the work as made up not of physical elements as such, but of elements like dance-steps or brushstrokes that are "informed by the purposiveness of the entire work." This point is also acknowledged by Levinson in a paper on the possibility and nature of "hybrid" art forms. Characterizing a hybrid art form as one that combines two or more media, he remarks that

> *medium* in the present context is *not* equivalent to *material* or *physical dimension*. Rather, by a *medium* I mean a developed way of using given materials or dimensions, with certain entrenched properties, practices, and possibilities. "Medium" in this sense is closer to "art form" than to "kind of stuff." (1984: 29)

Danto (1981: 159) similarly insists that we cannot identify the medium of a painting with the physical material of which it is composed, given the ways in which we talk about artworks. We might say that an artist characteristically works *in* a particular artistic medium when *working* a physical medium. To think of a painting as in an artistic medium is to relate its perceptible properties to the agency of a maker whose purposeful composition in that medium is the source of those properties.

Margolis' distinction between physical and artistic media is appealing, but it also requires clarification in at least two respects. First, we need a more precise account of the relationship between an artistic medium and that in which it may be realized. Second, we must ask whether all artworks are in an artistic medium in Margolis' sense, and, if so: (a) why is the existence of such a medium a precondition for something's being an artwork?; and (b) can a work be in an artistic medium without being in a physical medium?

In answering these questions, we may profitably return to Binkley's account of piece-specification. Binkley's more general project, which parallels some of our concerns in chapter 1, is to exhibit salient continuities and discontinuities between traditional works of fine art and late modern works. The primary obstacles to an understanding of late modern art, according to Binkley, are the subsumption of the artistic under the aesthetic, and, more particularly, a misunderstanding of the function of media in traditional fine art. He claims that philosophers have failed to understand the continuity between what may be termed "aesthetic" and "nonaesthetic" art because they have taken articulation in a medium to be the defining condition of art, and because they have misunderstood what it is to articulate an artistic statement in a medium. The medium is taken to be a kind of physical stuff through the manipulation of which an emergent *aesthetic object* comes into being – something whose appreciable properties are determinable through, and only through, a direct experiential encounter with the physical product of the artist's activity. What this misses, according to Binkley, is the essentially conventional nature of media in art. A medium is a set of conventions (or shared understandings) whereby performing certain manipulations on a kind of physical stuff counts as specifying a certain set of aesthetic properties as a piece, and thus as articulating a particular artistic statement. Once we recognize that the role of media in traditional fine art is to enable an artist to articulate an artistic statement in a manner graspable by receivers, however, we can see the eschewal of media, so construed, in late modern art as simply a decision to employ alternative means of articulating an artistic statement.

We can reformulate Binkley's central claim about media in aesthetic art in terms of the distinction between the physical medium and the artistic medium. Binkley's claim that media in art are properly regarded as *piece-specifying conventions* rather than as kinds of physical stuff can be seen as bringing out the contingent nature of the relation between a physical medium and an artistic medium. The point might be expressed in a modified version of the thought-experiment by Kendall Walton sketched in chapter 2. Imagine a culture C which has works – call them "C-paintings" – which are physically indistinguishable from our paintings, but where the topology of the painted canvas – most obviously realized in the thickness of the paint – is a crucial artistic property of a work. Appreciation of a C-painting *always* requires that one look at it not only from the front but also from the side. C-paintings share a physical medium with our paintings, but the artistic mediums differ. Thus if a C-painter and one of our painters both execute a given set of manipulations of the shared physical medium, they will almost certainly articulate different artistic statements. An artistic medium, then, cannot supervene upon a physical medium, because what is intuitively the *same* material or substrate can be worked in different artistic media. Rather, an artistic medium can be thought of as a set of shared understandings whereby an individual's acting in certain ways – for example, performing certain operations upon a physical medium – admits of particular descriptions in terms of which it can be seen as serving to articulate a particular artistic statement.[4]

If, like Binkley, we take an artistic medium to be something that permits the articulation of an artistic statement through the manipulation of a *physical medium*, then it will be difficult to think of purely conceptual works such as Robert Barry's *All the things I know but of which I am not at the moment thinking – 1:36 P.M.; 15 June 1969, New York*, or,

---

4 Levinson, in his paper on hybrid art forms, notes that the latter, "which merge different media, *may not* involve different materials or dimensions (e.g. prose-poems, 'fusion' jazz)" (1984: 29).

arguably, Duchampian Readymades and much late modern art, as involving artistic media. But we might characterize artistic media more generally as modes of artistic *mediation* that are necessary in order for there to be appreciable works. The artistic medium of a work, so construed, will be the means employed by an artist to articulate an artistic statement, and thereby specify a piece that is accessible to receivers. That in which the artistic medium is realized need not be a *physical* medium, however. In the case of much late modern art, the artistic medium may allow the articulation of an artistic statement through the execution of a particular action in a given cultural-historical context – this is plausibly what is going on in the sort of late modern art of concern to Binkley. We may adopt the term "vehicular medium" as a generalization of Margolis' notion of a physical medium in order to accommodate such works. The product of an artist's manipulation of a vehicular medium will then be the *vehicle* whereby a particular artistic statement is articulated in virtue, in part, of the *artistic medium* in which the artist is working in her manipulation of the vehicular medium. The vehicle may, as in the case of Picasso's *Guernica*, be a physical object, or, as in the case of Coleridge's *Kubla Khan*, a linguistic structure-type, or, as arguably in the case of Duchamp's *Fountain*, an action of a particular kind. The sense that many receivers have of not being able to "get" works of late modern fine art can then be explained as a failure to identify either the vehicle, or the artistic medium, or both. If one takes Duchamp's *Fountain* to be a work whose vehicle is a particular physical object and whose artistic medium is the one common in works of freestanding sculpture, then the resulting conception of the artistic statement articulated in the work may indeed leave one very puzzled. Similar remarks apply, mutatis mutandis, to Damien Hirst's *Pharmacy*, the performance pieces of Vito Acconci, and Warhol's film of the Empire State Building. We will say more about this in chapters 8 and 9 below.

An artistic medium mediates between what the artist does, naively construed, and what the work "says," in a broad sense, in virtue of what the artist does. To play this mediating role, an artistic medium must first bring the activity of the artist into the realm of art, where it can be taken to be the articulating of a particular artistic statement. For this reason, we can characterize the artistic medium in two different ways, something that was implicit in our discussion of Margolis and Binkley, who, it can now be noted, differ in precisely this respect. For Margolis, as for Beardsley in his account of dance, an artistic medium furnishes us with a way of characterizing the manipulations of a vehicular medium in terms that integrate the intentionality of the artist. In characterizing these manipulations in terms of "movings and posings," or in terms of "brushstrokes," we bring the artist's activity within the realm of art, which permits it to be understood as instrumental in the articulation of an artistic statement. Binkley, on the other hand, focuses on the shared understandings on the basis of which manipulations of a physical medium so characterized can be understood as articulations of *particular* artistic statements. An artistic medium so construed links the movings and posings of the dancer with a particular set of representational, formal, and expressive meanings. On both ways of characterizing an artistic medium, the latter is properly viewed as a matter of shared understandings of the import of what is done, and in each case attention to the artistic medium of a work necessarily refers us to the intentionality of a maker who acts in light of these supposed shared understandings in manipulating a vehicular medium with the goal of articulating an artistic statement. We need to grasp both aspects of the functioning of artistic media if we are to adequately represent the role of such media in the creation and appreciation of artworks, for an adequate understanding of each aspect refers us to the other.

3.2 Performance and Appreciation

Artworks, I have maintained, come into existence through the intentional manipulations of a vehicular medium. Through these manipulations, an artistic statement is articulated in virtue of shared understandings as to how those manipulations are to be characterized in the vocabulary of an artistic medium, and as to the import of particular manipulations so characterized. In our attempts to appreciate the artwork brought into existence through such activity, we are interested in the product of that activity in virtue of both the artistic statement articulated and the manner in which that statement has been articulated. Since the latter depends upon both the manipulations carried out in the vehicular medium and the shared understandings that the artist is able to utilize in performing those manipulations, our appreciative interest in the product of the artist's activity encompasses three interrelated elements: an articulated artistic statement, a vehicular medium, and an artistic medium. In brief, then, the focus of appreciation in our engagement with an artwork is *an artistic statement as articulated in an artistic medium realized in a vehicle.*

While I have spelled this out most fully in relation to the visual arts, I take this analysis of the focus of appreciation to apply to other art forms, although precisely how it applies to a given art form may be open to dispute. The challenge, in any given case, is to specify the nature of the vehicular medium, and to identify those shared understandings that make up the artistic medium. In the case of the literary arts in general, one might identify the vehicular medium with the resources available in a particular natural language at a particular time. The artistic media in the literary arts will then include a distinctive vocabulary for talking about ways of manipulating that medium – for example, talk about various verbal tropes and the putting together of words in ways that conform to certain metric requirements – and certain generic and "literary" conventions whereby particular artistic statements can be articulated through such manipulations. Such conventions will include a richer budget of symbolic functions than are in play in non-artistic uses of the linguistic medium, established "poetic" resonances of language, narrative conventions, and more narrowly generic expectations that are assumed in the reader. In theater and dance, the vehicular medium will include bodily movements, while the artistic medium will include a distinctive vocabulary for characterizing those movements and various conventions for representing or expressing particular mental states of the performer through bodily movements so characterized. The "artistic statement" articulated in a Japanese Noh play, for example, is determinable only when the prescribed manipulations in the vehicular medium are understood in terms of the artistic medium realized in those movements.[5]

In the cinematic arts, the vehicular medium consists of various means for exposing and developing lengths of film stock, and the exposed lengths of film stock joined to one another in a certain manner, where the artistic medium characterizes individual shots and their combinations in terms of such notions as framing, focus, depth, composition, and montage, and correlates particular manipulations of the physical medium so characterized with various contentful properties thereby realized. Arnheim's *Film as Art* (1964) provides a discussion of the articulation of artistic meaning in cinema that can be parsed in precisely these terms.[6] In music, the vehicular medium comprises various "instruments," conventional and unconventional,[7] the sounds that such instruments can produce, and a notation

---

5   The use of bodily movement as a medium in theater and dance is captured in Italian fifteenth-century paintings where the portrayal of gestures having an established significance in performance is used to articulate particular artistic statements. See, for example, Baxandall 1972.

6   See Arnheim 1964. See also Bazin 1967 for an alternative "classical" conception of film art that can be read in terms of the distinctions drawn above.

7   For example. the "noise music" proposed and performed by the Italian Futurist Russolo, inspired by his compatriot Marinetti, required the construction of special wooden "music boxes" which could reproduce the sound of a tram, or an exploding motor, or a foghorn,

in terms of which such sounds can be characterized, while the artistic medium comprises a vocabulary for describing the intentional composition – either as a performance or as a prescription for a class of performances – of a structure of sounds to be generated through the sequential manipulations of those instruments, and a set of shared understandings as to the artistic statement that would be articulated through such an act of composition.[8]

In analyzing the fine structure of the focus of appreciation, I have appealed either directly or indirectly to the ways in which – as critics or as ordinary receivers – we talk about artworks in our appreciative engagement with the products of artistic activity. If we accept the pragmatic constraint on theorizing about the arts, it is through reflection upon such ways of talking about and treating things in our receptive practices that we further our understanding of issues in the epistemology, ontology, and axiology of art. I shall now argue that such reflection should lead us to reject aesthetic empiricism and the strategies that aesthetic empiricists offer when faced with the kinds of arguments considered in the previous chapter. The issue, we may recall, is whether the proper appreciation of artworks requires that one take account of properties that fail to supervene on "manifest" properties of the product of the artist's activity, or upon manifest properties plus the category of art to which that product is properly assigned. A related issue is whether one can draw a principled distinction between those properties that are genuinely *artistic*, and therefore bear upon the proper appreciation of works, and those properties that are *art-historical*, and do not so bear.

It is readily apparent, I think, that, for each of the three elements that enter into the fine structure of the focus of appreciation, it may require considerable knowledge of the history of making of the product of artistic activity if we are to correctly assign to that product properties of the sort identified in the foregoing analysis. Furthermore, I shall argue, the intimate relationships that obtain between the three elements undermine any attempt to draw a principled line between properties that are legitimately artistic from an empiricist perspective and properties that are not. In fact, I shall suggest, our analysis of the fine structure of the focus of

among other things. The Dadaist Richard Huelsenbeck, influenced by Marinetti"s "Bruitism," envisaged such "instrumentation" as "a chorus of typewriters, kettledrums, rattles, and saucepan lids" (quoted in Goldberg 2001: 67).

8   Matters here are further complicated by the need to give an account of both the artistic activities of a composer of a musical piece and the artistic activities of one who gives a musical performance. For an attempt to develop such an account, see chapter 9 below.

appreciation permits us to defend the "strong counter-empiricist thesis" characterized in the previous chapter. And, if the strong counter-empiricist thesis is true, there can be no principled distinction between artistic and art-historical properties of the sort required by the aesthetic empiricist, or, more generally, between "manifest" artistic properties and those properties that are determinable only given a knowledge of provenance.

Most of the examples cited by those who oppose empiricism purport to show that aspects of provenance – in particular, the cultural-historical context in which a generative performance occurred – must be taken into account if we are to rightly characterize the artistic statement articulated by a manifest work. One general reason for thinking this to be so is that the generative activities through which artworks come into existence, while they frequently issue in objects, or instances of structure-types, which possess certain "manifest" properties, also serve to confer upon those entities certain "non-manifest" properties or values that seem central to the appreciation of the resulting works. Recall, for example, Danto's gallery of eight visually indistinguishable rectangular red canvases. Ex hypothesi, the artifacts possess qualitatively identical manifest properties. But, so Danto claims, viewed as constitutive of particular works, the canvases possess radically different "meanings." The first two canvases in Danto's "gallery" are: (a) a painting, suggested by Kierkegaard, of the Israelites crossing the Red Sea, representing the moment after the sea has closed over the pursuing Egyptian army; and (b) a painting entitled *Kierkegaard's Mood*, reflecting Kierkegaard's observation that the whole of his life is like painting (a), where everything that has occurred is melded into "a mood, a single colour." Here is the catalogue for the rest of Danto's "exhibition," with added indexing for easy reference in the discussion that follows:

> Beside these two, and resembling each as much as they resemble one another (exactly), we shall place [(c)] *Red Square*, a clever bit of Moscow landscape. Our next work is [(d)] a minimalist exemplar of geometrical art which, as it happens, has the same title, *Red Square*. Now comes [(e)] *Nirvana*. It is a metaphysical painting based on the artist's knowledge that the Nirvanic and Samsara orders are identical, and that the Samsara is fondly called the Red Dust by its deprecators. Now we must have [(f)] a still-life executed by an embittered disciple of Matisse, called *Red Table Cloth*; we may allow the paint to be somewhat more thinly applied in the case. Our next object [(g)] is not really an artwork, merely a canvas grounded in red lead, upon which, had he lived to execute it, Giorgione would have painted his unrealized masterwork *Conversazione Sacra*. It is a red surface which,

though hardly an artwork, is not without art-historical interest, since Giorgione himself laid the ground on it. Finally, I shall place [(h)] a surface painted, though not *grounded*, in red lead: a mere artifact. (1981: 1–2)

Danto's red rectangles provide a striking illustration of the non-supervenience of an articulated artistic statement upon the immediately perceivable properties of the product of the artist's activity. The hypothetical works differ quite dramatically in their representational, expressive, and formal properties. In four of the paintings (a, c, e, and f), the redness of the canvas plays a representational role, although in (e) it represents metaphorically rather than literally. In one of the paintings (b), the redness of the canvas functions as a means of expression. And in the remaining painting (d), the redness of the canvas is a property that, along with its squareness, it exemplifies. In virtue of these "first-order" meaning properties, the canvases possess certain higher-order "meanings," and are properly describable as ironic, witty, minimalist, allusive, or profound. One and the same "manifest" property of the product of artistic activity – its being a canvas painted red – plays very different roles in the articulation of an artistic statement in the six cases. We cannot explain this in terms of the titles of the paintings. For, even if (as is surely not the case) this were enough to account for the difference in articulated meanings in four of the cases, it fails to account for the quite radical difference between (c) and (d). Nor are the differences plausibly taken to be explicable in terms of belonging to different "categories of art," even if the paintings belong to very different *genres* in virtue of the ways in which they articulate their different artistic statements.[9] Rather, as we shall see shortly, a "category of art" is more like an artistic medium, something which all of the canvases share.

In the case in hand, the difference in articulated artistic statement is a function of the different art-historical contexts in which the canvases were generated. The artistic medium that all six painters share permits the articulation of different artistic statements in virtue of these differences in context. Analogously, users of a natural language can articulate quite different thoughts by uttering the very same string of words in different conversational contexts in virtue of the same "shared understandings" as to how utterances serve to articulate thoughts. The notion of "art-historical context" needs to be understood broadly, as a generalization of Levinson's characterization of a composer's "musico-historical context":

9 Danto 1981: 2 assigns the canvases to the genres of "historical painting, psychological portraiture, landscape, geometrical abstraction, religious art, and still-life."

The total musico-historical context of a composer P at a time t can be said to include at least the following: (a) the whole of cultural, social, and political history prior to t; (b) the whole of musical development up to t; (c) musical styles prevalent at t; (d) dominant musical influences at t; (e) musical activities of P's contemporaries at t; (f) P's apparent style at t; (g) P's musical repertoire at t; (h) P's oeuvre at t; (i) musical influences operating on P at t. (1980: 69)

Once we allow the art-historical context in which the activity generative of an artistic product takes place to play a role in determining the artistic statement thereby articulated, we can see this statement as having a richness denied to it by the empiricist. For example, Roy Lichtenstein's *Brushstroke*, a medium-size canvas depicting a single fat brushstroke, depends, for its cleverness and wit, upon the commentary it makes on the celebration of the brushstroke, as a mark of the agency and individuality of the artist, in the Abstract Expressionist painting current at the time. The wit of the piece requires that one see it as such a commentary, and also that one remark the complete *absence* of any evidence of brushstrokes in Lichtenstein's rendering of an Expressionist brushstroke. The brushstroke is represented in the extremely flat pseudo-pointilliste style employed by Lichtenstein in his large reproductions of frames from popular comic strips. One needs to bring a knowledge of the context of making of the piece to one's engagement with the canvas if one is to grasp fully the artistic statement articulated, and to do this one has to attend not only to *what* the painting represents but also to *how* it has been represented in the artistic medium.

More obviously, as noted in chapter 2, some of the differences remarked by Borges' narrator between Cervantes' *Quixote* and Menard's *Quixote* depend upon the art-historical contexts in which the two instances of the text were tokened. For example, both texts contain the following passage: "truth, mother of history, rival of time, depository of deeds, witness of the past, exemplar and adviser to the present, and the future's counsellor." But, whereas in Cervantes' text this is "mere rhetorical praise of history," in Menard's text it is much more significant:

History, the *mother* of truth: the idea is astounding. Menard, a contemporary of William James, does not define history as an inquiry into reality, but as its origin. Historical truth, for him, is not what has happened; it is what we judge to have happened. The final phrases – *exemplar and adviser to the present, and the future's counsellor* – are brazenly pragmatic. (1970: 69)

The inadequacy of empiricist accounts of the artistic statement articulated in a work can also be seen in our earlier discussion of Picasso's *Guernica* and Piero's *Baptism of Christ*. In both cases, it seems necessary to include at least some representational properties in the artistic statement that is part of the focus of appreciation of these works. But, in attending to a painting as a representation, our artistic interest is not merely in identifying the represented elements and the represented spatial relations between them. We seek to make some sense of these elements and relations, such that we feel we understand why the canvas represents *these* elements (rather than others) in *these* relations to one another (rather than others). This is crucial if we are to understand what might be termed the *thought content* of the representation, or what Roger Scruton (1983) terms the "thought embodied in perceptual form" about the subject of the painting. In the case of Picasso's *Guernica*, for example, a reception uninformed about the historical and artistic context of the painting may remark only a disordered assembly of crudely drawn figures, human and animal. Such a reception will yield neither a clear sense of the organization of the representational content of the picture, nor a sense of the thoughts expressed by the picture about its subject.

Similarly, as we noted, Piero's canvas, while a paragon of representational order, leaves the receiver puzzled about various features of the represented scene. Baxandall describes these features, which differentiate the picture from other representations of the baptism of Christ and which "demand explanation," as follows:

> One is the oddity, prominence and seeming separateness of the three Angels in the left foreground. A second is the shifting of the spectators, all but one man stripped for baptism, into the right background . . . A third is the change in the water around Christ's feet: in the background and middleground it is reflective but in the foreground it becomes transparent or, on some readings, dries up. (1985: 121)

Note that these puzzles, or close analogues of them, will arise even for a receiver who views the picture in ignorance of the identity of the portrayed figures or the significance of the event. Our interest in the painting as a representation will require that we make some kind of sense of these details of the pictorial order. Baxandall considers a number of "stories" that might be told, some of which explain the puzzling features of the representation in heavily symbolic terms, while others, like his own, explain these features in terms of Piero's idiom as a painter and various constraints imposed by the nature of the task set for him. While

Baxandall does not consider this option, we can also imagine a self-consciously highly anachronistic "story" that provides reasons for the pictorial order. What all of these explanations have in common is the assumption that the artistic statement articulated by Piero's painting can be specified only by referring manifest properties of the canvas to a history of making – whether historically accurate or not.

Put bluntly, an empiricist engagement with representational paintings would not be able to make sense of those paintings, or satisfy our artistic interest in those paintings, as representations. One response, here, is to hold that representational properties are relevant to appreciation of a painting only insofar as they contribute to its design. Indeed, this is the line that Clive Bell (1914) adopts in defending the idea that artistic value is purely a matter of significant form. But how the representational content contributes to the design depends upon what we take the marks on the canvas to represent – this is something that we noted in discussing the "symmetry" of the Piero painting. Thus Bell's strategy does not avoid the difficulty. An alternative response is to deny that representational properties have any part to play in the artistic statements articulated by the products of artistic activity. But it is very unlikely that this kind of strict formalist epistemology would be compatible with a rational reconstruction of our critical and appreciative practice.

The anti-empiricist claims that artistic appreciation must take detailed account of the history of making of a product of artistic activity. This is evident not only in respect of the artistic statement articulated, but also when we turn to the other elements that enter into the focus of appreciation – the vehicle and the artistic medium. In the first place, to correctly identify the vehicle, we need to identify the vehicular medium employed by the artist. This is not always apparent, even to an informed eye, from an experiential engagement with an instance of the product of the artist's activity. Our access to performances of musical works is usually mediated by recordings of those performances, but it may be impossible to determine, from listening to those recordings, whether the sounds were generated by human hands moving with dexterity over the keys or strings of standard instruments, or by a synthesizser (Dutton 1979). Even when we attend a live concert, it is often impossible to determine, without further research, how certain of the experienced sounds are produced, or how they are prescribed in the score from which the musicians are playing.

In film, increasing technical sophistication in computer graphic imaging has made it impossible to determine *merely by scrutinizing the projected image* how the representational content of the image has been generated. It is no longer, as in early science fiction films, by the *look* of monsters, aliens, and other impossible or unlikely elements in films that we determine them to be products of the ingenuity of designers and graphic artists. Rather, we infer from what we take to be the impossibility of filming what is imaged that the image must have been artificially generated – that is, we infer to a history of making. Such inferences are often supported by documentary footage telling us exactly *how* the trick was done – what manipulations of a vehicular medium generated the image which serves as the vehicle whereby the artistic statement of the film is articulated.

Consider, also, the many different techniques that are used in the production of animated films. A recent festival of animation included films containing one or more of the following techniques: 2D and 3D computer animation; claymation; sand; recyclomation; drawing on cels; cutouts; puppets; live action; ink, pencil, or gypsum on paper; pixilation; animated objects; paint on glass; engraving on film; and photography. One particular short animated film, less than 10 minutes in length, involves the following remarkable range of techniques: cut-outs, pixilation, 2D computer, animated objects, paint on paper, puppets, 3D computer, photocopies, photos, collage, mixed techniques, and internet software.[10] In such a case, it is to say the least unlikely that a receiver would be able to determine, by simply viewing the film, which vehicular media were employed and how they contributed to the resulting vehicle.

It is worth stressing that awareness of the vehicular medium is treated by artists and by critics as central to the appreciation of the works generated through the manipulation of that medium. One of the enduring themes in the work of the American artist Chuck Close, for example, is the different ways in which what is superficially the same representational image can be generated through distinct techniques involving the use of very different vehicular media. A receiver who looks at the images without taking account of the different vehicular media employed will see only repetition. Another example is the works of Richard Artschwager, who, having run his own furniture workshop, has chosen to create many of his sculptures from industrial materials used in making furniture – in particular, plywood, simulated wood formica, and Celotex, a coarsely textured compound made of pressed paper. Knowledge of the vehicular medium

10   The film in question is titled *(The Rise and Fall of the Legendary) Anglobilly Feverson*, edited by Rosto, and exhibited at the 2002 Festival at the Centre International du Cinéma d"Animation, at Annecy in France.

employed is even more crucial in the case of some of the Italian Arte Povera artists, in that properties of the vehicular medium directly affect the artistic statement articulated through the product of the artist's activity. Jannis Kounellis, for example, used materials such as iron, coal, coffee, beans, worn sacks, and live plants and animals for aesthetic effect in his works. One theme in these works is the relationship between nature and culture, which leads to the use of materials that pass from one realm to the other. And Piero Gilardi used synthetic materials – in particular polyurethane – to simulate the appearance and texture of such natural phenomena as riverbeds and leaves. Nor is this merely a feature of late modern art, and thus open to suspicion on Wolfean grounds. We already noted, earlier in this chapter, Clark's remarks about Turner's use of oil paints, and we may further remark that part of the artistic statement articulated by many Renaissance paintings depends upon the fact that, in painting certain parts of the canvas, the artist has used pigments that are both rare and very expensive. This also shows that to appreciate the way in which a vehicle has been used in the articulation of an artistic statement, we need to know something about the properties and history of the vehicular medium.

It is of course undeniable that information about the vehicular medium employed by an artist is usually available to receivers when they encounter a product of artistic activity in a gallery or a concert hall. The programme for a musical recital, or the notes that accompany a recording of a musical performance, usually inform the receiver about the instruments employed, or at least do so if there is anything unusual about those instruments. And the indexing of paintings and works of sculpture in galleries usually carries information about the materials employed. But this provides no succour to the empiricist, since this information is not available in an empiricist encounter with the product of the artist's activity. Such an encounter can take account only of the manifest properties of an instance of the work, and (presumably) of the title given to the work by the artist. Information about the vehicular medium employed by the artist is information about the history of making of the entity having those manifest properties, information not necessarily directly perceivable in that entity but supplied to receivers by the curators of the gallery, or the presenters of the concert, precisely because they feel that such information bears upon the appreciation of the work.

Second, even if the nature of the vehicular medium is apparent from informed attention to the product of the artist's activity, appreciation of the work may require knowledge of the resources available, in the art-historical context of generation, for the manipulation of that medium. Clark, in discussing how Turner was able to achieve certain representational effects in his depiction of the steamship in the *Snowstorm*, remarks on how Turner "drew from the recalcitrant medium of oil-paints these refinements and transparencies." In this comment, Clark not only alludes explicitly to certain properties of the vehicular medium that bear upon Turner's accomplishment in articulating a particular artistic statement by means of that medium, but also alludes implicitly to the lack of available techniques for achieving the sorts of effects sought by Turner in that medium. A similar example is furnished by Lucie-Smith's discussion of Morris Louis' experimental "staining" technique, which accounts for the distinctive manifest qualities of his canvases. Greenberg described this technique as follows: "Louis spills his paint on unsized and unprimed cotton duck canvas, leaving the pigment almost everywhere thin enough, no matter how many different veils of it are superimposed, for the eye to sense the threadedness and wovenness of the fabric underneath" (1960: 28). Lucie-Smith comments:

> In fact, Louis achieved his originality partly through the exploitation of a new material, acrylic paint, which gave his paintings a very different physical make-up from those of the abstract expressionists. The staining process meant a revulsion against shape, against light and dark, in favour of colour . . . One of the advantages of the staining technique, so far as Louis was concerned, was the fact that he was able to put colour into colour. His early paintings after the breakthrough are veils of shifting hue and tone: there is no feeling that the various colour configurations have been drawn with a brush. (1976: 106)

Interestingly, an artist may herself impose constraints on the vehicular medium in which she works, refusing to avail herself of various resources employed by others who share that vehicular medium, broadly construed. For example, Dogme 95, a collective of film directors founded in Copenhagen in 1995, formulated a "Vow of Chastity" requiring that participating film-makers eschew the use of certain available mechanisms, such as artificial light, props of certain kinds, and fixed cameras. While participants in Dogme 95 have expressed differently the motivations behind the adoption of this "Vow," two elements predominate. First, there is an ideological dissatisfaction with the move away from traditional skills and techniques of film-making, and toward the technological domination of the film-making process apparent in recent Hollywood cinema. But, second, there is also the sense that making films in accordance with the requirements of the "Vow" is a more challenging and interesting activity, and that it permits innovative use of traditional media to articulate novel artistic statements. If we acknowledge the two-foldness of artistic appreciation, our appreciation of, for example, the first official Dogme 95 film, Thomas Vinterberg's *Festen*, requires that we take account of how the artistic statement of the film has been articulated through manipulations performed in a more restricted vehicular medium. This necessitates that we refer the manifest work to the generative per-formance. If we did not do this, we might simply conclude that the illu-mination, mise-en-scène, or camera movement in certain scenes reflects incompetence. Once we take account of the self-imposed constraints under which Vinterberg is working, however, we both better assess the basic artistic statement articulated by the film and ascribe to the film meanings that derive from the deliberate choice to work under those con-straints. A similar analysis would apply to photographic images whose lack of sharpness stems from a deliberate decision on the part of the photog-rapher to work with longer exposure times, or to George Perec's novel *La Disparition* (1978), in which, by the choice of the author, the letter "e" is not used.

We may turn finally to the artistic medium in which an artist works in working a vehicular medium. Here we see most clearly the problems that confront an empiricist epistemology of art. As noted above, the most obvious component in the focus of appreciation for a particular work is the artistic statement articulated. But, as has been argued, an artist, in manipulating a vehicular medium, articulates a particular artistic statement only because these manipulations occur in the context of an artistic medium. It is only in virtue of the latter that the manipulations admit of a description in terms that can be correlated with particular "meanings" or "values" articulated. When we refer reflections upon a work's repre-sentational, expressive, or formal qualities to the product of artistic activ-ity in which those qualities are articulated, it is generally in terms of the artistic medium that we conceive that product. It is primarily in terms of brushstrokes, montage, contrasting of colors, and meaningful gestures that we talk about works, rather than in terms of arrays of paint, sequences of images, colored expanses, and bodily movements.[11]

---

11   This is not to say that reference to the vehicular medium is unimportant – indeed, as I have suggested above, it is a crucial element in the appreciation of works, and may play an important role in the articulation of an artistic statement, as in the Arte Povera exam-ples cited. But reference to the vehicular medium is usually significant insofar as it bears on how the artist has worked in a given artistic medium.

But to conceive a work as involving the articulation of an artistic statement in an artistic medium refers us beyond the manifest work to a performance issuing in it. For, as we have seen, an artistic medium is a set of presumed shared understandings upon which the artist draws in her attempt to articulate a particular artistic statement through manipulating a vehicular medium. An artistic medium, since it mediates between the observable properties of the vehicle and the artistic statement articulated through that vehicle, cannot, by its very nature, be manifest in the empiricist sense. It is, rather, that in virtue of which certain of the manifest properties of the vehicle count as artistic properties and contribute to the articulation of an artistic statement.

This can be seen if we return to the example with which I opened this chapter, Picasso's *Guernica*. In setting out that example, I offered two kinds of characterizations of the representational content of the picture. The first supposedly offers an empiricist account of the representational content of the picture insofar as the latter bears upon its artistic appreciation – the content ascribable by one who is ignorant of the canvas's history of making. The second characterization embodies the sort of knowledge that the empiricist proscribes. But even the representational content permitted by the empiricist bears upon the artistic statement articulated through the canvas only given assumptions about the artistic medium employed. Without those assumptions, we have only a vehicle upon which a particular representational design can be discerned. Suppose that the vehicle were not a painting but a guernica, in Walton's sense. In that case, it might plausibly be argued that the representational design of the vehicle was part of the vehicular medium itself, rather than part of the artistic statement articulated through the manipulation of the medium. All guernicas share that design, just as all oil paintings share the vehicular medium of oil paint. But guernicas need not have representational meaning in virtue of the design of their vehicles, any more than the artistic statements articulated by oil paintings generally have content purely in virtue of the fact that their vehicles employ oil paint.

It might be thought that this is merely to reiterate Walton's own argument for a *moderate* form of empiricism according to which artistic properties supervene on both manifest properties and category of art. But artistic media, while they in a sense subsume "categories of art" in Walton's sense, are broader and different in function, and cannot serve the purposes of moderate empiricism. A "category of art" is definable in terms of a distinction between properties that are standard, properties that are contra-standard, and properties that are variable. That having the representational design of Picasso's *Guernica* is standard for a guernica but variable for a painting is offered in explanation of the fact that the canvas produced by Picasso would be ascribed very different artistic properties if categorized as the former rather than as the latter. As Walton puts it, while we take Picasso's painting to be "violent dynamic, vital, disturbing," it would strike those who took it to be a guernica as "cold, stark, lifeless, or serene and restful, or perhaps bland, dull, boring" (1970: 347).

But an artistic medium performs a more basic function in making artistic properties, and the articulation of artistic statements, possible. Furthermore, while Walton's "categories of art" are intended to allow only limited information about history of making to enter into the appreciation of works – information about the category of art to which an art-object belongs – the mediatory role of artistic media allows no such empiricist segregation of admissible aspects of a history of making. Rather, as we have seen, the shared understandings that make up an artistic medium serve primarily to link manipulations of a vehicular medium *occurring in a particular art-historical context* with the artistic statements articulated by such manipulations in that context. This was one of the lessons to be drawn from reflection upon Danto's red rectangles.

A clearer recognition of the role of artistic media in the creation and appreciation of works allows us to make better sense of the claim, noted in chapter 2, that even ascriptions of what seem to be purely *formal* properties to works – for example, reference to the "firm design" of a picture – refer the manifest work to a history of making. More generally, we can now endorse, at least for those properties that enter into the artistic statement articulated in a work, the strong counter-empiricist claim that all ascriptions to artworks of properties that bear upon their artistic appreciation are in principle defeasible on the basis of non-categoreal facts about the provenance of the manifest work – in other words, that none of the properties of works that bear on their appreciation are "aesthetic properties" in the traditional sense. For, so it has been argued, one cannot determine any of the elements that feature in the artistic statement articulated by a vehicle by simply inspecting that vehicle. What artistic statement is articulated through those manipulations depends upon the artistic medium operative in such manipulations, and this, in turn, depends upon facts about the history of making of the vehicle not manifest to the receiver. Thus any claim about the artistic statement articulated in a work is in principle defeasible on the basis of information about provenance, which may lead us to revise our beliefs concerning the artistic medium operative in the manipulations of the vehicular medium. So the strong counter-empiricist thesis is true, at least for those sorts of properties traditionally taken by the empiricist to be the artistic properties of a work.

3.3 Ontology After Empiricism

In the first two sections of this chapter I have developed in a more systematic way the standard arguments for the weak counter-empiricist thesis, and, in so doing, have suggested how we might defend the strong counter-empiricist thesis. The latter, if correct, undermines the sort of strategy canvassed at the end of chapter 2 whereby one might acknowledge the inadequacies of empiricist epistemology of art but seek to preserve a pure structuralist ontology. This strategy, it will be recalled, maintains that those artistic properties which depend in some way upon a structure's context of instantiation are *relativized* properties. Wolterstorff proposes that we accommodate the fact that a given musical structure is Liszt-influenced as a composition by Brahms, but could not be Liszt-influenced as a composition by Beethoven, by ascribing to one and the same structure the relativized properties *being-Liszt-influenced-as-generated-by-Brahms* and *not-being-Liszt-influenced-as-generated-by-Beethoven*. The idea is that the work can then be identified with the structure without contradiction, thereby defusing the anti-structuralist implications of the anti-empiricist arguments.

If, however, we uphold the strong anti-empiricist thesis as argued above, then *all* aspects of the artistic statement articulated in a work will depend upon contextual and other features of the artistic activity generative of the artistic vehicle – all ascriptions of such artistic properties are defeasible in the light of information about provenance. Thus the structuralist who adopts something like Wolterstorff's strategy must hold that *all* such artistic properties of a work are relativized in the appropriate sense. If we follow this course, however, then we will have to ascribe, to a single work identified with a given structure, discrete internally coherent sets of artistic properties for each instantiation of that structure. In the case of the work identified with the sound-structure of Brahms' Piano Sonata op. 2, for example, there will be one set of properties each of which is relativized to the instantiation by Brahms and another set each of which is relativized to the instantiation by Beethoven. There can be no shared properties between these two sets because of their relativized nature, nor, if the strong anti-empiricist thesis is correct, can there be any unrelativized artistic properties pertaining to the artistic statement articulated in the work. Furthermore, these sets of artistic properties will fund quite distinct conceptions of the "work" in question – conceptions that need have no point of intersection whatsoever save for their being correlated with the same structure. It can then be urged against the structuralist that it makes more sense of our appreciative practice, in such a case, to take each set, unified by the common reference of its members to a given generation of a structure, as pertaining to a distinct *work*, rather than to hold that all of these sets of artistic properties are properties of a *single* work.

This point can be made in a slightly different way. In response to Wolterstorff's suggestion, which requires that we take works to be decontextualized objects or structures, we can ask whether these putative decontextualized entities are properly characterized in terms of predicates drawn from the vocabulary in which we describe the vehicular medium, or in terms of predicates drawn from the vocabulary in which we describe the artistic medium. As we have already seen, the artistic medium can vary across contexts of generative artistic activity without there being any corresponding variation in the manifest properties of the artistic vehicle. So, if Wolterstorff's strategy is to provide a generalizable answer to the epistemological argument against structuralism, then it seems he must identify the work with an entity characterizable in terms of the vocabulary in which we describe the vehicular medium. But, as already noted, our ordinary talk of works standardly employs the idiom of artistic media, and therefore prima facie validates the individuation of works by reference to features describable in that idiom. Thus we can bring the pragmatic constraint to bear against Wolterstorff without having to appeal, as do Currie and Levinson, to counterfactual critical judgments.

There is a second consideration that emerges from our analysis of the structure of the focus of appreciation. As was noted in the preceding section, the elements that enter into the focus of appreciation stand in very complex relationships to one another and to provenance, through the mediating role of the artistic medium whereby an artistic statement is articulated through the manipulation of a vehicular medium. If our attempts at appreciating a given work are to have a *coherent* focus, then it seems necessary that we tell a single story about the provenance of the different elements constitutive of that focus. We are unlikely to prosper in our critical and appreciative endeavors if we sunder our conception of how the vehicular medium was manipulated from our conception of the artistic medium operative in those manipulations, for example. But this again suggests that our critical and appreciative engagement with a structure as an artwork will be inextricably tied to our locating that structure in a particular art-historical context. To try to abstract the work from that context, so that we are to imagine *one and the same work* existing when an instance of the same structure-type is instantiated in a very different art-historical context, seems to do serious violence to the conception of a work that guides us in our appreciative endeavors.[12]

I shall therefore assume that we have good reason to reject not only empiricist epistemology but also the structuralism that is its natural ontological corollary. A manifest work's history of making, we may conclude, is in some way constitutive of the artwork we appreciate through our engagement with that manifest work. What kind of entity, then, should we take artworks to be? The answer to this question favored by almost all those who reject structuralism is best expressed in terms of two claims. First, structuralism is flawed even for most empiricists because, as noted in the final section of chapter 2, most empiricists and non-empiricists will insist that the question, "What is the ontological status of the artwork?" is fundamentally misconceived. It is misconceived because it assumes, wrongly, that there is a *single* ontological category to which works in the different arts belong. In repudiating this assumption, philosophers have appealed to salient differences in our treatment of works in the various arts to sustain an orthodoxy of ontological pluralism. In Wollheim's influential defence of such a pluralism, for example, paintings and sculptures and works of architecture are taken to be physical objects, while novels, poems, and musical works are structure-types. A more radically pluralist ontology is defended by Goodman, who maintains that

> in the different arts a work is differently localised. In painting, the work is an individual object; and in etching a class of objects. In music the work is a class of performances compliant with a character [that is, a score]. In

12   This also permits a response to "consumer-based" models of appreciation which maintain that a critical or appreciative appropriation of a work is to be measured not against any constraints stemming from provenance, but against the satisfactions yielded to the receiver by so taking the work. This view has a certain plausibility as long as we restrict the focus of appreciation to some "artistic statement" a work can be taken to articulate. For we can certainly imagine numerous such statements that *might* be made by a given vehicle. We can invoke a Foucaultian "author function" in offering a reading of a work without troubling ourselves as to the actual provenance of the text. Once we take account of the more intricate structure of the focus of appreciation in our engagement with something as an artwork, however, and once we recognize the rich complexity of the relations between aspects of that structure and a history of making (whether actual or invented), it becomes more difficult to motivate the activity of *fabricating* a history of making as a way of finding appreciable qualities in a work.

literature, the work is the character itself. And in calligraphy, we may add, the work is an individual inscription. (1976: 210)

Second, those authors who are persuaded that provenance is partly constitutive of works maintain that a work is to be identified with a *contextualized* object, structure-type, or instance of a structure-type, that is, such an entity *as having a particular provenance*. Perhaps the best-known ontology of this type is Levinson's characterization of musical works as "indicated structures," that is, as structures of sounds to be performed on specific instruments *as "indicated"* by a given individual at a given time, or perhaps as indicated in a given art-historical context, or some combination of the two (Levinson 1980: esp. 78ff). As Levinson makes clear in a later paper, the rather obscure notion of "indication" is to be understood along the lines of Nicholas Wolterstorff's notion of a "norm-kind" (Wolterstorff 1975, 1980). To "indicate" a sound/performance-means structure is to "[lay] some features down as required in order for a properly formed performance . . . to have occurred" (Levinson 1990a: 260). Others have provided variations on this ontological theme. Danto, for example, characterizes works in the visual arts as something like objects under an interpretation, where the relevant interpretation is given by features of provenance. Binkley seems to think of works in the "visual" arts as pieces intensionally specified through the manipulation of a physical medium. And Margolis maintains that works are culturally emergent but physically embodied entities.

Given our conclusions thus far concerning the manner in which generative performances enter into the appreciation of artworks, it seems natural to offer an epistemological argument in defence of a "contextualist" ontology of this sort – that is, an ontology which holds that works are to be identified with *contextualized* objects or structures, rather than with objects and structures per se. Such an argument might run as follows:

1 To appreciate a work is to appreciate a focus of appreciation, in the sense defined above, specified by the artist.
2 We can only grasp such a focus if we refer the "manifest work" to the performance whereby a focus was specified via that manifest work. For, as has just been argued, many if not all of the properties of the focus that bear upon the appreciation of the work are properties of an *indicated* structure, or an object with a particular history of making, not properties of a structure or object per se.

3 Given the pragmatic constraint, we should identify works with the focuses specified through appropriate generative performances, where such focuses can be characterized as "indicated structures," "pieces specified within artistic indexing conventions," etc.

On any such view, a performance generative of an object or structure that instantiates an artwork bears upon the appreciation of that work because it determines central features of the focus of appreciation specified through that performance. We might ask, however, whether this is sufficient to account for the role of performance in the appreciation of works, or whether there are features of the generative performance that bear on the appreciation of the *work*, but whose so bearing is not captured by an account of how that performance affects the properties constitutive of the *focus* of the work. In the following chapter, I shall argue that there are indeed such features. And, if so, this suggests that we cannot adequately account for the role of provenance in the constitution of works by taking the work to be a vehicle with a history of making in anything like Levinson's sense. Rather, we must entertain seriously the idea that the artwork is the focus-specifying performance, in some sense, rather than the specified focus.

In chapter 5 I shall offer a further argument in favor of identifying artworks with performances. The task in the following chapters will be to explore how such a conception of artworks might be developed and defended against various objections. In chapter 8, I return to the issues with which we began, and argue that the identification of artworks with generative performances provides us with the most promising framework for accommodating late modern art within a comprehensive philosophical theory of art. I also argue that contextualism is an unstable option, which, once we try to clarify its ontological theses, either collapses back into a non-contextualist position such as structuralism, or collapses "forward" into something like the view that I defend. For this reason, we should not be tempted by the prospect of revising contextualism to accommodate the sorts of considerations brought in support of what I shall term the "performance theory." Finally, in chapters 9 and 10, I further elaborate upon the broader philosophical framework for thinking about the arts that fits naturally with the performance theory. First, I develop a comprehensive theory of artistic performance which analyzes the different ways in which performance, in a more conventional sense, enters into the being and being appreciated of works. Second, I examine the ways in which artworks can be distinguished from other performances of the same generic kind. Finally, I defend an axiology of art that does justice to the ontology and epistemology of art defended in this book. As may be apparent from this outline, the case for the performance theory will be a cumulative one, and I ask readers to suspend judgment until it is clear what such a theory can offer us in our attempts to comprehend the complexity and diversity of our commerce with artworks both traditional and modern.

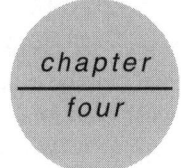

The Artwork as Performance: An Argument from Artistic Intentions

4.1 Overview

In this chapter, I begin to develop the ontological view to be elaborated and defended in the rest of this book. According to what I shall term the "performance" theory, artworks are performances. More specifically, they belong to the class of performances whereby a content is articulated through a vehicle on the basis of shared understandings. In chapter 3, in analyzing the focus of appreciation, I spoke of the articulation of an *artistic* statement by one who works in an *artistic* medium when working a vehicular medium. However, in talking of "artistic" statements and media, I relied on examples drawn from the different arts to clarify what I had in mind. To the extent that the performance theory is offered as an ontology of art rather than a definition of art, we may talk in the more general terms employed above, and leave the interpretation of the term "artistic" open, restricting ourselves in this way to examples of what would count as "artistic statements" and "artistic media" without specifying that in virtue of which these things are "artistic." I shall continue to talk in this way in the following chapters, where convenient. In the final chapter, however, I shall offer some suggestions as to how we might remedy this lacuna, and thereby develop a principled distinction between artworks and those performances belonging to the broader class specified above that are not artworks.

In chapter 3, I argued that, insofar as, in our critical and appreciative engagement with an artwork, we take account of the product of a generative act on the part of one or more individuals – a "focus of appreciation" in the sense defined – this product incorporates not only an artistic statement articulated through such a generative act, but also the manner in which that statement was articulated by drawing on shared understandings (an "artistic medium") as to what is done through acting upon, or manipulating, some material (the "vehicular medium"). To grasp the focus of appreciation for a given work, I further argued, requires that one identify relevant features of the art-historical context in which the making of a "manifest work" occurred. However, as I suggested at the end of the chapter, the bearing of a history of making on the appreciation of a work may not be exhausted by its contribution to the focus of appreciation thereby specified. In this chapter, I shall attempt to give substance to this claim. I shall begin by offering a couple of brief arguments that pick up directly on the discussion of the focus of appreciation in chapter 3. I shall then develop at considerably greater length an independent argument of the same general nature. Taken together, these arguments provide preliminary support for the view that the work itself, as the unit of criticism and appreciation, is to be identified not with a specified focus, but with a performance whereby a particular focus is specified – that is, preliminary support for the performance theory.

4.2 The Bearing of Provenance on Work and Focus

Consider, again, the bearing upon artistic appreciation of current debates about whether Renaissance and Baroque artists used various kinds of instruments to achieve certain representational effects in their paintings. Such debates bear neither upon *what* artistic statement was articulated, nor upon *how* the artistic and vehicular mediums enabled such an artistic statement to be articulated. They bear, rather, on *how the artist was able to use the vehicular medium* in order to produce a vehicle capable of articulating such an artistic statement, given the artistic medium. Thus our legitimate appreciative interest in the vehicle through which an artistic statement is articulated seems to encompass manipulations of the vehicular medium that confer properties on the resulting vehicle only in the trivial sense that the product of any process has the relational property of having been produced by that process.

If one is tempted to say that these sorts of details of the generative performance are not relevant to the *artistic* appreciation of the resultant works, one must either explain how this differs from the sort of interest cited by Clark in the "recalcitrant" properties of oil paint, or by Lucie-Smith in the technological basis for the "staining" techniques used by Morris Louis, or argue that the latter are equally irrelevant to artistic appreciation. The challenge, in other words, is to show how we can draw any kind of principled line once we accept that the focus of appreciation is to be construed in the manner proposed. Once we take the *properties* of the vehicle to be relevant, why shouldn't we also take the manner in which those properties were exploited by the artist to be relevant? For example, if it is relevant to know that oil paint is a recalcitrant medium, why wouldn't it be relevant to know of some particular technique used by Turner to overcome the recalcitrance of the medium?

A proponent of the view that works are contextualized entities might argue that she can accommodate the epistemological role of such aspects of provenance by holding them to be legitimate *relational* properties of the "focus of appreciation," in that they are directly involved in the generation of the properties actually possessed by the vehicle. Indeed, it might be said that the use of the camera obscura to produce an image in representational painting is analogous to the use of the different kinds of techniques noted earlier in the production of the images that make up an animated film. The camera obscura then is one of the things that enters directly into the manipulations of the vehicular medium through which the vehicle is produced.

Such a strategy is less plausible, however, if we inquire as to the relevance, for our appreciation of a work, of the various *preparatory* explorations that the artist went through. Recall Clark's claims about Turner's use of color to depict light in the *Snowstorm*. Clark continues: "To substitute colour for tone as a means of observing enlightened space could not be achieved by mere observation: it was a major feat of pictorial intelligence and involved Turner in a long struggle," a struggle involving what Clark describes as years of "experiments."[1] Note that it is precisely in virtue of the fact that Turner was able to do what he did only after such experiments that it constituted "a major feat of pictorial intelligence." But this fact is not reflected in the "focus of appreciation" as specified by Turner, nor is it a feature of the particular manipulations of the vehicular medium that produced the vehicle that hangs in the National Gallery in London. It pertains rather to what preceded those manipulations: Turner's achievement in finding novel ways of employing the vehicular

---

1   Clark 1960: 146. Once again, one might also consider Lucie-Smith's discussion of Morris Louis – see his 1976: 104ff.

medium of oil paint as an artistic medium in order to articulate a particular artistic statement.

Once we grant that our interest in these features of the generative performance enter legitimately into the artistic appreciation of Turner's painting, however, it seems that a parallel case can be made for the relevance of other manipulations of the vehicular medium, in the process of specifying a focus of appreciation, that do not leave any lasting mark on that focus – most obviously, sketches, drafts, revisions, etc. which don't appear in the final version of an artistic vehicle. Such activities on the part of the artist(s) are not directly generative of the final vehicle, nor do they affect in any way the artistic statement articulated through that vehicle, but they do bear on the use of *that* vehicle to articulate *that* artistic statement. A good example of this is the inclusion, in a recent exhibition of Picasso's erotic works, of a series of sketches preparatory to the painting *Les Demoiselles d'Avignon*. One might, of course, think of these sketches as appreciable works in their own right, but one can also see them as bearing directly on the appreciation of the painting itself, especially because they reveal quite dramatic changes in Picasso's conception of the organization of pictorial space in that highly original painting.

Finally, some of the properties cited by Levinson in his arguments against structuralism seem to be properties of a performance that specifies a focus of appreciation, rather than properties of the focus so specified. Consider, for example, the property of being "Liszt-influenced" ascribable to Brahms' Piano Sonata op. 2. There seem to be two elements involved in such a property. First, there must be some aspect of the focus of appreciation of Brahms' work that resembles a characteristic feature of the focuses of appreciation specified by Liszt. This, presumably, can be a property which a work possesses independently of its provenance. The best term for this might be "Liszt-like," or something like that. But, in order to be Liszt-influenced, the Liszt-like property must have resulted from a particular kind of intentionally guided process. It is because the generative performance stands in a particular historical relation to the work of Liszt that Brahms' work can be described as Liszt-influenced, given the Liszt-like features of its focus.

It is precisely this fact that has led critics of Levinson to argue that such "influence" properties are properties of the generative performance – the *specifying* of the focus – *rather than* being properties of the work – the *specified focus* – and that, as a consequence, such properties cannot enter legitimately into the artistic appreciation of the work. An alternative response to this line of reasoning, however, is to grant that influence properties are properties of specifying performances, but deny that they are therefore irrelevant to the artistic appreciation of works. Rather, to the extent that our interest in something as an artwork is always an interest in the specifying of a focus of appreciation, the influence properties are genuine properties of the work.

4.3 Artistic Intentions and the Ontology of Art

4.3.1 Interpretation and intention

In their much-cited paper on the so-called "intentional fallacy," Wimsatt and Beardsley (1946) bring two charges against those who would ascribe an essential role to the intentions of the artist in the understanding and appreciation of her works. Knowledge of what the artist intended is said to be irrelevant, first, to the *evaluation* of her work, and, second, to the *interpretation* of her work. The irrelevance of artistic intentions to the evaluation of works is defended on the grounds that, in evaluating a work, we are interested in assessing what the artist *achieved*, not what she attempted to achieve. Critics have generally granted this point, and debate has turned upon whether a proper interpretation of what the artist achieved requires attention to what the artist intended. Further, given a general consensus that what the artist achieved is the product of her activity, the issue has turned upon whether what the artist produced, qua *work*, is properly viewed as (1) a structure or physical object whose meaning is given by public conventions or institutionalized norms of interpretation, or (2) a structure as tokened, or a physical object as generated, on a particular occasion, where the meaning-properties of the structure or object, qua work, depend in part upon the circumstances of the tokening or generation in question.[2] If we confine our attention to literary works, we have the following two positions:

1 Literary works are "pieces of language" whose meanings are given by syntactic and semantic conventions, by more specific artistic and generic conventions, and by generally shared cultural knowledge . If so, then the artist's intentions concerning at least the basic meaning-properties of her work – such properties as literal meaning (of a text), representational content (of a painting), and fictional truth (in a narrative) – have no bearing upon what those meaning-properties are. We can term this a strict conventionalist theory of such meaning-properties.

2   See, for example, the papers collected in Iseminger 1992a.

2 Literary works are analogous to linguistic *utterances*, where "what is said" depends upon how language is being used on a given occasion. The artist's intentions are therefore at least partly determinative of the basic meaning-properties of works – "partly" because, as we shall see shortly, "actual intentionalism" (AI), which holds that artistic intentions do indeed play such a role in determining artistic meanings, may allow that such meanings are also constrained by the semantic and syntactic conventions of the linguistic medium employed.

To assess the plausibility of AI, consider the account that Iseminger (1992b) develops on the basis of the work of E. D. Hirsch (1967). On this account, which we may term "sophisticated AI," the meaning-properties of works are determined by two things. First, linguistic and artistic conventions establish a range of possible meanings for a text. Second, the actual author's actual intentions serve to "activate" one of these possible meanings. Because of the first constraint, the sophisticated AI account is not the "Humpty-Dumpty" view[3] which holds that intending to mean that p by an utterance of some sentence S is sufficient to make that utterance of S mean that p. But a basic failing in the Humpty-Dumpty view – that it cannot allow for a speaker to *fail* to say what she intends to say in uttering a sentence – applies in a more restricted way to sophisticated AI. For the latter cannot allow for the following possibility: even when a meaning-property that a speaker intends her utterance of a sentence S to possess is among the meanings of S permitted by the relevant linguistic conventions, the speaker's utterance of S may fail to possess that meaning-property. However, so I shall argue, there are circumstances in which this possibility would be realized, so the sophisticated AI thesis must be mistaken.

Given the subsequent argument, it will be convenient to focus on what may be termed an author's "narrative intentions" – what, as composer of a narrative, she intends to be true in that narrative. Currie (1990) talks here of the author's intentions concerning "story meaning." The following example[4] illustrates how an author may fail to realize her narrative intentions, even though the intended story meaning falls within the range consistent with her text. Consider an author, Smith, who generates a particular text T under a given set of circumstances. In T, various happenings are narrated concerning a number of characters, the upshot of which

3 So named by Alfred MacKay 1968, in honour of the Lewis Carroll character who famously opined that "when *I* use a word, it means just what I choose it to mean."
4 For a similar example put to different use, see my 1996.

is that the central character – call him Stanley – is reduced to a very unhappy state as a result of various choices that he has made in his relationships with others. Suppose that Smith's earlier novels express a general view about what motivates human behavior in interpersonal relationships – that what characteristically motivates individuals in such situations is a fear of emotional commitment. Suppose, further, that Smith intends that it be true in the story N told in T that Stanley's misfortune arises from actions so motivated.

However, a competent reader might be unable to reconcile this explanation of Stanley's actions with what is explicitly narrated in the text, not because such an explanation is incompatible with anything explicit in the text taken by itself, but because such an ascription of motives would violate the norms that standardly govern the ascription of intentional states to cognitive agents. These norms, applied to Smith's novel, would lead one to conclude that Stanley is motivated by (say) self-centered ambition. Such norms *may* be overridden by a competent reader in certain circumstances, if it is reasonable to assume that the world of the story is one in which standard principles of intentional ascription do not apply. We may take the author to be deliberately exploring alternative models of agency, or to belong to a culture that does not share our model of intentional ascription and explanation.[5] Let us stipulate, however, that no such reason for overriding standard norms of intentional ascription obtains in the case under consideration. In that case, I think a competent reader would and should conclude that what is true in the story is that Stanley's actions are motivated *not* by a fear of emotional commitment but by self-centered ambition. Smith therefore fails to realisze her narrative intentions.

If these are the right conclusions to draw in the circumstances, then sophisticated AI fails as an account of how the narrative properties of a text are determined. It is not sufficient, for a work to have a narrative property Pn, that the author intend it to have that property and that Pn fall within the range of narrative properties permitted by the linguistic and narrative conventions applicable to the text. While there may be some relevant disanalogy to block such an extension, it seems prima facie that the failure of a sophisticated AI theory of *narrative* properties calls into ques-

---

5   For an example of an author who shares our norms of intentional ascription but who deliberately presents a world in which some of those norms do not obtain, consider Russell Hoban's *Riddley Walker*, where certain emotional responses to death of kin do not seem to obtain. For an example of cultural differences in norms of intentional ascription, consider the behavioral implications of dishonour in Japanese literature and film.

tion the tenability of a sophisticated AI theory of meaning-properties more narrowly construed.[6] However, the general argument to be developed below would survive a demonstration that the foregoing analysis of the determination of narrative properties *cannot* be extended to meaning-properties in a narrower sense.

We have uncovered reasons to doubt whether an author's semantic intentions can play the role assigned to them by sophisticated AI in determining at least some of the meaning-properties rightly ascribable to her text, and to hold, rather, that what plays that role is "uptake" in some sense – how the text would be interpreted by appropriate members of the target audience. Philosophers who are unsympathetic to AI have usually endorsed a particular gloss on this claim. What has been termed "hypothetical intentionalism" (HI), as defended in different forms by Levinson (1992c), Currie (1995: ch. 8), and Nathan (1992), holds, with AI, that one can grasp the meaning of a literary work only by referring its text to the activity of an agent who has produced the text in a given context in order to realize certain aesthetic and artistic goals. HI also holds that a proper grasp of the meaning of a literary work requires that the text be referred to intentional activity that resembles in specific respects the manner in which the actual author generated the text. On the other hand, HI holds, against AI, that work-meaning is determined not by the intentions that the actual author actually had, but by the semantic intentions that a suitably competent and knowledgeable reader would *ascribe* to an author. While determining the meaning-properties of a literary text requires that we consider a particular utterance of a text, rather than the text by itself, work-meaning, according to HI, is to be identified with an "utterance-meaning" that is not determined by "utterer's meaning."[7] Work-meaning, as a kind of utterance-meaning, is taken by HI to involve the *ascription* of semantic intentions to authors.

The actual intentions of the actual author do play *some* legitimate role in determining the meaning-properties of a work, on at least some versions of HI. For example, Levinson thinks that it is such intentions that determine the artistic *category* to which a given work belongs.[8] As we noted in chapter 2, assigning a work to a particular category may affect the artistic statement articulated through the vehicle of the work, and thus

---

6 There is obviously much more to be said on this issue. See my forthcoming (a) for a more detailed critical assessment of sophisticated AI.

7 See Tolhurst 1979 and Levinson 1992c for this distinction.

8 Levinson 1992c: 232–3. Categorial properties of works, here, might include being fictional, in the case of literary works, or employing standard "perspectival" means of representing spatial arrays of objects, in the case of painting.

the meaning-properties rightly ascribed to it. Thus the actual author's actual categorial intentions can indirectly determine the meaning-properties of the work. HI theorists insist, however, that the actual author's actual *semantic* intentions can play no such determining role.

Iseminger (1996) identifies two distinct versions of HI. On the first of these, the meaning-properties of a literary work are those that a suitably informed reader would ascribe, as intended, to "an idealized, hypothetical author, an author who can be held responsible for everything in the text, being aware of all relevant features of context, conventions, and background assumptions, an author for whom we may imagine that everything is there by design, on purpose" (Nathan 1992: 199). On the second view, the meaning-properties are those that a suitably informed reader would ascribe, as intended, to the actual author, given the evidence such a reader would possess precisely in virtue of being "suitably informed." In this case, meaning depends on the ascription of hypothetical intentions to the actual author, whereas in the former case, we are ascribing intentions to a hypothetical author.

The argument presented above against AI, however, also challenges the "hypothetical intentions of the actual author" version of HI. If, as seems plausible, being "suitably informed" requires knowledge of an author's other works, then HI, so construed, may entail that Smith *realizes* her narrative intentions in respect of the story N told in T as long as those intentions are recognizable by the competent reader. But the reasoning presented against AI supports the conclusion that Smith does not realize her narrative intentions in such circumstances. This brand of HI cannot, it seems, account for cases where the receiver, in ascribing certain semantic intentions to the artist, will also take the artist to have failed to realize those intentions in virtue of failing to articulate what she intended to articulate (see further Dickie and Wilson 1995; Stecker 2003: ch. 2; Davies forthcoming (a)). The "Smith" example *can* be accounted for by "hypothetical author" versions of HI, where what is true in Smith's story is what an ideally competent author composing the text T in these circumstances – an author aware, inter alia, of the norms standardly governing intentional ascription – would intend to be true in the story. But it faces difficulties of its own. As Stecker (2003: ch. 2) points out, it seems to have no plausible story to tell about scenarios where the artistic vehicle is semantically or syntactically defective.

If HI is indeed flawed, the right response is not, as some propose, to add epicycles to actual intentionalism, for the latter cannot account for the role of "uptake" in interpretation. Rather we should question the assumption that an "uptake" account of work-meaning, or more generally of utterance-meaning, must identify the latter with ascribed semantic intentions of some kind. This assumption is grounded in a criticism of conventionalist accounts of utterance-meaning: only if we take a vehicle to be employed to realize the semantic intentions of an utterer can we bring our knowledge of conventions and context, and our more general interpretive skills, to bear upon it in a coherent manner. Given this criticism, it is natural to conclude that receivers are in the business of ascribing semantic intentions. But all that actually follows is that receivers only ascribe utterance-meaning to that which they regard as the product of an intentional act of utterance. This allows for an alternative formulation of the "uptake" view that identifies utterance-meaning not with ascribed semantic intentions of any kind, but with the meaning that a properly informed receiver, correctly applying the appropriate interpretive norms, would ascribe to a vehicle taken to be intentionally used to make a given kind of utterance. "Interpretive norms," here, may include linguistic and generic conventions, and more general heuristic principles. Let me term this kind of "uptake" theory "interpretive intentionalism" (II). II acknowledges that interpretive norms exist first and foremost to enable utterers to realize their semantic intentions. In the absence of such norms, an author could not expect her meaning to be grasped. But it is built into the understanding of interpretive norms that the meaning yielded by their correct application to a work-focus may not correspond to the author's intended meaning, and that this may be apparent to the interpreter. The interpreter ascribes meaning to a work-focus by bringing the appropriate norms to bear on what she takes to be an intentional use of a vehicle. But the criterion for correctness in ascription of work-meaning is conformity with the norms, not compliance with actual or hypothetical semantic intentions.

4.3.2 A role for actual intentions

I defend a version of II at greater length elsewhere (forthcoming (a), forthcoming (b)). In the present context, I shall simply assume, given the more general argument offered for an "uptake" account of at least some meaning-properties, that such an account will be a form of II rather than a form of HI. This will permit us to explore the implications of *accepting* such an account of certain meaning-properties of works. More specifically, I want to ask whether, if the actual intentions of the actual author with respect to certain kinds of meaning-properties of her work do *not* determine those properties of the work, these intentions have any role to play in the proper appreciation or evaluation of the work.

Given the general consensus that the proper object of critical evaluation is what the artist *achieved* rather than what was attempted, and that what the artist achieved is the product of the artist's creative activity, an "uptake" construal of a particular meaning property seems to entail that the actual semantic intentions of the actual artist in respect of that property have no bearing on the *evaluation* of her work. An argument to this effect might run as follows:

P1   The proper object of critical evaluation of a work is what the author achieves, not what she tries to achieve. (Assumption)

P2   What the author achieves is the product of her creative activities – what we may term the "work-product." (Assumption)

P3   The proper object of critical evaluation of a work is the work-product. (From P1 and P2, transitivity of identity)

P4   If the proper object of critical evaluation of a work is the work-product, then the author's actual semantic intentions can affect the critical evaluation of her work only by determining meaning-properties of the work-product. (Assumption)

P5   The author's actual semantic intentions can affect the critical evaluation of her work only by determining meaning-properties of the work-product. (P3, P4, modus ponens)

P6   For any type of meaning-property P for which an "uptake" analysis is correct, actual authorial semantic intentions with respect to P do *not* determine the P-type meaning-properties of the work-product. (Definition of "uptake")

C   For any type of meaning-property P for which an "uptake" analysis is correct, actual authorial semantic intentions with respect to P are irrelevant to the critical evaluation of works. (P5, P6)

"Work-product" here corresponds roughly to focus of appreciation in our sense. The foregoing argument is silent as to the structure of the work-product, but we may take it that what is at issue is the artistic statement articulated in a work. Other elements in the focus of appreciation enter into the argument only insofar as they can be thought to play a role in determining the artistic statement articulated in a work.

What I shall argue in the following pages is that the conclusion of the foregoing argument is incorrect. Even if we grant that certain kinds of meaning-properties of works are determined by "uptake" rather than by the actual author's actual semantic intentions in respect of such meaning-properties, a difference in such intentions, where all other relevant features of provenance are held constant, can affect the appreciation of a work. This, I shall further suggest, bears crucially on our conception of what artworks *are*, ontologically speaking. Certain recognizable differences in the artistic properties ascribable to works, when combined with an "uptake" theory of certain features of work-meaning, support the view that works themselves are more akin to processes than to their products – more akin to the tokenings or indicatings of structure-types, in the case of literary works, than to the structures so tokened or indicated taken by themselves. This suggests that we must distinguish not merely, as many commentators have rightly insisted,[9] between works and decontextualized structures ("works and texts," as this distinction gets drawn in the case of literary artworks), but also between works and the contextualized structures with which some writers propose to identify works.

Let me make one further clarificatory remark. The standard response to either conventionalism or an "uptake" theory, on the part of those who think that the actual semantic intentions of the artist have a part to play in the appreciation of her works, is to point to certain meaning-properties of the work-product that are claimed to depend upon such actual intentions. For example, it has been argued that such intentions determine the primary meaning-properties of works (Knapp and Michael 1992), or the "secondary" or implied meaning-properties of works (Ziff 1972; Juhl 1980), or specific illocutionary or perlocutionary properties of works, such as irony, allusiveness, or authorial assertion in propria persona (Carroll 1992; Hermeren 1992). These claims are not my present concern, however, since any such defense of AI establishes only that some of the meaning-properties of the product of the artist's activity – some aspects of the artistic statement articulated – are determined by the actual semantic intentions of the actual author. No obvious *ontological* implications attend such an intentionalist conclusion. My concern, rather, is the import of actual semantic intentions in contexts where, given an "uptake" theory, these intentions do not play a role in fixing the relevant meaning-properties of the work-product. To the extent that such actual intentions *do*, nevertheless, play a role in determining artistic properties of *the work*, we can, I shall suggest, draw certain conclusions as to the kind of thing that the work itself must be.

To clarify our intuitions, it will be helpful to have a range of closely related examples before us. We may begin by contrasting the "Smith" example with the case of Jones. Imagine that Smith doesn't author the text T, but that an identical text is authored in the same general cultural context by Jones, none of whose earlier works express the general thesis that human actions are motivated by fear of emotional commitment.

9 See, for example, Iseminger 1992b; Levinson 1992c: 235 ff; Currie 1991; and my 1991.

Jones, we shall assume, intends that it be true in the story that Stanley is motivated by self-centered ambition. Assuming no other salient difference between Smith's act of generating T and Jones' act of generating T that bears on the meaning-properties of T,[10] HI requires that we take "truth in the story N told in T" to be the same for T as generated by Jones as it was for T as generated by Smith. For future reference, I shall label the two cases SW1 and JW1. Their defining features may be summarized as follows:

SW1 Smith *intends*: it is true in the story N told in T that Stanley is motivated by fear of emotional commitment.

"Uptake" determines: it is true in N that Stanley is motivated by self-centered ambition.

JW1 Jones *intends*: it is true in the story N told in T that Stanley is motivated by self-centered ambition.

"Uptake" determines: it is true in N that Stanley is motivated by self-centered ambition.

Our question, then, is whether there can be a difference in the artistic properties ascribable to the work generated on these two occasions that is directly dependent on the actual intentions of the two authors.[11] But there are obstacles to providing an unambiguous answer to this question. Suppose we identify some respect in which the two generations of T differ in ascribable properties, and wish to conclude that this difference is a difference in artistic properties consequent upon the difference in the authors' actual narrative intentions. To justify such a conclusion, we must defuse two kinds of objections:

O1 If the difference in actual intentions that distinguishes SW1 and JW1 grounds a difference in ascribable properties, why shouldn't we say that the latter is not a difference in *artistic* properties but

10 This might strike the reader as an implausible assumption. However, as will be clear in the sequel, nothing rests on this assumption, since we shall be comparing SW1 and JW1 not with one another but with SW2 and JW2 (see below) respectively.

11 A further question is whether the two generations of T yield distinct works, or two instances of the same work. This question can be left open in setting up the example because the force of the example depends upon bringing out the dependence of certain appreciable properties of the resultant work(s) upon the actual intentions of the artist. However, if the individuation of works must respect sameness and difference in the properties bearing on their appreciation, the example will bear upon *resolving* the above question by bearing upon the nature of works themselves.

a difference that bears upon the relative merits of the artists, given the (shared) artistic properties ascribable to the works? One who subscribes to an "uptake" account of the meaning-properties of a work might insist that, whatever semantic intentions the actual author can be presumed to have, they can play no part in determining the meaning-properties of the work-product, and thus can make no difference to the properties of the work.

O2 If we try to compare SW1 with JW1, there is an obvious difficulty in determining whether any difference in properties that, we are persuaded, bears upon the appreciation of *the works* is really a function of the difference in actual intention, rather than a function of the contributions that the works make to the respective oeuvres of their authors in light of the meaning-properties possessed in virtue of an "uptake" analysis. For example, we may consider the product of Smith's generative activity to be relatively insignificant because it fails to develop the central theme in her other works, whatever Smith's actual narrative intentions. On the other hand, no such weakness is apparent in what Jones generates.

But O2 suggests how we might overcome both of these objections. The bearing of the actual semantic or narrative intentions of the author on the appreciation and evaluation of the work becomes clear if we imagine a situation that differs from our original scenario only in the following respect: in generating the text T, Smith intends that Stanley be motivated by self-centered ambition. We may characterize this case (call it SW2) as follows:

SW2 Smith *intends*: it is true in the story N told in T that Stanley is motivated by self-centered ambition.
"Uptake" determines: it is true in N that Stanley is motivated by self-centered ambition.

While "uptake" dictates that the linguistic vehicles generated by Smith in SW1 and SW2 are identical in narrative properties, the artistic properties of the work produced may differ as a direct result of the difference in actual narrative intentions on the part of the author. For SW2 represents a deliberate attempt by Smith to express a view of human motivation different from that developed in her other works, and may therefore have appreciable properties and a consequent value in virtue of enriching and rendering more nuanced our understanding of the oeuvre as a whole and the other works in particular. SW1, on the other hand, as a failed attempt to furnish one more illustration of a single thematic preoccupation, has no such virtues.

Similar observations apply if we contrast JW1 with JW2, identical to JW1 save that Jones' actual narrative intention is to represent a character whose misfortunes stem from a fear of emotional commitment. Schematically:

JW2 Jones *intends*:   it is true in the story N told in T that Stanley is motivated by fear of emotional commitment.
"Uptake" determines: it is true in N that Stanley is motivated by self-centered ambition.

While Jones' intentions do not make it true in JW2, any more than Smith's intentions make it true in SW1, that Stanley's actions are motivated by fear of emotional commitment, the works in JW2 and JW1 are open to different appreciations in virtue of the difference in actual narrative intentions. For example, JW2 may be interesting precisely in virtue of its relationship to the work of Smith, whom Jones may have intended to parody, or by whom Jones may have been influenced.

The above examples, despite their air of unreality, can be grounded in a very concrete critical context. If two critics, subscribing to an "uptake" account of how the semantic or narrative properties of a given work are determined, disagree as to the actual narrative or semantic intentions with which a given linguistic structure was generated in a given context, they may as a direct consequence legitimately disagree as to the artistic properties and values of the work in question. Two critical accounts of the generation of T by Smith may completely agree as to what is true in N but offer different evaluations of Smith's work because one takes this generation to instantiate SW1 while the other takes it to instantiate SW2.

The general lesson to be drawn from these examples is, I hope, relatively clear. The sorts of artistic properties and values that we ascribe to a work reflect, among other things, how that work stands in the larger context of the artist's oeuvre. But the place of a work in the artist's oeuvre – as a major work, a minor work, or an aberration – depends crucially not just upon what meaning-properties the work-product possesses, but also upon what properties it was *intended* to possess. Thus the actual semantic or narrative intentions of the author, even if they do not determine the meaning-properties of the authored text, do enter crucially into the appreciative evaluation of the *work*.

This helps to clarify, I think, how we should respond to the sorts of arguments that have led many philosophers to embrace some form of sophisticated AI (see, for example, Hirsch 1967; Iseminger 1992b; Livingston 1998; Carroll 2000; Stecker 2003). Defenders of AI appeal to examples where conventionalist resources of the sort allowed by Beardsley, applied to a literary text, leave certain meaning-properties indeterminate. The author's intention that the text be read in one of the ways consistent with such conventions is taken to resolve this indeterminacy. This strategy speaks to the strong intuition that authorial intention, in such cases, is relevant to the appreciation of the literary work. Indeed, it seems to be assumed that this intuition can be satisfied only if authorial intention determines the meaning-properties rightly ascribed to the artistic vehicle. Philosophers moved by such considerations have embraced sophisticated AI, even though the capacity of authorial intentions to fix the meaning of otherwise ambiguous utterances might seem, prima facie, no less mysterious than the capacity of Humpty-Dumpty's semantic wishes to do the same.

Iseminger, for example, cites the opening lines of Gerald Manley Hopkins' poem *Henry Purcell*: "Have fair fallen, O fair, fair have fallen, / so dear / To me, so arch-especial a spirit as heaves / in Henry Purcell, / An age is now since passed, since parted / . . ." In correspondence with Robert Bridges, Hopkins made it clear that, while he intended the opening line to express the wish that fair fortune have befallen Purcell, it not only lends itself to an alternative reading, but may even require that reading on grammatical grounds: "I *meant* "fair fall" to mean *fair (fortune be)fall*; it has since struck me that perhaps "fair" is an adjective proper and in the predicate and can only be used in cases like "fair fall the day," that is, *may the day fall, turn out, fair*" (John Pick, ed., *A Hopkins Reader*. New York, Oxford University Press, 1953: 141; cited in Iseminger 1992b: 77). On this alternative reading, the wish expressed is that Purcell should have done good things, rather than that good things have happened to him.

Iseminger contends that, given Hopkins' expressed semantic intentions, we should overlook the possible grammatical infelicity and take the first of the above readings as giving the true meaning of the text. An "uptake" theory of the relevant kind of meaning-property, on the other hand, might agree with a strict conventionalist like Beardsley that it is the *second*, unintended reading that correctly represents the meaning-properties ascribable to Hopkins' linguistic vehicle. But our sense that Hopkins' semantic intentions are relevant to the appreciation of the poem should not lead us to embrace the sort of sophisticated AI for which Iseminger is arguing. For, even if we adopt an "uptake" account of such meaning-properties, Hopkins' semantic intentions may still bear upon the appreciation of the poem, qua *work*, in that they affect the thematic implications of the poem for Hopkins' broader oeuvre, and also, perhaps, our more general sense of Hopkins' literary achievement in writing the poem.

In light of the discussion in chapter 2, it might be objected that the sorts of critical judgments upon which I have relied in the preceding pages are not properly *artistic* judgments, but *art-historical* judgments on a work's contribution to the development of an artist, a school, a movement, etc. Even if this distinction be granted, however, it does not undermine the foregoing argument as long as both artistic and art-historical judgments are taken to be elements in the appreciation of *the work*. For we may still ask what works must be if such judgments are to be true of them. However, it might be maintained that art-historical judgments bear not upon the *work* as an object of critical appreciation, but upon the artist's activity in creating the work. But, even if this point be granted with respect to some of the judgments that might be classified as "art-historical," it is surely not applicable to the sorts of judgments that feature in the above discussion. If we exclude from appreciation of the work all judgments that refer implicitly or explicitly to the place of a work in an oeuvre, we will have to relegate much of what is accepted as "art-criticism" to the realm of biography, something difficult to reconcile with the pragmatic constraint. And, it should also be noted, the principal target in the current context is the contextualist, not the structuralist, and the former rejects the sort of distinction between artistic and art-historical considerations to which the above objection appeals.

4.3.3 Ontological implications

Let me summarize the argument thus far and relate it to the anti-intentionalist claims with which we began this section.

1 We have two acts of generating a structure T by a particular author. In each case, by the nature of the example, an "uptake" theory is committed to ascribing the same narrative property Ma to the story N told in T, for in each case this is the interpretation that a properly informed receiver would give if she rightly applied the relevant interpretive norms.

2 Further, ex hypothesi, in one case the author intended the story told in T to have the narrative property Mb rather than Ma, whereas in the other case the author intended the story to have the narrative property Ma.

3 There may be a difference in the artistic properties of the works resulting from these generations of T that is directly dependent on the actual intentions of the author.

4 This establishes one of the two intentionalist claims rejected by Wimsatt and Beardsley while at least partially granting the case against the other. If, granting an "uptake" theory for a given class of meaning-properties, we reject the idea that the actual semantic or narrative intentions of the author with respect to these properties play a role in determining such meaning-properties of *the work-product*, we nevertheless affirm that such actual intentions on the part of the author may play a role in determining certain of the artistic properties of *the work* relevant to its being appreciated as the work it is, and thus in determining the artistic value of that work.

I now want to suggest a further implication of this analysis. Recall the argument sketched earlier to the effect that the relevance of the actual author's semantic intentions to the *evaluation* of her works depends upon the relevance of such intentions to the *interpretation* of those works. This argument, we noted, rests on two generally accepted assumptions, and a third assumption that also seems plausible. These assumptions are, respectively:

P1 The proper object of critical evaluation of a work is what the author achieves, not what she tries to achieve;

P2 What the author achieves is the product of her creative activities, the "work-product."

P4 If the proper object of critical evaluation of a work is the product of the author's creative activities, then her actual semantic intentions can affect the critical evaluation of her work only by determining meaning-properties of the work-product.

Given the further premise

P6 for any type of meaning-property P for which an "uptake" analysis is correct, actual authorial semantic intentions with respect to P do *not* determine the P-type meaning-properties of the work-product,

it follows that

C for any type of meaning-property P for which an "uptake" analysis is correct, actual authorial semantic intentions with respect to P are irrelevant to the critical evaluation of works.

If the argument developed above is correct, however, C is false, for it fails to hold for the sorts of narrative properties that featured in the examples given. Furthermore, since P6 is true by definition, it seems that at least one of the other three assumptions (P1, P2, P4) must be incorrect. I assume that we should give up P1 only under duress. I believe that what we should do is give up P2, which, I further claim, is tantamount to giving up the idea that the work is the *product* of the creative process and saying, rather, that the work – what the artist achieves – is the *process* eventuating in that product. Works themselves are neither structures nor objects simpliciter, nor are they contextualized structures or objects. They are, rather, intentionally guided generative performances that eventuate in contextualized structures or objects (or events, as we shall see) – performances completed by what I am terming a focus of appreciation. To the extent that the performances that are artworks are usually generatings of an object or structure, the latter, as the product generated, is partly individuative of the work, and partly determinative of the work's properties, for the process in question is the generating of a *particular* focus with particular properties relevant to the appreciation of the work. But this fact about the individuation of processes and the determination of their properties should not lead us mistakenly to identify the generated work-product with the work.

In support of this proposal, let me sketch how giving up P2 and identifying works with generative performances solves the problem at hand, and also counter the supposition that this problem is easily solvable *without* giving up P2. It is tempting to think that one can retain P2 and accommodate the bearing of the actual author's actual semantic intentions[12] on the appreciation of a work by simply rejecting P4 on the following sorts of grounds:

> We can ascribe to the work-product not merely meaning-properties but also such properties as "having been created with the intention that it mean x." The theorist who identifies the work with the work-product can therefore maintain that the artist's achievement is to be identified with the work-product, as P2 requires, but that an adequate evaluation of the artist's achievement requires that we take into account its property of having been created with a certain intention. The latter, it might be claimed, is simply

---

12 For consistency with the initial analysis, I talk here of "semantic intentions," rather than of "narrative intentions," one species of the broader genus. If the foregoing argument concerning narrative intentions does not extend to semantic intentions of other kinds, the case for giving up P2 and retaining P4, and the subsequent ontological argument, could be reformulated in terms of narrative intentions alone.

one more property that the work-product possesses in virtue of its provenance.

The problem with such a strategy is that it fails to explain why such relational properties of work-products are properly taken to be artistically relevant. Granted that the work-product *has* among its properties the property of being generated with the intention that it articulate a particular artistic statement, how can such a property bear on the appreciation of the work if an "uptake" theory is correct? To see why this is a problem, consider what one adopting this strategy, who is obviously committed to P2, will say about P1. There are two options here. First, as in the above exposition of the strategy, one might uphold P1 and maintain that what is at issue in evaluation is what the artist *achieved*. But, if (by P2) what the artist achieves is the work-product, and if the actual artist's actual semantic intentions play no role in determining the meaning-properties of the work-product, then the latter's relational property of being generated with particular semantic intentions surely relates to what was *attempted*, and therefore (by P1) has no bearing on evaluation of the work. If, second, one rejects P1, maintaining that, while what the artist achieved – the work – is the work-product, what was attempted also bears upon critically evaluating the work, some rationale for the latter claim must be provided. Why would an interest in what the artist attempted have any bearing upon evaluating the *work*, if that latter is the product of the artist's activity? Would it not bear, rather, upon evaluating the *artist*?

No such difficulties arise, however, if we respond to the falsity of C by retaining P1 and P4 and rejecting P2, identifying the work with a generative process rather than with its generated product. The proper object of critical evaluation is what the author achieved, and what the author achieved is the work, conceived as a generative performance which specifies a focus of appreciation (work-product) having certain meaning-properties. Since both the actual semantic intentions of the actual author and the meaning-properties of the work-focus (as elements in the artistic statement articulated) are aspects of the work so conceived, we can explain how the actual author's semantic intentions can be relevant to the appreciation of the work even if they are not determinative of meaning-properties of the work-product.

Note that one who identifies works with generative performances has no difficulty giving content to the distinction, in P1, between what an artist *attempts* and what she *achieves*, where the former may not coincide with the latter. A novelist, for example, attempts to articulate a particular artistic statement through manipulating language in light of certain presumed shared understandings. Her intention may be to thereby compose a novel in which it is true that p, but her achievement may consist in thereby writing a novel in which it is true that q. What the author *intends* is what she tries to achieve. When she realizes her intentions, what she achieves is identical to what she tries to achieve, namely, the writing of a novel in which it is true that p. Both what is attempted and what is achieved are *performances* of the appropriate sort. The proper object of critical evaluation in the case surmised is, as P1 requires, what the artist achieves – the specifying of a particular focus of appreciation whose artistic statement includes its being true in the story that q – not what the artist attempted – the specifying of a focus of appreciation whose artistic statement includes its being true in the story that p. It is a feature of both performances, however, that the author intends to write a novel in which it is true that p.

4.4 Conclusions

In the preceding section, I have argued that actual authorial semantic intentions bear upon the appreciation and evaluation of works even on an "uptake" construal of the meaning-properties articulated through work-vehicles. This further illustrates a more general feature of our critical and appreciative practice discussed in section 4.2 – the role played in the appreciation of a work by aspects of provenance that are neither directly responsible for features of the work's artistic vehicle nor determinative of the artistic statement articulated through this vehicle. Other phenomena of this type are erased or covered elements in pictorial designs whose presence can be revealed only by X-ray photography, preparatory sketches of paintings, and early drafts of literary works and musical scores. All such cases, I suggest, present the following challenge to accepted views in the ontology of art: why should such features of provenance bear upon the appreciation of works if works are to be identified with work-products – focuses of appreciation – whether or not such focuses are understood contextually? And all such cases, I have argued, are easily explained if we identify the work – the unit of criticism and appreciation – not with a focus per se but with the performance whereby a focus is specified.

I noted at the end of chapter 3 that the argument advanced for the performance theory is a cumulative one. The individual considerations adduced in its favor may acquire more weight as it becomes clear how they fit into an overarching theoretical framework for thinking about artistic practice and our discourse about art. This framework will become fully apparent only in the later chapters, after the notion of artistic performance that is central to the performance theory has been spelled out in greater detail. However, one should not underestimate the challenge presented to contextualist ontologies of art by the argument developed in this chapter. In particular, it would be wrong to think that the contextualist can easily dismiss the phenomena in question as peripheral and of interest only to the art historian. For, as was argued in chapter 3, the contextualist's case against structuralism rests upon a recognition that our properly appreciative interest in an artistic vehicle, and in the meanings articulated through that vehicle, requires that we attend to the performance whereby that vehicle was crafted and to the art-historical context in which that performance took place. The contextualist enthusiastically endorses the idea that attention to such a generative performance is crucial to the artistic appreciation of the work brought into existence through that performance. But the contextualist insists that this is compatible with the identification of the work with the contextualized *product* of that performance because the artistic vehicle has the relational property of having been produced by such a performance, and the articulated artistic statement is a function of this relational property of the artistic vehicle.

This move on the contextualist's part is plausible to the extent that our interest in the generative artistic performance is restricted to those features of the performance that directly affect the focus of appreciation specified through it – that is to say, manipulations of the vehicular medium that are responsible for the finished form of the artistic vehicle and aspects of the context in which such manipulations take place that affect the artistic statement thereby articulated. But the phenomena addressed in this chapter suggest that no principled distinction of the sort required by the contextualist can be drawn between artistically relevant and artistically irrelevant features of the generative performance. Preliminary sketches of Picasso's *Les Demoiselles d'Avignon* enter into an overall account that would explain why the final vehicle has a given form no less than the actual manipulations of the vehicular medium directly productive of that form. Analogously, an author's intention that certain things be true in a story enters into an overall account of why she constructed a given linguistic structure quite independently of whether or not her intentions were realised in that structure.

It is, of course, always open to the contextualist to accommodate such facts in terms of more complex relational properties of the work-product. But, as stressed above, this seems to misrepresent the object of our appreciative interest in the work. Consider the following analogy. Suppose I have a (non-artistic) appreciative interest in Sir Edmund Hillary's climbing of Everest. My interest would lead me to examine the details of the climb, including various strategic decisions made in the planning stages, some of which were revised and therefore failed to manifest themselves in the actual ascent. Each of these details could be reformulated as a relational property of the "product" of the ascent, that is, Hillary's standing on the summit of Everest. Then it might be said that, in spite of my interest in Hillary's performance in climbing Everest, the real object of my interest is the product of that performance – Hillary's standing on the summit of Everest as achieved by these means. Because of the logic of process/product talk, there is no property of Hillary's climb that could be cited to prove that such a view was mistaken. But it surely *is* mistaken: we are interested in a particular performance or doing completed by a particular state of affairs, not in the state of affairs as achieved by such a performance. Once we recognize the different ways in which our appreciative interest in an artwork requires that we take account of a generative performance, the burden of proof shifts to the contextualist to show why we should nonetheless think of the work as a contextualized product. In subsequent chapters we shall see why contextualists have felt that they need not discharge such a burden of proof. The claim, as we shall see, is that there are independent reasons to reject the performance theory or any similar theory that takes works to be process-like rather than product-like entities. But, I suggest, our preliminary conclusion should be that the logic of the contextualist argument against structuralist ontologies of art calls contextualism itself into question. In the following chapter, we shall consider a further challenge to contextualism, and a further step in the cumulative argument for the performance theory.

Provenance, Modality, and the Identity of the Artwork

5.1 Preliminaries

Some readers may have noticed that, in formulating the pragmatic constraint in chapter 1, I incorporated an unelaborated reference to "the
modal properties that are reasonably ascribed to 'works'" in our critical
and appreciative practice. "Modal properties" of a work identify ways that
the work might or might not have been in counterfactual situations. For
example, it may be claimed that a particular work – say, *Les Demoiselles
d'Avignon* – could (or could not) have been produced by a different artist
– say, Braque – or by the same artist under different art-historical conditions – say, 20 years later. In fact, our critical practice incorporates very
few modal judgments of this sort, since we are rarely interested in how a
given work might have been, but only in how it is. Many philosophers,
however, have taken our modal *intuitions* about artworks very seriously,
assuming that these intuitions serve as an indication of the sorts of principles that guide us in our actual critical and appreciative practice. Certainly an appeal to our modal intuitions is often made in the sorts of
hypothetical examples that philosophers propose in either challenging the
artistic theories of others or arguing for their own alternatives.

On a structuralist conception of the artwork, modal properties of works
seem relatively clear. The structuralist identifies a given work with a particular structure-type. The work can then be supposed to exist in any
counterfactual situation in which that structure-type is instantiated.[1]

---

1 *If* labels for artworks are "rigid designators" rather than "cluster" concepts – see below.

Perhaps the structuralist would restrict this analysis to *appropriate* instantiations that result from the intentional activity of an agent. For she may wish to exclude the generation of an instance of a given artistic structure-type by a confluence of non-intentional events – for example, an instance of the verbal structure *Kubla Khan* generated by the random agency of wind blowing in the Sahara Desert, or through the activity of the infamous monkey let loose on the keys of a typewriter.

Once we allow aspects of provenance to enter into our conception of what works are and how they are to be individuated, however, matters become less clear. In this chapter, I want to argue that, given certain assumptions as to how our modal intuitions stand in relation to our actual practices of individuating artworks, we can bring general structural features of our modal intuitions to bear in critically assessing different ontologies of art that accord a place to provenance in the identity of the artwork. To the extent that the assumptions about modality and individuation to which I appeal are open to dispute, so will be the argument predicated upon them. On the other hand, to the extent that the reader finds these assumptions plausible, the argument that follows is intended to provide further support for the performance theory, and further ammunition against contextualist alternatives.

My argument appeals to a range of examples of modal judgments about works. In bringing these examples to bear upon the ontological issues, I shall draw upon what I term the "modality principle." I shall not provide a detailed defence or elaboration of this principle in the body of this chapter, because the necessarily technical nature of the discussion would present difficulties for readers who lack a background in the relevant literature. I refer the interested reader to a fuller treatment of the issues in an appendix at the end of this chapter. The following simplified exposition should, however, prove adequate for the comprehension of the ensuing argument.

The modality principle relates what I term the "constitutive features" of an entity to what can be termed its "essential properties" – the features it must have in any counterfactual situation in which it exists. The constitutive features of an entity are those features in virtue of which it is a particular instance of the type of thing that it is. So, for example, the constitutive features of Rover are those features in virtue of which he is a particular dog – being a dog, first, and perhaps having a particular genetic heritage, second. Other dogs share with Rover their dogginess, but differ with respect to those properties by reference to which we individuate dogs – what we may term the "individuating conditions" for things belonging to the type "dog." Individuating things of kind X, here, is a matter of determining when we have the same X on two different occasions, and when we have different Xs. The constitutive features of an entity, then, are, first, the particular type of thing that it is, and, second, those individuating conditions in virtue of which it is a particular thing of that type. According to what I term the "modality principle," an entity's essential properties are all and only its constitutive properties so conceived – the properties that make it a particular instance of the type of thing that it is, given the way in which such things are individuated. If we assume that the labels that we use to identify and index artworks – labels such as *Guernica*, *King Lear*, and *the Hammerklavier Sonata* – name particular entities in the world and thereby permit us to talk about *those* entities in counterfactual situations – if such labels are what Kripke (1980) termed "rigid designators" – then, according to the modality principle, the essential properties of an artwork are all and only its constitutive properties. In the argument to be developed below, I shall assume that the modality principle indeed applies in this way to artworks, and consider what this entails.

5.2 The Work-Relativity of Modality

There are two questions which must be addressed by any theorist who rejects a purely structuralist conception of the artwork. First – call this the "ontological question" – to which more general ontological category (or categories) do artworks belong? Second – call this the "individuation question" – if aspects of provenance play a role in the individuation of artworks, *which* aspects of provenance serve as individuating conditions for, and are therefore constitutive properties of, those works? It is instructive to consider how these questions present themselves to perhaps the most discussed contextualist ontology of art, namely, Levinson's thesis that works in at least some media are "indicated structures."

Levinson, as noted earlier, maintains that musical and literary works are *indicated structures*. To indicate a structure-type S, we may recall, is to make S normative for a work, so that correct instances of the work must comply with that structure-type. On the canonical version of this view, all such works fit the following schema: *S-as-indicated-by-A-at-t*, where "S" is a particular structure-type, "A" a particular individual, and "t" a particular time (1980: 79). However, Levinson also considers an alternative version, where the values of the variables in the schema are not a particular individual and time but a particular artistic/cultural context of creation. The schema, on this version, is *S*-as-indicated-in-art-historical-context-*C* (1980: 82).

The versions may differ concerning the *modal* properties of works. The values of the variables in Levinson's schemas are clearly constitutive properties of individual works in our sense. If the modality principle applies to artworks, then a work's constitutive properties are also its essential properties. Thus, if, as in Levinson's alternative version of the indicated structure theory, we make the artistic/cultural context of creation one of the elements entering into our work-schema, then the work can exist only in possible worlds that reproduce that context. Further, works will also possess essentially those of their appreciable properties implied by structure-type and context of creation.

Levinson's preferred formulation of the indicated structure theory avoids this consequence while also satisfying his own constraints on the individuation of works within a world.[2] According to Levinson's anti-structuralist argument, examined in chapter 2, works, in virtue of their histories of making, possess fine-grained aesthetic and artistic properties, and must be individuated so that any difference in such appreciable properties in the *actual* world entails that we have distinct works. These requirements for individuation can be met as long as each work has a unique location in the cultural-historical space of the actual world, such that all of its appreciable properties in the actual world are determinate given that location. But this can be done without building an explicit reference to that cultural-historical space into our conception of a work's identity. We can uniquely determine all of the relevant parameters that define a work's place in actual cultural-historical space by tying the work constitutively to an individual and a time. For, given historical facts about the actual world, the relevant individual/time coordinates, when mapped onto that world, will pick out a particular art-historical context as partly determinative of the work's artistic properties. For example, the coordinates {Sibelius, 1904–7}, mapped onto the actual world, identify the art-historical context in which Sibelius composed his Third Symphony. But this allows the work to possess different properties in other possible worlds insofar as the cultural and historical facts can differ in those worlds. When we map a work's individual/time coordinates onto a possible world whose cultural history differs from that of the actual world, we pick out a location in cultural-historical space different from the one that the work occupies in the actual world. As a result, the work may possess a very different

2   Levinson notes this as a virtue of the preferred formulation – see his 1980: 84, fn. 29.

set of appreciable properties in that possible world from the properties it possesses in the actual world.

A problem with this strategy, however, is that it may place too *few* constraints on the counterfactual existence of works. For it allows that any specific historical fact bearing on the appreciable properties of a work may vary in other possible worlds in which that work exists, so that none of the appreciable features of the work that are not determined by time, structure-type, and indicator alone can be an essential feature of the work. This is problematic for a contextualist ontology such as Levinson's because, while it makes *some* features of a work's provenance essential (time, indicating individual), the essential features are not the ones that seem important for our sense of what the work *is*, as reflected in those aspects of our appreciative and individuative practice stressed in Levinson's own arguments against structuralism. The counterintuitive implications of such a view will become clearer below.

More significantly, the canonical version of Levinson's indicated-structure theory faces a further problem given its implicit assumption that certain general features of provenance, like the identity of the indicator and the time of indication, are always work-constitutive. If a work's constitutive features are its essential features, as the modality principle requires, then, if certain general features of provenance are always work-constitutive, these features must always be essential properties of works. But, as I shall now argue, reflection on our modal practice suggests that whether a given general feature of provenance is essential or non-essential depends upon the particular *work* in question – or, as I shall say, is "*work-relative*."

Let me rehearse a few examples of modal claims about works in order to tease out more general features of our modal judgments.[3] The reader will almost certainly not share all (and may not even share any) of the particular modal intuitions expressed in the following examples. However, the purpose of the examples is to bring out a salient *structural* feature of our modal thinking about works. This feature should hold for the reader's own modal thinking even if her specific intuitions differ from the ones expressed.

Consider, first, the *time* at which a work comes into existence. Given that the actual time at which a work W came into being was t, could *that*

3 Since these examples all relate to features of provenance, they will not impress structuralists, whose intuitions might nonetheless be shown to have the same feature if we focused on kinds of differences in *structure*.

very work have come into being at a different time t', other features of
the world remaining broadly unchanged? In certain cases, I think, there
is a strong inclination to answer this question affirmatively. Take the case
of a hypothetical work *Prairie Snowscape*, painted by a "naive" occasional
painter living in the Midwest at the very same time as Warhol was producing his first *Brillo Boxes*. Barring any unusual features of the context
of its creation, it seems that *Prairie Snowscape* could have been executed
a few years earlier or later. If there are distinctive properties of this work
that depend upon its relation to other works in the painter's own oeuvre,
let us assume that these would be unaffected by the envisaged change in
the date of execution of *Prairie Snowscape*. On the other hand, a work
like Warhol's seems much more closely tied to a particular time of execution, if we hold constant developments in American art in the 1950s
and 1960s. Produced either substantially earlier or substantially later, the
"point" of the work would be different. Certainly Warhol could have
exhibited a pile of Brillo boxes at another time but it is tempting, at least,
to say that, in so doing, he would have been creating a different work.
The "artistic statement" articulated would be quite distinct.[4]

This sort of example highlights a problem that confronts any proposed
answer to the individuation question that, like the canonical version of
the indicated-structure theory, makes time of execution constitutive of
(and hence essential for) the work, while leaving context of creation non-
constitutive (and non-essential). Such an account, generalized to the
visual arts,[5] entails that a world in which the canvas of *Prairie Snowscape*
is produced at a different time is a world in which we have what we may
term a "critical counterpart" of the work,[6] but not the work itself. Equally
troubling, it entails that *Brillo Boxes* can sensibly be supposed to exist in
a world in which the entire New York art-scene of the 1950s and 1960s
doesn't exist as long as Warhol, in that world, executes a piece having the
same outward appearance as *Brillo Boxes* at the same time as he executed
the piece *Brillo Boxes* in the actual world.

---

4   See Danto's discussion of Picasso's "tie" in chapter 2 of his 1981 for another example
of the bearing of temporal location on the identity of works.
5   Levinson's account, of course, is only intended to apply to works in the musical and literary arts, but the general point being made in the text admits of examples drawn from the
latter. Consider, for example, Perec's *La Disparition* and a historical romance penned at the
same time by an occasional novelist in the French provinces.
6   This is analogous to the Kripkean response to recalcitrant modal intuitions (see Kripke
1980: 140ff). He suggests that, in such cases, we are really talking about an "epistemic"
counterpart of the entity in question, an entity indistinguishable from the latter in terms of
its manifest properties.

What the example also brings out, however, is that one doesn't resolve this problem by making context of creation, rather than time of execution, constitutive of the work. For, if we do this, we cannot sensibly imagine that *Prairie Snowscape* exists in a world which differs strikingly in its general art-historical features from the actual world. What matters, as I shall argue below, is not the context of creation per se, but the manner in which the context enters into the generative activity of the artist.

Before turning to this, however, we may note another respect in which our sense of the identity of certain works may be tied very precisely to their actual time of creation, other things remaining unchanged, whereas our sense of the identity of other works is not so tied. It is arguably a constitutive and essential feature of a work that it is "finished" or "unfinished," "complete" or "incomplete." As Paisley Livingston has recently argued, critical practice treats a work's being finished or complete as a function of the work's history of making, rather than as an aesthetic feature of a work.[7] A work's being aesthetically or artistically complete, in the sense of possessing certain prescribed aesthetically or artistically valued features, is neither necessary nor sufficient for its being a completed or finished work of art. It is not necessary because we are quite prepared to criticize what we regard as finished works of art for their failure to achieve aesthetic or artistic completeness. It is not sufficient because a work left unfinished at an author's death might, in the eyes of receivers, be aesthetically or artistically complete, yet it would still be viewed as an unfinished piece. A work is deemed to be finished or complete in virtue of some kind of decision on the part of its creator, not subsequently revised, that no further work is called for.

If this is what it is for a work to be complete, it is readily apparent that this property plays an important role in the individuation of works, and is plausibly taken to be work-constitutive in the designated sense. For, in our individuative practice, we appeal directly to this property in distinguishing between works and parts of works, and in classifying a series of disparate episodes or entities as stages in the production of a single work, rather than as distinct works. We take it that an author returns to *the same work*, rather than begins a new one, insofar as there is no prior appropriately authoritative decision that a work is complete.

7 Livingston argues for this point in his 1999. In developing my argument in the following paragraphs, I have drawn heavily on Livingston's analysis of how judgments of what he terms "genetic completeness" enter into our critical practice.

Further, the assumption that a work is incomplete may have important repercussions for our interpretation of the work, depending upon the circumstances we take to be responsible for its being incomplete. A work-focus may be unfinished because of some external factor that prevents the artist from carrying out certain anticipated modifications of what she conceives to be a fragment or draft. Most dramatically, an artist may die, or be swept up in personal or worldly affairs. On the other hand, an unfinished work-focus may be one that the artist has returned to and revised on many occasions, but that she has never brought to what she views as a satisfactory resolution. If the fashioning of a work-focus was terminated under externally grounded conditions, we proceed differently in our attempts to interpret the work. For example, we are less inclined to seek a more comprehensive interpretation if an otherwise satisfactory reading requires that certain "promissory notes" in the piece be regarded as unfulfilled.

In these ways, the assumed reasons for a work's being unfinished bear upon our sense of a work's *identity*. A work unfinished because of the sudden death of the artist, or because of an unexpected event such as the arrival of the infamous person from Porlock,[8] cannot be expected to manifest the kind of narrative or aesthetic closure that we will at least try to find in a work to which an artist has returned many times without ever being willing to think of the work as complete. In the case of a work-focus left unfinished because of the intrusion of some external circumstance, we may be reluctant to think that the very same work could exist in circumstances where no such cause of the focus's being unfinished was forthcoming. A work by Coleridge textually indistinguishable from *Kubla Khan* but upon which work ceased a couple of hours before or after the arrival of the person from Porlock would, if unfinished at all, be unfinished in a way that would carry a different sense of what the author had done.[9] Arguably, in such a case, coming into existence at a particular time, other relevant things remaining unchanged, is an essential and a

8   A surprise visit by a "person from Porlock" was identified by Coleridge as the reason for the purportedly fragmentary nature of the poem *Kubla Khan*.

9   There are features of the historical example that complicate matters here. For example, Coleridge maintained that he awoke from an opium-assisted dream with the entire text of the poem complete "in his head," and that what was interrupted by the person from Porlock was not so much the *composition* of the text as the *transcription* of an already completed text. Suppose, however, that we change the example such that there is no pre-existing "ideal poem" merely in need of transcription, and that what is terminated by the arrival of the person from Porlock is the composition of the text of the work.

constitutive feature of the work. In the case of completed works, on the other hand, there is usually nothing about the precise time of completion relative to other environing events that we would take to be work-constitutive.

We may now consider more directly our modal intuitions concerning cases where what are changed are features of the art-historical *context of creation* of a work. One way in which particular features of the context of creation may enter into our sense of the identity of a work is if the work is conceived to be a response to what has been done in other works, often by other artists. For example, it might be said that Picasso's early Cubist works could not exist in a world in which none of Cézanne's works existed.[10] For Picasso's early Cubism is taken to be in large part a response to the manner of representing spatial volumes in the later works of Cézanne. There is therefore good reason to say that, if provenance is to bear on work identity, it should bear in such a way that *Les Demoiselles d'Avignon* could not exist in a world bereft of Cézanne's works, even if Picasso were to generate an instance of the same embodied design in that world. In terms of our analysis of the structure of the "focus of appreciation" in chapter 3, we can say that the artistic statement articulated in the hypothetical work would differ quite significantly from the artistic statement articulated in the actual work. To take another example, Michael Nyman's score for Peter Greenaway's film *Drowning by Numbers* is, by Nyman's admission, a series of variations on the melody that closes the slow movement of Mozart's *Sinfonia Concertante* for violin, viola, and orchestra.[11] It is questionable whether the same work could sensibly be supposed to exist in a world in which Nyman generates an identical score, but neither Mozart nor anyone else ever composed a piece structurally identical to the *Sinfonia Concertante*. The identity of a work may also be tied to non-artistic features of its context of creation. It might be argued, for example, that Orwell's *Animal Farm* could not exist in a world in which an event like the Russian revolution never occurred, and that Picasso's *Guernica* could not exist in a world in which events like those depicted in the picture did not take place. In all of these cases, our sense that we could not have the same work in the hypothesized circumstances is analyzable in terms of a drastic difference in the artistic statement artic-

10   Or perhaps we need to consider a world in which no works exist with the relevant properties of Cézanne's works. We might be willing to allow that Picasso's works could exist in a world in which *someone other than Cézanne* did what Cézanne did.
11   See Nyman's liner notes for the soundtrack to the film – Virgin Records 1988, VE23.

ulated, combined with the centrality of an articulated artistic statement to our sense of what a given work is.

Other aspects of the context of creation, however, seem irrelevant to the modal properties of a work, even if clearly known to the artist. To the extent that we find no evidence that Picasso's work engages in any way with the work of Turner, for example, we may be willing to locate *Les Demoiselles d'Avignon* in a world in which Turner's oeuvre does not exist, whether or not Picasso was, in a more general sense, aware of that oeuvre. This point seems even clearer if we consider features of provenance of which the artist was not aware, even if such features bear upon what the artist actually achieves through her works. For example, consider a situation in which, unknown to Picasso or anyone else in the artworld, an artist in provincial Spain, influenced by Cézanne, anticipates early Cubism in a series of works in the later nineteenth century, but both the canvases and all memory of the canvases are lost in an earthquake in 1900. Can the early works of Picasso exist in such a world? If we take what a work achieves to be an essential property of that work,[12] we must say no. But this seems to run counter to our practice both in the arts and elsewhere. If all of the "achievement-properties" of a work are essential properties, then we can never say, of a work, that it might have been a greater or lesser achievement than it was. However, we certainly talk in this way, and it is unlikely that we would reject such ways of talking if we reflected upon our practice.

As noted above, I do not intend that the dialectical force of the above reflections should rest upon the reader's sharing the particular intuitions expressed concerning the cited examples. What is to be noted, rather, is the manner in which *aspects of provenance bear upon our modal judgments with a variable force that reflects our overall sense of what is to be appreciated in a given work*. It is this feature of our modal judgments about works – what I term their "work-relativity" – to which I wish to appeal in assessing competing provenance-sensitive ontologies of art. In the case of certain works – for example, much mid-to-late-twentieth-century visual art – it is difficult to imagine how *those very works* could exist in a world that did not very closely reproduce the actual artistic and cultural context of generation. In the case of other works – for example, "naive" paintings – very little of the actual engendering artistic and cultural context seems to be required in order for the work to exist in a world.

---

12 Currie takes achievement properties of this kind to be constitutive but *not* essential properties of works. See chapter 6 below.

If we are correct in identifying a work's essential properties with its constitutive properties, however, the work-relativity of our modal judgments about works entails that the *constitutive* properties of works are also work-relative. This presents a problem for a contextualist ontology like Levinson's because the latter incorporates a solution to the problem of individuation that is *not* work-relative. The contextualist is not without strategies with which to address this problem, but the more obvious strategies are not promising. Consider the following two options:

1 Given a particular contextualist ontology that takes certain features of provenance to be work-constitutive, it may be claimed that, in a given possible world, only an entity that possesses the designated work-constitutive features can instantiate the work in that world. If something lacks any of those features, then we have a different work. For example, the canonical version of the indicated-structure theory takes the time of indication of a structure-type to be a work-constitutive feature. The proposed strategy dictates that, in a world in which Coleridge finishes a work textually identical to the *Ancient Mariner* slightly earlier or later, we have a "critical counterpart" of the *Ancient Mariner*, but not the latter work. This strategy, however, simply fails to address the problem posed by work-relativity, and requires that we take what seem to be "insignificant" details to be work-constitutive in certain cases (for example, the "naive" painting).

2 Levinson's own response to the problem is more accommodating. In considering a version of the indicated-structure theory which takes structure, title, and context of creation to be the constitutive elements of works, he suggests that "the most appealing view is probably to regard the constituents of the type as indeed essential to it – structure, context, title – while recognising a measure of looseness in what counts as the *same* structure, *same* context, *same* title" (1990a: 163). Generalizing from this suggestion, it might be claimed that, given a particular view about how provenance enters into the individuation and constitution of works, any *slight* difference in the work-constitutive features of provenance can be overlooked when we ask about the essential properties of a work. The problem with this strategy, however, is that sometimes slight differences in the constitutive features of works *are* relevant to work identity, as the examples discussed above may demonstrate. The proposed strategy lacks the resources to provide us with principled constraints on our willingness to be flexible in our judgments of sameness and difference.

5.3 A Strategy for Accommodating the Work-Relativity of Modality

As we have seen, a significant challenge for any theorist who wishes to factor provenance into the identity of works is to give an account of the modal properties of works that is both (1) principled, and (2) compatible with the work-relativity of our modal judgments. Our discussion of work-relativity, taken in conjunction with the analysis given in chapter 3 of the structure of the focus of appreciation, suggests that we should approach the issues in the following way. We may think of an artwork as an entity that originates in a performance whereby a focus of appreciation is specified, that is, where an artistic statement is articulated in an artistic medium realized in a vehicle. We may then take the ascription of modal properties to an artwork to be grounded in part in a judgment as to which features of the art-historical context of creation must be directly or indirectly incorporated into what we would take to be an adequate characterization of the originating performance. To the extent that this performance is an exercise of practical rationality, we can expect many of the relevant aspects of the context of creation to be implicated in a description of the performance in virtue of their being implicated in a characterization of the intentional states guiding that performance. But other aspects of the context of creation may be implicated in an adequate description of the originating performance because they are necessary if the activity of the artist is to specify a particular focus of appreciation. For example, certain conditions of light may be necessary for the production of an image articulative of a particular artistic statement by means of a given photographic device.

This strategy allows us to accommodate the work-relativity of modality, as can be seen if we reanalyze some of the examples set out in the previous section. Consider first the "naive" artist. Her naivity entails that an adequate characterization of the generative performance resulting in a piece like *Prairie Snowscape* will make little if any reference to the more general art-historical context in which she acts. In particular, no reference to such a context will be either explicit or implicit in the intentional states that we take to have guided her in her manipulation of the vehicular medium. As a result, we can easily imagine such a performance taking place in a very different art-historical context, or, ceteris paribus, at a different time. Consider, on the other hand, Picasso's *Les Demoiselles d'Avignon*. The manipulations of the vehicular medium resulting in the canvas of this painting, I suggested, were guided in part by a concern with problems of pictorial design or of representation arising out of Picasso's responses to certain paintings by Cézanne. If so, then an adequate representation of Picasso's performance must refer to Cézanne's paintings (or perhaps to a body of work having the same qualities as that of Cézanne). Given the proposed strategy, we thereby explain our reluctance to allow that the work could exist in an art-historical context that lacked paintings having the pictorial and design qualities of Cézanne's works. For in such a world, a performance having the characteristics we ascribe to the making of the canvas titled *Les Demoiselles d'Avignon* could not occur. Such considerations apply with even greater force in the case of many later modernist pieces, where the artistic statement is in part a commentary on other art. Only in an art-historical context very similar to the one in which such pieces were created could the conditions built into an adequate representation of the performances generative of such pieces be satisfied.

Suppose, on the other hand, that an artist, in creating a work W, is unaware of other existing paintings which nonetheless bear upon his achievement – as, for example, is the case with Picasso's ignorance of the oeuvre of our hypothetical Spanish Cubist. Or suppose that other works that are part of the larger cultural context in which an artist created W, while known to the artist, are not implicated in his intentional manipulations of the vehicular medium. Then there will be no reference to the existence of such works in an adequate representation of the artist's generative performance, and our strategy allows that W could exist in a world in which the other works do not.

A similar analysis applies to our modal intuitions about the temporal properties of works. It might be maintained that an adequate description of the manipulations of the linguistic medium that resulted in the text of the *Ancient Mariner* does not locate Coleridge's performance at any precise moment in a broader temporal interval. If so, then we have no difficulty in imagining that this very performance occurs at different times in that temporal interval, other relevant matters remaining constant, and, given our strategy, we can sensibly consider counterfactual situations in which the *Ancient Mariner* comes into existence at those times. On the other hand, an adequate description of the manipulations of the linguistic medium generative of the text of *Kubla Khan*, it might be argued, *does* precisely locate the performance relative to other events in the world. If so, then we cannot imagine that the very same performance occurs at a different time relative to those events, and this accounts for our intuition that *Kubla Khan* could not have come into existence at such a time.

In the last couple of paragraphs, I have appealed to the idea of "an adequate representation" of the performance generative of an artistic vehicle, and the reader may be wondering whether this notion can carry the dialectical weight here assigned to it. In particular, it might be asked what basis there is for the assumption that certain features of provenance are to be included, and others excluded, from an adequate representation of the performance generative of the vehicle of a given work. What principle constrains such claims about "adequate representation" so that they can serve as independent confirmation of the proposed strategy for accommodating the work-relativity of modality? And, perhaps equally worrying, how are generative performances being conceived if their time of occurrence is to be treated as, in many cases, a non-essential property of those performances? On standard philosophical treatments of events, the time of occurrence of an event-token is *constitutive* of, and thus, by the modality principle, an essential property of, that event-token. So, it would seem, the performances generative of artistic vehicles are not to be conceived as events so construed. But what, then, is their ontological status?

These questions will be addressed in chapter 7, where I clarify the constitution and ontological status of the performances with which I propose to identify artworks. To briefly anticipate what I shall argue there, an adequate representation of an artistic performance generative of an artistic vehicle is one that takes full account of those manipulations of a vehicular medium, on the part of one or more agents, the aim of which is to specify a focus of appreciation. Such performances are what I term "happenings" or "doings," particular occurrences that might have transpired otherwise. Happenings, I shall argue, are required to make sense of much of our modal talk about events in general, and artistic performances, as happenings, have the properties required to make sense of the work-relativity of our modal judgments about artworks. Finally, we can clarify the idea of an "adequate representation" of the performances generative of particular artistic vehicles without begging any questions concerning the work-relativity of modality. For the proposed strategy affirms that, *whatever* one takes to be an "adequate representation" of the performance generative of an artistic vehicle, it is this that determines what one takes to be the modal properties of the resulting work.

The suggestion, then, is that (1) in appreciating a work, we arrive at a perspicuous representation of the performance whereby the work focus was specified; (2) it is relative to that representation that we decide when we have *the same performance* in counterfactual situations; and (3) it is these judgments about sameness of performance that ground and explain the work-relativity of our modal judgments about works. According to this strategy, the question of which features of provenance we regard as essential for a given work depends upon how we would characterize the manipulations of the vehicular medium through which the work-focus is specified. Our intuitions about "same work" in modal contexts track our intuitions about "same specificatory performance," which, in turn, reflect our construction, in appreciating the work, of a perspicuous representation of that performance. In giving a characterization of the kind of performance through which works come into existence, this answer is principled, while allowing appropriate flexibility in virtue of the sorts of considerations that enter into determining whether we have *the same performance* on two occasions. The underlying idea is that our intuitions as to the modal properties of works are of the form: "Could this have been *done* under those circumstances?," where "this" refers to a generative performance rather than the product of such a performance.

If this is the right story to tell about the ascription of modal properties to works, however, and if, as the modality principle maintains, a work's essential properties are also its constitutive properties, then the motivated manipulations generative of a work-focus must also partially determine the *constitutive* properties of a work. If this is at least part of the answer to the *individuation* question, we can return to the *ontological* question: what kind of thing must works be if generative performances so construed at least partially determine their constitutive properties?

Unsurprisingly, the answer to this question that I wish to urge upon the reader is that works should be identified with the generative performances themselves, on some construal of those performances that requires further analysis. But, if the work-relativity of the modal properties of works is indeed to provide an argument in favor of the performance theory, it is important to be clear how the argument runs. More specifically, the argument for the performance theory cannot rest merely on the claim – central to Levinson's own arguments for his brand of contextualism – that the manner in which an artistic vehicle came into existence is partly constitutive of the resulting work, in virtue of the role it plays in the individuation of works. As Davidson has stressed, we must not conflate questions of ontology and questions of individuation.[13] Sunburn, for example, is a physical condition of the skin, but what makes such a physical condition count as sunburn is the process whereby the skin came to be in that condition. It would be wrong to conclude, however, from the fact that the process whereby a skin condition is caused is one of the individuating conditions of sunburn, that the latter, when we ascribe it to John, is itself a process. Of course, there *is* a process termed sunburn, but the sunburn we ascribe to John is the product of such a

---

13   Davidson's argument is discussed in more detail in the first section of chapter 8.

process, not the process itself. Sunburn, then, might be identified with skin-condition-SK-as-caused-by-a-particular-physical-process-SP.

Analogously, we can acknowledge that the performances whereby focuses of appreciation are specified enter into the individuation of art-works without identifying the works themselves with such performances. Thus, it might seem, Levinson could modify his contextualism to take account of the work-relativity of modality by identifying a work with a structure-type-*S*-as-indicated-by-a-particular-performance-*P*. The consti-tutive and essential properties of a work, so conceived, will depend upon *which* aspects of provenance are built into the characterization of *P* for that work. Thus, it seems, it is our intuitions as to what would be an ade-quate characterization of the generative performance *P* that ground our modal intuitions about works, just as the proposed strategy for dealing with the work-relativity of modality requires. In this way, it might be argued, a modified contextualism can accommodate the work-relativity of modality, even if, as argued earlier, standard versions of the indicated structure theory cannot.

The problem with this response is that it fails to preserve the insight, expressed in the earlier characterization of the work-relativity of modal-ity, that aspects of provenance bear upon our modal judgments with a *variable* force that reflects *our overall sense of what is to be appreciated* in a given work. The claim is not merely that provenance plays a role in the individuation of, and the ascription of modal properties to, artworks, but that it is particular aspects of the supposed history of making of an indi-vidual artistic vehicle that significantly determine our sense of what the resulting work *is* and what its essential properties are. There is no ana-logue, in the sunburn example, of the *variable* bearing of aspects of provenance on our sense of what a work *is*. Rather, we can give a univo-cal characterization of the causal process that enters into something's being sunburn, furnishing us with necessary and sufficient conditions for something's being sunburn in counterfactual circumstances. The univo-cal characterization will be given by a description of the "particular" causal process SP cited in our analysis of sunburn.

In the case of the proposed revision of Levinson's account, however, no such univocal characterization is forthcoming. The *particularity* of "a-particular-performance-*P*," for the revised contextualist account, can only consist in its being a performance which specifies a focus of appreciation through the manipulation of a vehicular medium, this being the relational property shared by those indicated structures with which the contextual-ist wishes to identify works. But this gives us no insight into our modal intuitions about works. What drives our modal intuitions, I have suggested, is our sense of what is significant in the particular performance whereby a given artistic vehicle is generated, where the "particularity" of the performance is *its individual nature*, not some general property it shares with other generative artistic performances. Thus we should not respond to the work-relativity of modality by identifying musical or literary works with structure-types that share the relational property of being the products of a particular kind of performance.

It might seem that it is still open to a contextualist to argue that manipulations of a vehicular medium bear upon the constitutive and modal properties of works only because they bear upon *the nature of the focus of appreciation specified* by the artist. The aspects of provenance that we need to take into account, in providing an adequate representation of a performance generative of a work-focus, are, it might be claimed, just those that affect the focus thereby specified. This bears upon the modal properties of works because a difference in the specified focus – in particular, a difference in the artistic statement articulated – entails a difference in work. This reiterates an aspect of the contextualist view noted in the previous chapter. The contextualist, as we have seen, takes features of provenance to be work-constitutive because, if they are *not*, then work-focuses cannot possess the sorts of determinate properties ascribed to them in our critical and appreciative practice. It is because many of the aesthetic and artistic properties of the work-focus supervene not on structure alone, but on structure and certain features of provenance, that the relevant features of provenance must be constitutive of works.

But nothing in our discussion of the work-relativity of modality entails that only features of provenance that bear in this way on appreciable features of a specified focus of appreciation can enter into the sort of adequate representation of a generative artistic performance that grounds our modal intuitions about works. In fact, it was argued in the previous chapter that there are indeed features of provenance that bear upon our sense of what has been done, artistically speaking, by means of a generative performance, but that do not affect the focus of appreciation specified through that performance. If there are constitutive and essential features of a work's history of making that cannot owe this status to their bearing on the work's focus of appreciation, the contextualist lacks an explanation of why this should be so.

As a further step in my cumulative argument for the performance theory, therefore, I suggest that we can best accommodate the work-relativity of modality if we avail ourselves of a strategy that identifies works with generative performances of some sort, rather than with their contextualized or uncontextualized products. But, as the reader is surely protesting, the relative novelty of this ontological proposal, coupled with the amount of philosophical energy expounded in recent years on ontological matters, suggests that there must be good reasons why philosophers have pursued structuralist or contextualist alternatives rather than adopt the sort of strategy I am proposing. Are there not obvious, and serious, obstacles to an ontological view like the performance theory?

There are certainly *thought* to be such obstacles, and whether they can be overcome will depend upon *how* one seeks to develop the potential insight that artworks are to be conceived as performances. To clarify the perceived failings of views that, like the performance theory, conceive works to be generative performances of some description, it will be instructive to examine the reception of the only such theory to be seriously advanced in the recent analytic literature. Therefore, in the next chapter, I shall present and critically analyze the theory in question – Gregory Currie's so-called "action-type hypothesis," whose "boldness," lauded by its critics, did not save it from a blistering critical response. After assessing the virtues and failings of Currie's view, and after identifying a number of crippling problems that it faces, I shall argue, in the following chapters, that the "performance theory," when spelled out more fully, can avoid such problems.

5.4 Appendix: A Defense of the "Modality Principle"

First, let me set out what I take to be the relationship between ontology and individuation – that is, the relation between something's having a particular ontological status and its being individuated in a certain way, where individuation is a matter of determining when we have the *same* thing on different occasions. I shall assume, following David Wiggins,[14] that the following account of individuation is broadly correct. We judge whether, in two given situations, we have the same entity e or different entities e and f, by bringing e under a sortal that characterizes the kind of thing that e is. Matters of sameness or difference are to be decided relative to a judgment "e is a *P*," where *P* is the sortal that characterizes the kind of thing that e is. The sortals under which entities can be brought for the

14 I draw here on David Wiggins' discussion of such matters in his 1980. The central thesis, for current purposes, is what Wiggins terms the "sortal dependence of individuation" (15).

purposes of individuation express "substance concepts." Where *P* is a sortal expressing a substance concept, it carries with it a criterion according to which P-type things are individuated – by reference, let us suppose, to their φ-properties. We may term the latter the "individuating" properties of e, given that e is rightly classified as a *P*. e, then, is this *P*, that is, the *P* having these φ-properties.

Ontology bears upon individuation in that it is the broader ontological classification of *P*-type things that determines what kinds of individuating conditions are appropriate. For example, in the case of physical objects like chairs and tables, we individuate particulars by reference to the presence or absence of some spatio-temporally continuous path connecting an entity encountered on one occasion with entities encountered on other occasions. If e is a table, and is also the table at which I was writing yesterday, then it is in virtue of the existence of such a spatio-temporally continuous path, rather than in virtue of visual resemblance, that the entity at which I am writing today is the same entity e rather than a different entity f. As is well known, things get much more complicated when the particulars in question are persons, but we need not go into such matters.

A similar analysis holds if we consider the classification of entities as *instances* of some generic entity, such as a kind or a universal – that is, where our sortal is brought to bear in determining whether we have "instances of the same *x*" rather than "the same instance of *x*." Suppose, for example, that we subscribe to the view that something belongs to the ontological category "natural kind" in virtue of behaving in certain lawlike ways in virtue of its microstructure. e and f are the same instance of a natural kind K just in case they are both instances of K and they stand in the sort of spatio-temporally continuous relation to one another by reference to which K-type instances are individuated. But e and f are instances of the same kind K in virtue of the fact that they have the same microstructure. This allows us to talk about the individuating conditions of the natural kind K itself. Relative to the sortal "natural kind," having a specific microstructure is the individuating property of K, the property in virtue of which entities are classified as instances of K: K is *this* natural kind, namely, the one whose instances have *these* microstructural properties.

We can apply these somewhat abstract reflections to more immediate concerns by considering the individuation of literary works on structuralist and "contextualist" construals of the ontological status of the work. For the structuralist, literary works are linguistic structure-types, texts, and we have an instance of a literary work whenever we have an (appropriate) instantiation of the relevant structure. We therefore have two instances of the *same* literary work when we have two (appropriate) instantiations of the same text. Assuming that texts, as linguistic structure-types, are themselves individuated in terms of sameness of spelling and sameness of language, we have two instantiations of the same literary work when we have two (appropriate) generations of identically spelled tokens of a linguistic structure-type in a given language. For this reason, the structuralist will insist, Cervantes and Menard do not produce distinct literary works, but only produce two instances of the same literary work (assuming that both texts are in the same language). Being in a particular language and being spelled in a particular way are then the *individuating* conditions of the literary work, the conditions by reference to which something qualifies as an instance of the work.

For a contextualist like Levinson, however, things look very different. If literary works are "indicated linguistic structure-types," then they belong to a very different ontological category from structure-types themselves – albeit a rather puzzling ontological category, as critics have pointed out.[15] How literary works are individuated, on such a view, will depend upon how the notion of indicated structure is cashed out, as we saw above. Suppose, for example, we build into our characterization of an indicated structure some reference to a particular individual who does the indicating and a particular time at which the indicating takes place. Then we have an instance of a given literary work, qua indicated structure, just in case the relevant structure-type is instantiated by the individual in question at the assigned time. We would have two instances of the *same* literary work just in case (per impossibile) this feat is performed in the actual world on two distinct occasions. Trivially, therefore, Cervantes and Menard do not produce two different instances of the same literary work. On this ontological story, the individuating conditions of the literary work will be much more complex, depending, as noted above, on what we build into our understanding of the notion of an "indicated structure."

We may now ask how the *individuating* conditions of an entity e bear upon the *modal* properties of e, and, in particular, on the vexed question whether e possesses any *essential* properties, properties it must possess in every counterfactual situation in which it exists. Before offering an answer to this question, let me introduce one more piece of terminology. I have defined the individuating conditions of an entity e as those conditions which individuate it as a thing of type P, assuming that "P" is the sortal

---

15   See Currie 1989: 58. We shall return to this charge in chapter 8.

appropriate for e. I shall define the *constitutive* properties of an entity e as the ordered pair comprising its individuating conditions and the sortal under which it is properly individuated. The constitutive properties of e specify what we are saying of e when we say it is *this P*. I shall now offer and try to defend the following principle, which I refer to as the "modality principle": all and only the constitutive properties of an entity e are *essential* properties of e.

The modality principle can be applied to our modal talk about artworks if the terms that we use to label artworks – terms like *Ulysses, Guernica*, and the *Enigma Variations* – serve to pick out particular entities in the actual world and thereby enable us to talk about those very entities under counterfactual conditions. More technically, the modality principle will apply to our modal talk about artworks if such labels function as "rigid designators." A rigid designator is a term that designates the entity designated in the actual world in every possible world in which it designates anything at all. Kripke (1980) and others have claimed that certain classes of expressions in a language function as rigid designators, rather than as disguised descriptions of some sort. In particular, it is claimed, proper names and natural kind terms such as "gold" and "water" are rigid designators. If, as seems plausible, the terms that we use to denote works of art are proper names, and function in modal contexts in the way proper names are claimed to function by Kripke et al., then it would follow from the modality principle that all and only the constitutive properties of an artwork are essential properties of that work. This restriction on the application of the modality principle to modal discourse about artworks is significant, however. For one might challenge the argument developed in this chapter by denying that the terms used to classify artworks are rigid designators. Indeed, as we shall see, Currie adopts just such a strategy as a way of avoiding the problems that I develop by appeal to the modality principle.

Here is the intuition that underlies the modality principle linking constitutive and modal properties as it applies to artworks. First, if work-denoting terms are rigid designators, then what we are asking, when we ask about the modal properties of a work – say, Turner's *Snowstorm* – is which properties of the entity e* denoted by "*Snowstorm*" in the actual world must be possessed by e* in every possible world in which it exists. Since the constitutive properties of e* are just the properties that distinguish it as a painting and individuate it from other works of its kind, however, they are presumably the very properties that allow us to make sense of talking counterfactually about one work, *Snowstorm*, rather than another work that differs from this in some constitutive property. So, if work-denoting terms function as rigid designators in modal contexts, the essential properties of a work are the constitutive properties of the entity that is the work in the actual world.

It is crucial to note that this argument does *not* depend upon what might, following Kripke (1980), be termed the "telescope" view of how real-world entities are located in counterfactual situations. Kripke maintains that, in our talk of possible worlds, we *specify* which real-world entities are in a world. A world contains Napoleon, for example, in virtue of such a specification, not because an individual independently identifiable in that world, as if by looking through a telescope, satisfies the criteria for being Napoleon. The matter at issue in the present context, however, is: what are we doing when we specify that *this* individual (for example, Napoleon) rather than some other individual (for example, Napoleon's twin brother) exists in a given possible world? This question bears upon our modal claims, because, in answering it, we bring out certain constraints on such acts of specification. For example, I cannot specify that Napoleon exists in a given world but that in that world he is an aardvark; nor, if Kripke's further suggestion is right, can I specify that Napoleon exists in a world but has different parents. Napoleon, in another possible world, must be the very individual denoted by "Napoleon" in the actual world, and there are constraints on specification that derive from the nature of the individual in question. My claim, then, is that talk of the "nature" of the individual, here, is talk of the individual's constitutive properties, as defined above. It is the constitutive properties of Napoleon that must hold of him in any possible world in which we specify him to exist.

If a work-denoting term "*S*" is *not* a rigid designator, however, but a definite description, then the modality principle need not apply to our modal discourse about works. In such a case, we need to ask whether, in a modal claim of the form "*S* could have been Θ," the claim is to be understood in terms of *de re* or *de dicto* modality. On a *de re* reading, we are asking about the modal properties of the entity denoted by "*S*" in the actual world, and the same analysis will hold as given above. In other words, to say that a modal claim containing a description should be read *de re* is to treat the description as a rigid designator in that context. On a *de dicto* reading, on the other hand, we are asking about the properties that are necessarily shared or contingently possessed by those entities in different possible worlds that are *S* in those worlds in virtue of satisfying a suitable number of the descriptions associated with the label "*S*." In this case, it is very unlikely that we can evaluate the modal claim by attending to the constitutive properties of the entity that is *S* in the actual world.

Its constitutive properties, apart from its being a given type of work, are presumably those that individuate it as, for example, a particular canvas upon which is inscribed a particular design. But none of these properties, save the constitutive property of generic identity, need be shared by every member of the class of entities that are S in their respective worlds, if we take the term "S" to function as a genuine cluster term.

Consider, for example, the following modal claim (MC): "the tallest defenseman in the National Hockey League could have been Welsh." If we read the modality in MC *de dicto* rather than *de re*, we evaluate the claim by reference to different possible worlds in which different individuals satisfy, in a world w, the description "the tallest defenseman in the National Hockey League in w." So, if the individuals in question are $\{a, b, c, \ldots n\}$, the claim is true if at least one of these individuals is Welsh. But it may throw no light on the truth of the modal claim to ask about the constitutive properties of the individual who is the tallest defenseman in the National Hockey League in the actual world. In fact, it might be held that ethnic origin is an essential property of persons, so that, if the tallest defenseman in the National Hockey League in the actual world is *not* Welsh, this may be a constitutive property of that person, and thus one he possesses essentially. Nonetheless, MC, read *de dicto*, is presumably true.

Let me briefly respond to a couple of possible sources of disquiet with the foregoing defense of the modality principle. In the first place, it might be suggested that, to the extent that we are willing to talk about essential properties of entities, we must allow that entities have essential properties not included in their constitutive properties. For example, it might be said, it is an essential property of a table that it have, at any given moment that it exists in a given world, a determinate spatio-temporal location in that world. I grant this point, but assume it can be easily handled by modifying the characterization of "constitutive property" to include not only the sortal under which e is properly individuated but also any properties that are entailed by that sortal, given the more general ontological category under which it falls. Given this modification, the inference from something's being an essential property to its being a constitutive property seems sound. If p is a property that e must have in any world in which it exists, then it is a property e must have in the actual world if e actually exists. If it is not a property directly pertaining to the more general kind of thing that e is (say kind K), then, given that it is *variable* for things of that kind, it is reasonably taken to be among e's individuating properties in virtue of which it is differentiated, as *this* K, from other Ks.

The inference from being a constitutive property to being an essential property might seem more problematic. It might be thought that a commitment to e's having essential properties is being directly inferred from our ability to individuate e in the actual world. If this were indeed the structure of the argument, it might be responded that our ability to individuate in no way presupposes that there are specifiable "individuating conditions." We may, in the manner proposed by Wittgenstein, proceed by reference to "family resemblances" between the things already individuated as particular *K*s and novel cases which we now so classify. If there are no such identifiable "individuating conditions," then the latter cannot serve as the basis for the ascription of essential properties. I fully grant this objection, but take it that my argument is unaffected, since I was not assuming that all individuation must proceed by reference to determinate individuating conditions. All I require is that (1a) how we individuate entities reflects more general ontological considerations as to the kind of thing an entity is and how such things might be individuated, and (2) where we *can* identify determinate individuating conditions relative to a given entity, those conditions may furnish us with essential properties of the entity in question.

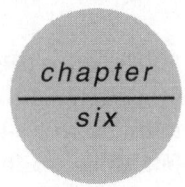
Artwork, Action, and Performance

6.1 The "Action-Type Hypothesis"

As we noted in chapter 3, it has been a rarely questioned article of faith in analytic aesthetics over the past 30 years that the question, "What is the ontological status of the work of art?," is misconceived, resting on the mistaken assumption that there is a *single* ontological category to which works in the different arts belong. In repudiating such an assumption, philosophers have upheld an orthodoxy of ontological pluralism. In Wollheim's original defense of such a pluralism, as we saw, paintings and sculptures are taken to be physical objects, novels and musical works to be structure-types. Subsequent work within this tradition, however, has needed to avail itself of a more ambitious ontology in its attempts to shore up the basic Wollheimian framework in the face of a growing recognition of the place of provenance in the individuation of works. As a result, we inherit a philosophical bestiary containing such creatures as culturally emergent but physically embodied entities, objects-under-interpretations, pieces specified intensionally within artistic indexing conventions, and indicated structures. In matters of ontology, it might be thought, contemporary philosophy of art has almost no shame!

Responding to this situation in *An Ontology of Art* (1989), Gregory Currie argues that all artworks belong to a single and relatively respectable ontological category: they are all *action-types*. Critics of Currie's book, while expressing admiration for the boldness of this claim, cavilled at the idea that artworks are to be classified as action-like entities,[1] as generative processes rather than the products of such processes. In the face of these

---

1 See, for example, the reviews of *An Ontology of Art* in Budd 1990; Wolterstorff 1991; Shields 1995; and the critical notice in Levinson 1992a.

criticisms, Currie appears to have given up on his proposed ontology of art, or, at least, to have given up the project of promoting it. Within a year, one finds him writing on ontological matters without alluding to the so-called "action-type hypothesis,"[2] and he has never, to my knowledge, attempted to answer his critics in print. This has led many to assume that the project of identifying artworks in general with processes of some kind, rather than with the contextualized or decontextualized products of those processes, has been conclusively undermined. Since I am proposing an ontology of art that, like Currie's, takes works to be process-like rather than product-like entities, it will be valuable to examine at some length Currie's position and the criticisms it generated. This will clarify those respects in which the performance theory differs from Currie's view. It will also help us to determine whether, to the extent that Currie's critics were right in their attacks on the action-type hypothesis, the performance theory can evade such criticisms.

According to Currie, an artwork is an action-type. An action-type is a generic entity that can in principle be multiply realized, or enacted by different agents on different occasions. An enactment of an action-type by an agent is a *token* of that type. For example, attending a screening of *Gone With the Wind* is an action-type which has been tokened by many people on at least one occasion and by some people on many separate occasions. Currie maintains that an artwork, as an action-type, is a discovering of a particular structure-type (*S*) by a particular method. A particular way of discovering a given structure-type is what Currie terms the *heuristic path* (HP) utilized by the discoverer. To characterize the heuristic path is to identify all relevant features of the method whereby the structure-type was discovered. To token such an action-type – to "enact" the work in question, as Currie puts it – is to discover the structure-type in question by the means prescribed in the heuristic path. Schematically, then, an artwork, as an action-type, can be represented by an expression of the form: the discovering of S_n via HP_i by x at t, where "x" and "t" are variables taking as values an individual and a time respectively. We will say more about the constitutive elements of Currie's "action-types" shortly.

Currie defends the action-type hypothesis (ATH) by means of epistemological arguments of the sort characterized at the end of chapter 1 above. An epistemological argument, we may recall, draws an ontological conclusion from an epistemological premiss and a methodological premiss. The epistemological premiss identifies the kinds of properties ascribable to

2   See his 1991, for example.

works in our reflective appreciative and critical practice, and the method-ological premiss – the "pragmatic constraint" – asserts that ontology of art must fit with such practice. Currie develops his epistemological premiss through the critique of aesthetic empiricism sketched in chapter 2 above. He argues that "the appreciation of artworks is the appreciation of a certain kind of achievement" (72), where the "achievement" is the action per-formed by the artist, and not merely the entity generated through that action. The methodological premiss requires that the term "work of art" be elucidated in the context of "an overall aesthetic theory which describes and analyses the sorts of relations that hold between us as critics and observers, and the works themselves" (11–12). Works are to be assigned to a particular ontological category only if it can accommodate "the ways in which works are to be judged and appreciated" in our critical and appre-ciative practice.

Given the epistemological and methodological premisses, Currie argues as follows:

1 "Achievement properties" – properties that pertain to what the artist achieved in executing a work – must be attributed to the *work*, and not just to the creative activity of the artist.
2 These properties, as properties of the work, are relevant to the artis-tic value of the work, and not to some separable "art-historical" value.
3 Given the pragmatic constraint, artworks must be assigned to an ontological category, or to ontological categories, whose members can possess such achievement properties.
4 The best overall theory of art consistent with (2) takes artworks to be action-types: "In general, an art work will be an action type with two 'open places' (one for a person, one for a time) and having three constitutive elements: a structure [y], a heuristic [z], and the rela-tion *x discovers y by means of z*" (70).
5 It is therefore crucial to distinguish artworks from "instances of art-works," that is, "those concrete things we come into contact with when we experience a work of art" (5), such as canvases hanging on walls of galleries, copies of novels, and performances of musical works. To avoid confusion, I shall henceforth talk of "Currian instances" of works when "instance" is used in this sense. Signifi-cantly, though artworks are types, on Currie's account, tokens of those types are not Currian instances of works but the action-tokens that individual artists enact in generating the structures partially con-stitutive of their works.

We have already examined, in earlier chapters, the sort of reasoning that can be offered in support of (1) and (2). I shall focus, therefore, on the argument offered in support of the conclusion, drawn in (4), that, if achievement properties are artistic properties of works, then the ontology of art that best satisfies the pragmatic constraint is the ATH. Currie argues for this conclusion by elimination: none of the plausible alternatives to the ATH, he maintains, can do justice to the role that achievement properties play in the appreciation of works. Two alternative accounts are considered and found wanting. First, as we saw in chapter 2, Currie rejects "structuralism" – the view that "the work itself is a certain pattern of lines and colours, structures of sounds, or sequences of words" (47) – on the grounds that it cannot allow for the possibility of distinct works with a common structure. Such a possibility would be realized if a given structure-type were to be multiply discovered in a given world, where the different art-historical contexts of discovery conferred distinct and incompatible properties on that structure. If, in such a situation, we identify the work with the structure, then the work will have incompatible properties in a world.

According to Currie, however, not every discovering of a given structure-type eventuates in a distinct work, as would be claimed by those whom he labels "creationists." Creationism is wrong, he argues, because all works admit of multiple realization. For example, suppose that Twin Beethoven, on Twin Earth, discovers the structure of the *Hammerklavier Sonata* in a cultural environment, and by methods, qualitatively identical to those involved in Beethoven's discovery of that structure on Earth. In such circumstances, Currie claims, Beethoven and Twin Beethoven independently produce the same work, given that they "solve the same musical problems in the same way, under the same influences and with the same degree of originality, coming up with that sound structure" (62). For, he claims, given that appreciating a work is appreciating the artist's achievement, "if two artists achieve the same thing, why should we count their works as distinct?" (63). He further maintains that the *work* is not to be identified with the product of the artist's activity, but with the action-type whose tokens are discoverings of the pattern or structure of the *Hammerklavier Sonata* via a particular "heuristic path." A composer's heuristic path comprises the aesthetically relevant facts about his or her actions in coming to a particular sound structure: such facts will include "ways the artist drew on existing works for his inspiration," and "problems the artist had to resolve in order to achieve his end result." Specifying the artist's heuristic path is "a matter of rationally reconstructing the detailed history of his creative thought, insofar as the information available allows this to be done" (68–9).

6.2 Assessing the ATH

Given the argument of earlier chapters, I shall assume that, with further elaboration, the case against structuralism can be sustained. Currie's anti-creationist argument, however, and the positive thesis for which it is an argument, require closer scrutiny. The argument may be reconstructed as follows:

A To (artistically) appreciate an artwork is to appreciate the kind of thing achieved by the artist. (Epistemological claim, based on an appeal to features of critical practice)

B The kind of thing achieved by the artist is the discovering of a certain structure-type via a particular heuristic path. (Premiss)

C To (artistically) appreciate an artwork is to appreciate the discovering of a particular structure-type via a particular heuristic path. (From A and B)

D The discovering of a particular structure-type via a particular heuristic path is an "action-type" which different artists can "enact." (Premiss, re "action-types")

E To (artistically) appreciate an artwork is to appreciate a certain action-type which different artists can enact. (From C and D)

F So

a artworks are action-types. (E)

b if two artists achieve the same thing, that is, enact the same action-type, they produce the same work. (E)

Even if we grant (B) that the kind of thing achieved by the artist is the discovery of a structure-type via a heuristic path, the final step in this argument, from (E)to (Fa), is invalid. From the fact that to appreciate *x*s is to appreciate certain kinds or types, it does *not* follow that *x*s are themselves kinds or types. For appreciating an action- or object-*token* generally presupposes appreciating some kind or type that it instantiates – the kind or type in virtue of instantiating which it is appreciated.[3] Suppose, for

3 Generally, but not perhaps always. If something like the Kantian analysis of pure aesthetic judgments is correct, we must allow for the possibility of appreciating a token object or event "for its own sake," without bringing it under some concept.

example, that John takes a hat-trick in a cricket test match. My appreciating John's doing what he did requires that I subsume his action-token under the action-type in terms of which I would express my appreciation – here, let us assume, the action-*type* "taking a hat-trick in a cricket test match." But my appreciating John's performance *as* a token of this type presupposes that I appreciate the action-*type* "taking a hat trick in a cricket test match," of which type John's performance is a token. It is only insofar as I regard the taking of a hat-trick in a test match as a remarkable *type* of achievement, of which John's performance is a *token*, that I can appreciate John's particular action *as* a token of this type. But this doesn't make John's performance a type. If (E) is true, this reflects both the historically situated nature of artworks and the logic of appreciation, but it entails, by itself, nothing about the ontological classification of works. Another way of bringing out this problem with Currie's anti-creationist argument is as follows. On the most plausible reading of premiss (C), the referent of "the discovering of a particular structure-type via a particular heuristic path" is an action-*token*. The truth of premiss (D), however, requires that the referent of this expression be an action-*type*. In that case, the derivation of (E) from (C) and (D) involves an equivocation.

Similar objections can be raised against the inference from (E) to (Fb). If Twin John takes a hat-trick under qualitatively identical circumstances in the Twin Test on Twin Earth (dismissing the Twin Earth counterparts of the batsmen dismissed by John, by means of qualitatively identical deliveries, etc.), then, to parallel Currie's reasoning, every judgment we would make about John's achievement, qua athletic achievement, we would also make about Twin John's achievement. But, although they have "achieved the same thing," in accomplishing the same athletic feat, they have done so by taking two distinct hat-tricks. Analogously, even if the actions of Beethoven and Twin Beethoven instantiate identical kinds of artistic achievement, it does not follow that they produce the same work, unless we have independent reasons to identify works with *kinds* of achievement, rather than with particular actions that exemplify those kinds. But this is the very identification that the anti-creationist argument is supposed to establish.

Not only do we have reason to question Currie's anti-creationist argument, there are also good reasons to resist Currie's proposal that works are action-types. In the remainder of this section, I shall present four charges against the ATH:

1 The notion of "heuristic" cannot bear the ontological burden placed upon it by the ATH.

2 The notion of "structure" is of limited application in the ontology of art.
3 Neither a realist nor a nominalist construal of "action-types," as that notion is understood in the ATH, can furnish us with an adequate ontology of art.
4 The ATH faces difficulties accounting for the work-relativity of modality as argued for in chapter 5.

6.2.1 Problems with the "heuristic path"

Currie builds the heuristic path whereby a structure-type is "discovered" into the action-type identified with the work. The notion of a heuristic path is based upon influential work in the philosophy of science by Imre Lakatos (1970), as is the idea that specifying the heuristic path is "a matter of rationally reconstructing the detailed history of [the artist's] creative thought, insofar as the information available to us allows this to be done" (Currie 1989: 68–9). Lakatos, attempting to develop a philosophical model of scientific rationality, famously insisted that "rational reconstructions" of particular episodes in the history of science are not fully accountable to the actual historical facts. What matters is that such episodes "come out" as rational when recast in terms of a particular model of rational belief-fixation which permits us to arrange the general historical circumstances (problems, resources, etc.) into an appropriate "narrative." Since rational reconstruction, so construed, is not fully accountable to the actual sequence of events leading a scientist to a given conclusion, alternative and incompatible rational reconstructions of a given episode in the history of science, involving different heuristic paths, might be equally satisfactory when measured against all relevant criteria included in our model of rational belief-fixation. While some have argued[4] that rational reconstruction of this sort is bad epistemology of science, the possibility of alternative rational reconstructions of a given historical episode is not itself a difficulty for Lakatos. For his concern is epistemological: he does not build the heuristic path into the very individuation and identity of episodes in the history of science.

Currie, however, *is* proposing to build the heuristic path into the individuation and identity of artworks, and this presents a serious problem. Suppose we ask the following question: is it a *specification* of the artist's heuristic path, assessable in terms of various criteria for rational recon-

4 See, for example, Kuhn 1970.

struction, that enters into the individuation of artworks as action-types, or are all such specifications accountable to an independently existing heuristic path which itself serves as one of the elements that makes up the artwork itself, qua action-type? We may label these two conceptions of the nature of the heuristic path "heuristic interpretationism" and "heuristic realism" respectively Suppose Currie opts for heuristic interpretationism. Then he must hold that, where we have different, equally acceptable, rational reconstructions of the action-token whereby a particular structure-type is discovered, we must recognize *distinct* action-types that incorporate the distinct heuristic paths posited in these rational reconstructions, and thus, given the ATH, distinct *artworks*. But surely neither actual critical practice nor a "codification" of that practice will license the idea that the creative activities of artists routinely issue in multiple works – for example, that Leonardo produced a number of different works in generating the arrangement of pigment on canvas exhibited as the *Mona Lisa*.

If Currie opts for heuristic realism, then he must clarify the nature of the heuristic path that exists independently of our interpretive endeavors. It cannot be all or even some of the actual events whereby the structure-type was discovered. For, if it were, then the artwork, in having the heuristic path so construed as one of its constituents, would not be multiply instantiable in Twin Earth situations as Currie requires. Twin Earth, here, is supposedly another planet existing in the same world as Earth, and a given token sequence of events can be instantiated at most once in a world.

Currie's discussion of the "Twin Beethoven" example suggests that we should identify the heuristic path with the actual sequence of events *qualitatively construed*. The heuristic component of the work, then, is given by the description, "a manner of discovery qualitatively identical to *this*," where "this" picks out the actual sequence of events whereby the structure is discovered. But this will build into the work, as constitutive features, qualitative features of this sequence of events that are surely quite irrelevant to the identity of the work – for example, the buzzing sound emitted by the fly that sported unnoticed in the corner of the artist's studio while she painted the canvas. Indeed, a primary motivation for speaking of action-types rather than action-tokens is presumably to help to isolate *relevant* features of an action-token which might plausibly be construed as constitutive properties of the work. If, however, we attempt to overcome this problem by delimiting those qualitative features of the actual sequence of events that are properly included in the heuristic path, we seem to be thrown back onto the first horn of the dilemma – the heuristic interpretationist reading of the heuristic path.[5]

6.2.2 Problems with the "structure"

The other principal constitutive element of the artwork, on Currie's account, is the structure-type which is discovered through a particular heuristic path. However, as he is aware, while the thesis that artworks incorporate discovered structures seems well suited to art forms such as music and literature, where works have standardly been viewed as con-textualized or decontextualized structure-types, it is unclear how this thesis is to be extended to the visual arts. He proposes that, in the case of painting, the discovered structure-type is to be identified with the visual pattern or design instantiated by a painted canvas. Similar analyses are intended to apply to sculpture and other visual arts. But this is problematic in a number of respects. First, as Nelson Goodman argued a number of years ago,[6] it seems impossible to specify which features of the overall visual design of a painting are definitive of the structure-type supposedly instantiated by a particular canvas, except by "pointing," literally or metaphorically, to the canvas itself. This is a result of what Goodman terms the "syntactic density" of the pictorial medium. There is no minimal significant element in an artistic pictorial design such that we could come up with a vocabulary for individuating such designs in terms of the order of their component parts. In the case of instances of literary or musical works, we can rely on a notation to capture those features that define the structure-type partly or wholly constitutive of the instantiated work. In the case of pictorial artworks, however, we can appeal to no such notational means of characterizing the artistically relevant features of the design embodied in a painted canvas. To identify the design properties of a work, the best we can do is gesture toward the canvas itself.

Nor is there any obvious way in which this "gesture" could be characterized so as to define a structure-type discoverable on different occasions by a given heuristic path. For example, it will not suffice to represent the structure-type as "a pattern that *looks just like that one*," where "that one" picks out the distribution of pigment on a particular canvas. For whether a given canvas is a token of such a structure-type will depend

5   It is worth noting that Michael Baxandall, whom Currie credits (1989: xi) with employing something like the notion of a "heuristic" in his 1985, understands the notion in a Lakatosian manner but, like Lakatos, accords it only an *epistemological* role.
6   See his 1976, especially 194–9.

upon *whose judgments of similarity in appearance* are at issue. A connois-
seur will be sensitive to differences in design that a lay person will miss,
and they will therefore disagree as to which other canvases exhibit patterns that "look just like" the pattern of a given painting.

Even if there were some of way of solving this problem for traditional
works of visual art, the ATH faces a further difficulty in accounting for
many of the late modern works discussed in chapter 1. On the one hand,
there are works in the late modern tradition that are unhappily construed
as involving discovered structures, even if there is an art-object that possesses particular structural features. We do little to facilitate our appreciation of a work like Duchamp's *Fountain* if we construe it as the
discovering of the structural properties of the exhibited urinal by a particular heuristic path. On the other hand, there are conceptual works, such
as Barry's famous piece, that seem completely resistant to a characterization in terms of discovered structure-types.[7]

6.2.3 Problems with "action-types"

One of the supposed virtues of the ATH is that it identifies artworks with
entities of an ontologically unproblematic nature. But the "action-types"
with which Currie wishes to identify artworks are less ontologically innocent than he would have us believe. The work, we are told, "is the action
type that [the artist] performs in discovering the structure of the work,"
and this action-type is "enacted" by the artist (75). We may ask, however,
whether action-types, so construed, exist independently of their tokens,
as a "realist" about such generic entities would maintain, or whether they
exist only when tokened, as a "nominalist" about types would say. Neither
of these answers is promising in the present context. On a realist construal of action-types, artworks exist independently of the action-type
being enacted. This commits us to the existence of an indefinitely large
number of "undiscovered" artworks, which seems an unfortunate consequence. Some might happily countenance a realism or Platonism according to which the different musical or verbal structures licensed by a given
symbol system timelessly exist independently of their realization in the
practice of users of that symbol system.[8] But there is surely something
ontologically profligate in the claim that, for each such structure-type and
for each possible way of discovering that structure-type by a heuristic path,

---

7   As noted in chapter 1, the seriousness of this problem is apparent if one considers the
pieces catalogued in Lippard 1973.
8   See, for example, Kivy 1983, 1987.

there timelessly exists an entity (a work) corresponding to that discovering of that structure-type.

A nominalist about action-types might protest that the preceding argument conflates action-types and action-type descriptions. While our stock of action-type descriptions is unaffected by unfolding events (except for those involving relevant neologism), the same does not hold for the class of action-types: an action-type exists through, and only through, its tokens, the nominalist will maintain. Action-types are like natural kinds in this respect. To decide whether a language contains a given natural kind description, for example, a unicorn-description, we consult a linguist. To decide if the corresponding kind, that is, unicorns, exists, we determine whether there are any instances of the kind. In discovering a certain structure-type by a certain heuristic path, then, the artist may perform an action-token that satisfies a hitherto unsatisfied action-type description, thereby bringing the action-type into existence.

But, if our appreciative interest is really in the action-type rather than in a particular enactment of that action-type, why should it matter to us whether that action-type "exists" in the proposed sense? Why shouldn't "hypothetical" action-types, such as those canvassed in Currie's imaginative examples, interest us, as artworks, as much as, or even more than, those related action-types that "exist"?[9] More significantly, we face, in even sharper form, the difficulty canvassed above concerning the specification of the heuristic. *Which* artwork(s), qua action-types, I bring into existence in discovering a particular structure-type on a particular occasion depends upon which are the artistically relevant action-type descriptions true of my action-token, and *this* depends upon the constraints governing the heuristic component in the type description. The ATH, construed nominalistically, seems to entail that an artist's creative activities may simultaneously generate multiple works, where we surely want to say that such activities generate a single work allowing of different right interpretations. And, we may also note, the ATH, construed realistically, confronts a related difficulty, in that an artist's activities may involve the simultaneous *discovery* of multiple works.

6.2.4 Problems with modality

Finally, Currie faces difficulties in accommodating the work-relativity of modality, as presented in the previous chapter. To see why, we need to

9 We could imagine setting up the Borges chair of comparative literature to study imaginary literary works of the former kind!

examine one further, apparently peripheral, feature of Currie's account. As we have seen, Currie argues, against aesthetic empiricism, that to appreciate a work is to appreciate a certain kind of *achievement*. But he further maintains that, in characterizing the "kind of achievement" with which the work is to be identified, we must take account of *all* features of the history of making that determine appreciable features of the work in the actual world, including features of the art-historical context of making of which the artist was unaware. All such features of provenance are to be included in the heuristic path, and are thereby constitutive properties of the work. Since, as we shall see, this effectively prevents Currie from accounting for the work-relativity of modality in the manner proposed in the previous chapter, we need to understand why the identification of artworks with action-types leads Currie to adopt such a position.

Currie has to incorporate all features of provenance bearing on the achievement properties of a work into its heuristic path because, if he *doesn't* do this, then some aspects of what we intuitively take to have been achieved in a work will have no bearing on its appreciation. This follows from the identification of artworks with *types* of events. If the work is an action-type whose constitutive elements include a structure-type and a heuristic path, then appreciating the work is appreciating that *type*. Suppose that, as in our "hypothetical Spanish Cubist" example in chapter 5, there are features of provenance unknown to the artist A that bear on what is achieved through her creative activity. If we exclude such features of provenance from the heuristic path, they are thereby excluded from the constitutive elements of the action-type with which we identify the work. For any achievement property that depends upon these excluded features of provenance, the property will not belong to the work, qua action-type. The work will have the relativized property of being such an achievement as enacted by A, but not the property of being such an achievement simpliciter.

Now, however, we can appeal to the assumption that underlies Levinson's anti-structuralist argument – an assumption shared by Currie (1989: 11ff). If works are rightly ascribed achievement properties that depend upon features of provenance unknown to the artist, then works cannot be action-types whose heuristic paths exclude such features of provenance, because action-types so construed possess only relativized versions of these properties. If Currie is not to fall foul of such an objection, he must identify works with action-types whose heuristic paths include all features of provenance bearing on what the artist can rightly be said to have achieved in discovering the structure in question. Thus the heuristic path must incorporate any features of context that are relevant to appreciating the artist's achievement, whether or not such features were known to the artist. So, if appreciating a work just is appreciating what has been achieved, as Currie maintains, then the heuristic path together with the discovered structure-type will determine all of a work's appreciable properties.

But, if a work's constitutive properties are ones it possesses in every possible world in which it exists, as the modality principle requires, then all of the appreciable properties of a work that supervene on structure and heuristic path will be *essential* properties of the work, on Currie's account. This is not to say that all features of the context of creation of a work are constitutive, and therefore (we are assuming) essential, for Currie. The composition of Currie's heuristic path reflects the operation of the same sort of principle as was employed in our proposed resolution of the problem of work-relativity in the previous chapter. The heuristic path includes only those features of the context of creation that actually bear upon what is achieved by the work. Thus Currie, unlike Levinson, can account for the work-relativity of our modal judgments in respect of works like *Prairie Snowscape* and *Brillo Boxes*. But the ATH also seems to entail that all of a work's appreciable properties are essential, which is strongly counter-intuitive.

Currie certainly wants to resist such a consequence, and he attempts to do so by denying that the modality principle applies to our talk about artworks. While he has to say that all features of provenance bearing on a work's appreciable properties are "constitutive" in our sense, he maintains that the work can exist in worlds where such features of provenance are lacking. For, so he claims, the labels that we use to classify works function not as "rigid designators" but, rather, as disguised descriptions which refer to whatever in a given world complies to a sufficient degree with a cluster of descriptions associated with the label (80ff). Thus, even though the heuristic path for a work like *To the Lighthouse* may refer to precise details of the literary context of discovery of the text, and even though the structure-type specifies to the letter the linguistic structure of that text, the work *To the Lighthouse* can exist in counterfactual situations where both the literary context and the structure of the text differ, with consequent differences in the achievement properties. It can do so because such differences may obtain in the case of the entity that qualifies as *To the Lighthouse* in those situations in virtue of complying to a sufficient extent with the cluster of descriptions associated with the label *"To the Lighthouse."* If Currie is correct, then this would undermine my attempt, in chapter 5, to bring the work-relativity of modality to bear on questions in the ontology of art. For reasons spelled out in the appendix to chapter

5, the modality principle applies only to modal discourse that employs labels that rigidly designate particular entities in the world. If Currie is right, then the principle will not apply to modal discourse about artworks. But, without the principle, there is no way of bringing structural features of our modal intuitions to bear on the individuation of artworks and thus on the ontological issues.

However, Currie's claim that artistic labels are disguised descriptions rather than names is not convincing. First, the sorts of problems traditionally associated with the idea that proper names are really disguised descriptions resurface as problems for our grasp of the modal properties of works. In particular, we may ask what makes certain descriptions more salient than others in determining what counts as a particular work – say, *To the Lighthouse* – in a counterfactual situation. Second, unless we have a principled answer to this question, Currie's proposal will entail that *none* of a work's properties is essential, not even structural ones. For every property P that a work possesses in the actual world, there will be a possible world in which the entity that qualifies as that very work in that world in virtue of superior compliance with the associated cluster of descriptions *lacks* P. Currie accepts this consequence, but this commits him to such claims as the following: Picasso's *Les Demoiselles d'Avignon* could exist in a world in which there are no paintings like those of Cézanne, and Nyman could have created his music to *Drowning by Numbers* in the absence of Mozart's *Sinfonia Concertante*. If we think such claims are false, we cannot endorse Currie's proposal. The ATH will then be an option only if we are prepared to forsake Scylla for Charybdis and accept that a work has all of its appreciable properties essentially.

6.3 Currie and his Critics

There is one crucial difference between the four criticisms of Currie's ATH outlined in the previous section and the majority of the criticisms leveled at Currie in the reviews of his book. For Currie's critics, the principal target was the idea that artworks are to be identified with generative processes rather than with the products of those processes, and the principal argument, sketched below, was intended to show that no such identification of artworks with processes can satisfy the pragmatic constraint on the ontology of art. None of my criticisms, however, challenges in any obvious way the general project of identifying artworks with processes. Rather, they address specific features of Currie's interpretation of that project. In particular, the third and fourth criticisms attack the idea that artworks can be identified with *types* of processes, while the first and second criticisms question the adequacy of the elements taken to be constitutive of those process-types.

There is therefore no prima facie reason to think that the performance theory will be vulnerable to the same four criticisms. For the performance theory identifies works with particular performances, which are process- or event-*tokens* rather than process- or event-types. Further, in characterizing those performances, as manipulations of vehicular media in the interests of specifying focuses of appreciation, there is no reference to heuristic paths, and no suggestion that structures are necessary for the existence of artworks. Of course, as may already be clear, the Currian notions that are conspicuously absent from our talk of artworks as performances were included in the formulation of the ATH for a reason. Such notions do philosophical work that must be done somehow in any adequate ontology of art. We will have to ask, therefore, whether the notions which do the same philosophical work in the performance theory lay that theory open to criticisms that parallel the ones directed at the ATH. A principal objective of the next chapter will be to answer this question in favor of the performance theory.

Before turning to such matters, however, we must take preliminary account of those criticisms of the ATH that target the latter's identification of artworks with processes, and that might therefore seem to bear with equal weight upon the performance theory. As just noted, these criticisms are the ones most often sounded in reviews of Currie's book, and perhaps the ones that persuaded Currie to abandon ontology of art for the more fruitful pastures of fiction, film, and cognitive science. The charge is that the ATH is wildly *revisionary* of our actual critical and appreciative discourse about art, and that it thereby fails to satisfy the pragmatic constraint on ontologizing about the arts. The ATH, it is claimed, entails that much of our talk about art is either false or hopelessly imprecise, for (1) we say all manner of things about artworks that cannot sensibly be said about discoverings of structures via heuristic paths; and (2) the identification of works with process-like entities commits us to the coherence and possible truth of claims about works of art that violate standards of accepted linguistic usage. If well grounded, these charges seems equally telling against any attempt to identify artworks with action- or event-*tokens*, and therefore against the performance theory.

Revisionary examples of type (1) seem worryingly plentiful. We say of Turner's *Snowstorm*, for example, that it hangs in the Tate Gallery in London, has lost some of the brightness of its original color, is protected against acts of vandalism by an elaborate security system, is distinguishable from forgeries by suitably trained experts, and, were it ever to be offered for sale, might be expected to fetch a very tidy sum. To ascribe any of these properties to an action-type or a token performance is surely to commit the sort of mistake that philosophers used to describe as a logical "howler," a category mistake that only a speaker unclear about the rules of correct usage of the English language would ever commit. Similarly, we assume that it might truly be said that Beethoven's Fifth Symphony is currently being performed by the Berlin Philharmonic Orchestra and has many dramatic passages; that Burgess's *Clockwork Orange* contains 27 chapters in its original English edition but only 26 in its American edition; and that Godard's *Weekend* juxtaposes image and sound in a revolutionary manner and, so Godard claimed when charged with producing an unnecessarily violent work, "contains a lot of red." Again, it is unclear how these properties can coherently be ascribed to action-types or to performances (other than performances *of* works). In all of these examples, it seems *obvious* that the bearer of such properties must be the product or outcome of a process or event, not the process or event itself. If artworks are actually action-types or performances, then it seems that these properties that we standardly predicate of works in our critical and appreciative talk about art are not really properties of artworks at all.

Relatedly, critical and everyday discourse about the arts seems predicated on the assumption that works are accessible to receivers in standard contexts of reception. One can look at pictorial works and sculptures, read literary works, listen to or perform musical works, etc. But neither Currie's action-types nor the generative performances of artists are usually accessible to receivers.[10] The Currian instances that *are* standardly accessible to receivers – objects in galleries, performances of musical works, and texts of novels, for example – are neither works nor tokens of works, if works are identified with either action-types or performances that specify focuses of appreciation. Of course, it might be claimed that, in such ordinary talk about artworks, speakers refer in an elliptical way to (Currian) *instances* of works rather than to the works themselves. But actual critical discourse seems quite capable of drawing a distinction between works and their Currian instances in those art forms traditionally regarded as "multiple" – it is *copies* of books that suffer such fates as burning, not books. If a process-centered ontology is to have recourse, here, to a distinction between "talk of works" and "talk of (Currian) instances of works," this distinction cannot itself be motivated by a simple appeal to "actual critical practice."

10   Budd 1990; Levinson 1992a; Wolterstorff 1991 all make this point.

Purportedly revisionary examples of type (2) are less obvious, but equally serious in the eyes of those who bring them against ontologies of art that take works to be process-like rather than product-like entities. A token performance takes place at a certain time, normally has a particular spatial location, endures for a certain time, and may be interrupted a number of times before its completion. If *Le malade imaginaire*, for example, is a particular generative performance, then it can both coherently and perhaps truly be claimed that *Le malade imaginaire* occurred in 1673, in France, took a number of months, and was interrupted by bouts of tuberculosis. But, so the objection goes, these properties are plausibly predicated not of the *work*, but only of the *writing* of the work. To say that the *work Le malade imaginaire* (and not, for example, the action described in the work) has a particular spatio-temporal location and duration is, once again, to commit a category mistake. The ATH is not open to precisely the same purported counter-examples, since action-types lack the distinctive spatio-temporal properties of their tokens. But action-types stand under the condition *that their tokens have such determinate spatio-temporal properties*, and this presents analogous problems.

A beginning of an answer to the "revisionism" objection reiterates a point first stressed in chapter 1. It is not our actual practice as it stands that is to serve as the tribunal against which ontologies of art are to be assessed, under the pragmatic constraint, but, rather, a theoretical representation of the norms that *should* govern the judgments that critics make concerning "the ways in which works are to be judged and appreciated." Of course, any such representation is assessed against its implications for our actual practice, and is open to criticism if it entails revisions in that practice that we would be unwilling, after rational reflection, to undertake.

But, if the relationship between ontological proposal and actual critical practice is so mediated, it is clear how the proponent of the ATH or the performance theory should proceed in responding to the revisionism objection. Ontology, she will point out, is not accountable to the plurality of judgments in actual critical practice but, rather, to a theoretical representation of that practice that argues for the propriety of some, and the impropriety of other, sorts of critical judgments in contexts of rightly appreciating works of art. The task, then, is to motivate, in the context of such a theoretical representation, a distinction between "talk of works" and "talk of instances of works or of work-products." She must argue that features of actual critical discourse that, taken at face value, are incompatible with the idea that works are process-like rather than product-like entities are best reinterpreted as discourse about (Currian) *instances* of works or work-products, rather than discourse about works themselves. In so arguing, she will point to the explanatory virtues of the distinction between works and their Currian instances or work-products, citing general features of our critical and appreciative commerce with artworks that are better explained in terms of such a distinction than in terms of alternative ontologies.

Both the performance theory and the ATH can clearly avail themselves of such a distinction between works, on the one hand, and the kinds of entities with which we come into contact in appreciating works, on the other. Currie, indeed, stresses the distinction between works – action-types – and ("Currian") instances of works – physical objects such as canvases and carved lumps of stone, copies of novels or poems, performances of musical works, etc. The performance theorist, in turn, has available a distinction between generative performances and "work-products" – the *focuses* specified through those performances. Given such distinctions, it can be argued that artistic and critical ascriptions of properties that cannot coherently be predicated of process-like entities – properties such as hanging on the wall of a gallery or being cleaned – do not count against the view that works are process-like entities, because these properties are not ascribed to works at all, but to the *instances* or *focuses* of works or to their constituent elements. Similarly, the purportedly problematic properties of type (2) *are* genuine properties of works, because the writing of *Le malade imaginaire* is the process of *producing an instance of the text* or of *generating a focus that incorporates the text as vehicle*, and this just is the work if one endorses either the ATH or the performance theory.

However, while this is obviously what a defender of either the ATH or the performance theory must say, this is not in itself an adequate response to the objection. For clearly, in sentences in which certain properties are ascribed to Turner's *Snowstorm*, or in which we seem to be talking about the *writing* of *Le malade imaginaire*, there is the appearance of talking about *works* in the first case, and of merely talking about the *creation* of works in the second case. If these appearances are to be discounted by appeal to a distinction between talk about works and talk about their instances or focuses, we are owed some principled account of when a particular claim is rightly taken to be about the work itself and when it is not. It is hardly satisfactory to baldly maintain that, although large segments of our discourse about art are clearly about things that are product-like rather than event-like entities, this doesn't count against the view that works are event-like entities because such discourse is not really about works at all. To put the point in its sharpest form, such discourse seems to be a *paradigm* of talk about works. Thus it seems to be precisely the sort of thing against which any proposed ontology of art must be tested. If a theorist is allowed to dismiss such talk as not being about works, against what touchstone are ontologies of art supposed to be measured? What body of discourse *does* express genuine claims about works, if not our talk about paintings as hanging on walls of galleries, etc.? If the proponent of the performance theory or of the ATH is to meet the charge that her account entails an untenable revisionism in our discourse about art, she must provide some reason, other than its congeniality to her ontology of art, for accepting her analysis of the situation, in terms of a distinction between talk about works and talk about work-instances or work-focuses.

As we noted at the beginning of this section, Currie never explicitly responds, to my knowledge, to the revisionism objection as levied against the ATH, so it is unclear precisely how he would proceed at this point. I shall address the revisionism objection from the perspective of the performance theory in chapter 8. The task now before us is to further elaborate upon the schematic idea of a performance that specifies a focus of appreciation. This will help us to determine whether the identification of artworks with such performances can overcome not only the revisionism objection but also the sorts of criticisms of the ATH that I developed earlier in this chapter.

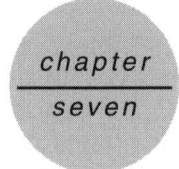
Art as Performance

7.1 Elaborating the Performance Theory

In chapter 3, after analyzing the structure of the focus of our critical and
appreciative attention to artworks, I introduced the performance theory
as an alternative to the structuralist and contextualist ontologies already
in play. According to the performance theory, an artwork, in any of the
arts, is a performance that specifies a focus of appreciation. The latter can
be understood to comprise an articulated content in a broad sense, a
vehicle by means of which the content is articulated, and a set of shared
understandings – an "artistic medium" – which mediates between the
vehicle and the content, permitting the artist to articulate a particular
content through carrying out certain manipulations (in a broad sense) of
the vehicular medium.

In the previous chapter, I critically examined an ontology of art that
in many ways seems similar to the performance theory. Critics have argued
that Currie's ATH fails to provide us with a viable ontology of art, a conclusion with which I concur, although my reasons differ from those that
have moved other commentators. The task before me, therefore, is to
show that the performance theory can succeed where the ATH fails. This
requires that I further elaborate the performance theory, to show how it
can evade the sorts of objections that undermine the ATH. In particular,
more needs to be said about the nature of the performances with which
I propose to identify artworks, the manner in which they are individuated, and the sorts of modal properties they possess. This will require,
once again, that I trespass upon broader philosophical terrain and take
stances on issues that I cannot hope to fully defend in this context. As in
the case of the discussion of the relationship between modality and indi-

viduation in chapter 5 above, I shall try to say enough to render my assumptions plausible to the reader.

In chapter 5, I argued that a theorist who wishes to factor provenance into the identity of the artwork must give an account of the modal properties of works that is both (1) principled and (2) compatible with the work-relativity of our modal judgments. I suggested that such an account can be given if we think of our modal judgments about works as having the following grounding:

1 In appreciating a work, we try to construct a perspicuous representation of the performance whereby the work-focus was specified.
2 It is relative to that representation that we decide when we have *the same performance* in counterfactual situations.
3 It is these judgments about sameness of performance that ground our modal judgments about artworks.
4 This explains the work-relativity of such judgments.

However, so I claimed, if this is the right story to tell about the modal properties of works, and if a work's essential properties are also its constitutive properties, then the performance that specifies the work-focus must also partially determine the *constitutive* properties of a work. This raises the *ontological* question: what kind of thing must works be if artistic performances so construed are partially determinative of their constitutive properties? The performance theory is, in a sense, the most straightforward answer to this question. A work just is the performance whereby a work-focus is specified, the very performance to which we have just appealed in accounting for the work-relativity of the modal properties of works. A work is not, as Levinson might argue, a work-focus *as specified* by such a performance, or, as Currie maintains, an action-type that is instantiated by that performance.

This already indicates how the performance theory can meet two of the objections brought against the ATH. I raised four difficulties, apart from the "revisionism" objection, for Currie's account:

1 The notion of a "heuristic" cannot bear the ontological burden placed upon it.
2 The notion of "structure" is of limited application in the ontology of art.
3 Neither a realist nor a nominalist construal of "action-types," as that notion is understood in the ATH, can furnish us with an adequate ontology of art.

4 Currie is unable to accommodate the work-relativity of modality, since he holds, for reasons intrinsic to his overall account, that work-denoting terms express "cluster" concepts rather than being rigid designators, and he denies that there are essential properties of works.

By identifying works with *token* performances whereby work-focuses are specified rather than with action-types, the performance theory can accommodate the work-relativity of modal and constitutive properties in the manner just sketched. The work just is the performance, completed by a particular work-focus, whose perspicuous description determines the work's modal properties. We also, obviously, avoid the third kind of difficulty faced by the ATH, since the notion of action-type does not figure in our conception of what a work is.

Indeed, the first two difficulties for the ATH do not arise for the performance theory either, since the latter does not take heuristic paths or structures, in Currie's sense, to be constitutive elements in the performances that are artworks. But talk of "heuristics" and "structures" in the ATH *does* do philosophical work. More specifically, in identifying artworks with action-*types* whose constitutive elements are heuristics and structures, the ATH not only provides an account of what is common to the action-types with which we are to identify works of art, but also seeks to exclude from artworks seemingly extraneous features of the artist's activity in "enacting" a given work. If the performance theory eschews such resources, what is to do the philosophical work of the rejected notions?

7.2 Structure and Focus

Something functionally equivalent to Currie's notion of a "structure" is clearly needed if we are to say anything of a general nature concerning the performances that are artworks. As we saw in chapter 6, while the creation of many artworks can plausibly be described in terms of the notion of "discovering a structure," this notion cannot play the role accorded to it in Currie's theory for two reasons: (1) the ATH requires that we associate works with *types* of structures as constituents of those works, but any such correlation of paintings and sculptures with structure-types seems problematic; and (2) in the case of many late modern works, it is not clear that there is a structure plausibly taken to be a constituent of the work.

The first kind of difficulty will not arise for the performance theory, for we can pick out indexically the token-structure generated in the case of a given visual artwork – it is the structure of the very object painted or sculpted by the artist. But any attempt to rehabilitate Currie's notion of structure would be misguided, for the notion is flawed in a more fundamental way. "Structure," as we have seen, is one of three constituent notions that enter into Currie's conception of the artwork, the other two being "heuristic path" and "discovery." The structure is *that which is discovered* by a particular heuristic path. As such, it is supposed to provide us with a general characterization of the *product* or *outcome* of a creative process, insofar as that product or outcome bears upon the appreciation of the artwork. In other words, the notion of structure is offered as an account, partial or total, of what we have termed the "focus of appreciation." But, as we have seen, the internal constitution of the focus of appreciation is complex, and needs to be elaborated in terms of an articulated artistic statement, a vehicle by means of which that statement is articulated, and an artistic medium.

The problem with Currie's notion of "structure" is that it does not map in a useful way onto any of these constituent elements in the focus of appreciation. In the case of a painting, for example, the discovered structure will presumably include certain elements in the articulated artistic statement (the formal elements) since those elements can be seen in the arrangement of pigment on canvas (the vehicle) by one who shares with the artist certain understandings of the art form (the artistic medium). Presumably, on Currie's account, the other elements in the articulated artistic statement are jointly determined by the "structure" in the formal sense and those aspects of provenance that enter into the specification of the heuristic path. If we are convinced that our interest in the product of a generative artistic performance is an interest in a focus of appreciation constituted in the manner for which I have argued, and that the work is to be identified with the performance through which that focus is specified, then we will see no useful role for this notion of "structure" in our ontology of art because (1) it blurs the crucial distinction between vehicular and artistic medium, and (2) it artificially divides the artistic statement articulated in a work. The only way in which we might preserve an ontological role for the notion of "structure" in the face of this criticism is by identifying it with the artistic vehicle alone. But then our original criticism becomes more telling, for in the visual arts, and especially in much late modern visual art, it is unhelpful, at best, to think of the artistic vehicle as a structure.

In elaborating the performance theory, therefore, we should talk not of "discovering a structure" but of "specifying a focus of appreciation," and characterize artworks as performances whereby such focuses are specified. The notion of "specifying a focus of appreciation" is broader than that of "discovering a structure" in two important respects. First, it allows us to accommodate art forms in which the articulation of an artistic statement does not, in any obvious sense, involve the manipulation of a vehicular medium in the interests of discovering or realizing a structure, or an artistic medium that correlates vehicular structures with articulated artistic statements. While the performance theory offers a monistic conception of the artwork – as a particular kind of performance – it permits considerable variation in the elements that realize the constitutive roles in the focus of appreciation, and, in particular, in the vehicular medium. The performance theory preserves an ontological pluralism at the level of the *artwork-focus*, while proposing a monistic view of the work itself. And in espousing a pluralistic conception of the work-focus, the performance theory is able to preserve many insights of contemporary philosophy of art as to *differences* between the arts and their implications for our artistic practice.

Second, in according a central role to specified work-focuses rather than to discovered structures, we are able to accommodate cases where a generative performance issues not in any structure or object capable of entering essentially into the appreciation of a work, but in an action on the part of the artist. In some cases, such as standard works of performance art, the vehicle by means of which a content is articulated is an action-token, and it is the manifest properties of that action-token that must be placed in the context of an artistic medium if one is to grasp the artistic statement articulated by the work. In other cases (conceptual art, and perhaps Readymades), as will be argued in chapters 8 and 9, one need only apprehend the kind of action being performed on this particular occasion.

Note that this does not make a conceptual artwork or a Readymade an action-*type*. The work is a particular performance which specifies a focus whose vehicle is itself the (distinct) performance of an action of a given type in a particular cultural-historical context. Such a construal of the artistic vehicle in many conceptual pieces also differs significantly from the proposal that conceptual *works* are to be identified with the action-tokens in question – that, for example, the work *Fountain* is Duchamp's action (token) of exhibiting a mass-produced urinal. A problem with the latter sort of claim is that we lack the resources to account for the sort of internal complexity in the structure of intentions and actions that may bear upon the appreciation of a conceptual work. Another problem is that, as just suggested, it may be the *type* of action performed that is relevant to the appreciation of a conceptual work, rather than distinctive properties of the particular *token* of that action-type performed. Again, we shall return to these questions in a more systematic way in the following two chapters.

7.3 Heuristics and the Individuation of Artworks

An artwork, we are claiming, is a performance whereby a focus of appreciation is specified. To specify a focus is both to make that focus *specific*, and to make it *intersubjectively available*. It is in virtue of the need for shared understandings that mediate between manipulations of a vehicular medium and the articulation of a determinate content that specification in the first sense involves specification in the second sense. The focus specified through a generative performance *completes* that performance in three senses. It is, first, the thing whose specification is the aim of the performance, this aim being what animates and motivates the performance. It is also the thing whose specification, when accomplished, marks one of the temporal boundaries of the performance identified with the work. Third, and perhaps most significant, as the product of the performance it is central to our appreciation of the performance construed as a doing which achieves something determinate. The work, as performance, is the particular performance through which *this* focus of appreciation is specified. This is why the product of the artist's labors, while not itself the work, is still the *focus* of our appreciative interest in the work. It is the manipulation of the vehicular medium in the interest of specifying *this* focus that we appreciate.

Talk about delimiting the temporal boundaries of the performance identified with the work, however, raises a more general question. How does the performance theorist propose to individuate artworks, as performances? What elements of an artist's overall activity at the time of creating a piece enter into the identity of the work, qua performance? Take, as an example, Jane's first novel. If works are generative performances, then this particular work is the performance whereby she specifies the work's focus of appreciation – a performance which articulates a given content through the manipulation of a linguistic vehicular medium. But which features of Jane's overall activity are constitutive of the artwork so conceived? Suppose that, from the moment when she first conceived the idea of writing her novel to the moment when she completed the final revisions of her text, five years elapsed, during which time there were periods of frenetic activity and other periods when she despaired of the whole idea and applied herself to other pursuits. Presumably, during those five years, a vast number of things occurred in the world, and more particularly in the world of culture, having more or less obvious causal and intentional links to what Jane was doing. Surely much that she did, and much that happened, in that five-year period is completely irrelevant to both the identity and the appreciation of her work. If the work is to be identified with a generative performance, then, it would seem, it must be made up of some subset of the things done by Jane within the relevant temporal span. Also, it seems, it must incorporate, in its identity as a work, some small fraction of the things making up the total socio-cultural context in which Jane's creative activity occurred, if we take provenance to be partly constitutive of artworks. But what principled means do we have for "carving" such an entity out of the relatively seamless continuity of Jane's life during that period, and out of the entire socio-cultural context in which that life unfolded?

Consider another example. We surely do not want to say that a painter's pausing to make and drink a cup of coffee while executing a canvas has any place in either the identity or the appreciation of her work, let alone that it is partially constitutive of the work and therefore a condition on the work's existing in counterfactual situations. But what principled reason can the performance theorist give for excluding this action from the work conceived as generative performance? What I termed in chapter 5 the "individuation question" for a contextualist ontology of art – the problem of determining which features of provenance enter into the identity of the work – presents itself to the performance theory in precisely this form.

In wrestling with this problem, we may be tempted by something like Currie's notion of a "heuristic path," whose principal role in his theory is to make the sorts of distinctions we currently require. The heuristic path contains just those actions on the artist's part and just those features of context that play a role in determining what the artist achieved in the discovery of a particular structure. On a Currian analysis of Jane's novel, we determine which features of Jane's activity and the context in which it occurred bear upon what we take to be her artistic achievement. These features, qualitatively construed, are then incorporated into the heuristic path that is one of the constituent elements in the work, the other principal element being the linguistic structure-type that Jane discovered through such a heuristic path. A performance theorist, it might seem, could tailor Currie's strategy to her own purposes by identifying Jane's work with a particular token, as enacted by Jane on the relevant occasion, of the action-type with which her work would be identified on a Currian analysis (appropriately modified so that the notion of a "focus of appreciation" replaces the notion of a "structure-type," as argued above).

One obvious objection to this strategy is that we inherit many of the difficulties that, so I argued in chapter 6, are inherent in the ontological role ascribed to heuristic paths in the ATH. Suppose that we allow for *alternative* and possibly incompatible characterizations of what the artist has achieved that are equally defensible given the norms that govern right critical practice. Then, given that the heuristic path incorporates all and only those aspects of provenance taken to be relevant to the artist's achievement, the proposed strategy – identifying the work with a token-ing of the Currian action-type – seems to commit us to the existence of different *works* arising out of what is intuitively a single creative performance, where it seems much more plausible to say that we have a single work admitting of different *interpretations*. To spell this out more clearly, many have argued that (1) there can be distinct and sometimes incompatible interpretations of *the same work*.[1] It also seems reasonable to maintain, however, that (2) where we have incompatible interpretations, they differ as to *what the artist has achieved*. But, if we appeal to the notion of what the artist has achieved to "carve out" the work, as specifying performance, from the larger agential context in which a given focus of appreciation has been specified, then (2) seems to entail that (3) where we have incompatible interpretations, they must differ as to *what the work is*. For, as positings of different achievements, they will "carve out" different performances. And this seems to conflict with (1). We cannot reconcile (1) and (3) by interpreting the latter as a disagreement about the qualities of a common object, "the work," because this is ruled out by our appeal to "the artist's achievement" in identifying the work.

Note that this problem is not avoided by espousing what we termed heuristic realism, according to which there is a "fact of the matter," independent of our rational reconstructions, as to what the artist's real achievement is. For not only is heuristic realism somewhat implausible, requiring as it does that there be independent facts not simply as to what Jane did, but as to what she achieved in her doing; but, as we just saw, any ontology of art that individuates works by reference to a specific artistic achievement seems incompatible with the intuition that works admit of distinct and sometimes incompatible right interpretations. Thus the notion of "heuristic path" is no more serviceable than the notion of "structure-type" for an ontology of art that treats works as being process-like rather than product-like entities. The problem with Currie's ATH is

1   See, for example, Goodman and Elgin 1988: ch. 3.

not merely that it identifies works with action-*types* rather than with token performances. It also misidentifies the constituent elements in the actions themselves.[2]

However, the performance theorist can avail herself of an alternative solution to the problem of individuation, one prefigured in our earlier discussion of the work-relativity of modality. The key to accounting for the latter, it will be recalled, is to see our modal intuitions about works as reflecting our judgments as to when we would have the same focus-specifying performance. Such a performance is taken to involve the manipulation of a vehicular medium, in light of shared understandings, with the aim of articulating an artistic statement through the resulting vehicle. Our modal intuitions about works track our sense of what would count as an adequate characterization of these motivated manipulations – an adequate characterization of *what was done* in a particular creative performance. Taking this as our guide in addressing the problem of individuation – which we may do if a work's constitutive properties are identical to its essential properties – we may say that a work, as a performance, comprises just those actions on the part of the artist(s), and just those features of the performative context, that would be incorporated into such an adequate characterization of the motivated manipulations resulting in the artistic vehicle of the work. It is, again, our sense of what was done, as this sense emerges in our appreciative engagement with a work, that determines what the work's constitutive properties are.

It is because our sense of what was done, as this notion was elucidated in chapter 5, is distinct from our sense of what was *achieved* through that doing that we can allow, as Currie cannot, for appreciable properties of a work that are not essential properties of that work. An adequate characterization of what was done, we may recall, must take account of those aspects of the art-historical context that are implicated in the mental states ascribed to the artist as partly *motivating* her manipulations of the vehicular medium. But it will not include other features of the art-historical

2   It should perhaps be stressed here, to avoid possible misunderstanding, that the performance theory is proposed as an independent theory in the ontology of art, rather than being, in any sense, an attempt to patch up Currie's ATH in the face of objections. My interest in the ATH is in whether anything can be learned from the difficulties it faces that may be of use in elaborating the performance theory. The present moral is that very little of the detail of the ATH can be of use to us, even though, as should be clear, I share many of Currie's reasons for seeking an account of artworks that views them as process-like entities. It is also perhaps worth noting that the core idea of the performance theory was first advanced in my unpublished MA thesis, "The Aesthetic Relevance of Artistic Acts," University of Manitoba, 1979.

context, even if they bear upon what the artist may be thought to have achieved through her performance. So we can locate the work, qua performance, in counterfactual situations in which *these* features of the art-historical context differ, and in which the work possesses, as a consequence, different appreciable properties from the ones possessed in the actual world. For example, *Les Demoiselles d'Avignon* can exist in worlds where Cubism is anticipated by our hypothetical Spanish painter, or where the mode of representation initiated in the painting is not further pursued by Picasso or by anyone else. We can also allow, as Currie cannot, for different and even incompatible interpretations of a given work which disagree as to what the work achieved. Critics who offer such interpretations, it may be said, disagree as to what was achieved in executing a particular sequence of motivated manipulations. But the work, characterized as the performance identified with that sequence of manipulations completed by a work-focus, provides a shared subject for the critical disagreement. Thus we are able to say that the critics disagree over the interpretation of a given work, not that their disagreement engenders, or addresses, different works.

It is also instructive to see how the proposed account would handle the "painter's coffee break" example sketched above. Suppose that the painter has a high susceptibility to caffeine, and paints in a much more agitated manner after consuming the cup of coffee. The coffee then has a material affect on the manipulations of the vehicular medium by the artist, such that we might be willing to say that the distribution of pigment on the canvas would have been different in subtle but perhaps aesthetically important ways if the coffee had not been consumed. Or, to vary the example, suppose that the painter is very aware of the manner in which caffeine consumption affects his manipulation of the vehicular medium, and, wanting to execute a given canvas in the sort of "speedy" way elicited by caffeine, takes the coffee break for just that reason. In fact, there are obvious examples of actual works that present just this kind of problem. Consider, for example, the relationship between Coleridge's use of opium and the identity and appreciation of the poem *Kubla Khan*. To what extent does Coleridge's use of opium at the time when he wrote the poem enter into a proper characterization of the performance with which we are to identify this work? Here, as in the above example, we can distinguish between cases where Coleridge deliberately takes the drug as an aid to composition, and cases where he does not.

Let me suggest that, while there are interesting differences between the two scenarios sketched for each of the examples, in none of these cases should we take the ingestion of the relevant drug as entering into either the identity or the appreciation of the work. Rather, in each case, it is part of a *causal explanation* of features of the performance that is the work, of how that performance came to be enacted, and thus, on the performance theory, of how the work came to be. In our appreciative interest in such works, we need first to clarify the nature of the performance which serves as the object of critical evaluation and appreciation. This allows us to identify the work. Once we have identified the work, we can inquire how this work came about. The object of critical evaluation and appreciation, we are claiming, is the motivated manipulation of the vehicular medium, in light of shared understandings, with the aim of articulating an artistic statement, and completed by a particular work-focus. The motivations that enter into the identity of the work, and thus bear upon its appreciation, are those that directly relate to the goal of articulating an artistic statement – they thereby have the general form "manipulate the vehicular medium in this manner in order to produce a vehicle that will articulate an artistic statement having a particular content p." There are many other motivations that bear upon the manipulations of the vehicular medium that do not enter into the identity of the work – for example, the desire to pay off outstanding debts by selling the resulting canvas. This desire is not part of the work, though it may enter into a larger story which explains how the work came to be.

The same, I would argue, applies to the artist's consumption of coffee, even when the artist is fully aware of its effect upon the ensuing manipulations of the vehicular medium. That the artist ingests a stimulant or narcotic before painting a canvas or writing a poem, deliberately or not, does not affect *what the work is* – "*what was done*" in the sense that bears upon our grasping something as an artwork. It may, however, bear upon whether we take the work to have been a singular personal achievement in the circumstances. Indeed, it is by reference to the work construed as a performance in the prescribed sense that we determine when a given aspect of provenance pertains to *what the work is* and when it pertains to *how we regard the coming into being of such a work*. When provenance bears upon the first of these things, it can affect the evaluation of the work, whereas when it bears on the second, it relates only to our evaluation of the artist. In the *Kubla Khan* case, for example, Coleridge's use of opium bears not upon our evaluation of the work, but only upon our assessment of Coleridge relative to his being the author of the work. It thus belongs in the same general category as reflections on the capacity of morally bad people to write great literature –

Céline being the standard example, or, if one adopts the conventional view of this, Joyce. An author's psychology and personal habits presumably enter into a causal story about how her works came to be produced, but the works themselves must be distanced from these features of their provenance.

There may be a reluctance to grant this in the case where the artist deliberately chooses to alter her states of consciousness in a particular way as a prelude to manipulating a vehicular medium. For how does this differ, in principle, from the artist's looking for new ways to employ the medium to obtain a particular effect? In fact, the two things are importantly different because, in the former case, none of the constituent elements in the *artistic* performance are changed – it is just that the artist adopts special means to enable her to enact that performance and thereby bring into being that work. The work, for the performance theorist, to repeat, is a performance whereby an artistic statement x is articulated in an artistic medium y realized in a vehicle z. We have seen that, in order to evaluate this performance, we must determine what the values of its constituent variables are and by means of what motivated manipulations of the vehicular medium those constituent variables are themselves brought into being as elements in the work-focus. Further, to appreciate the performance in virtue of these values of the constituent variables, we also need to locate these values in a context of artistic making – only in so doing can we assess how great an artistic achievement it was to articulate such a statement in such a manner. We need to refer the statement articulated, the use of the artistic medium, and the use of the vehicular medium to the relevant tradition of artistic making – this, for example, is just what Clark is doing in his discussion of Turner. But the artist's partaking in various kinds of stimulants, or having a particular kind of personal life, seems to have no bearing on evaluating the work as artistic performance so construed. It bears only on how we assess the artist relative to her act.

This is not to say that there could not be examples where the artist's use of certain stimulants *might* enter into the identity and appreciation of the work. But there can be such cases only where we think of the work itself as a kind of "performance work," where it is the actions of the artist themselves, including the posited ingestion of stimulants, that function as the vehicle whereby an artistic statement is articulated. I shall say more about the notion of "performance works" in chapters 8 and 9. But what may be remarked here is that, in the face of such an example, we would have two options: (1) the act of ingesting the stimulant could be figured, as such, into the performance; or, more plausibly, (2) that the manipulations of some stuff[3] were carried out in a state of stimulation could be an important part of the characterization of the manipulations themselves, where the latter explicitly figure as the vehicle in the focus of the resultant work. The second option is preferable for at least one reason. Since, on this option, no specific action of drinking coffee enters into the characterization of the performance constitutive of the work, there is no problem about the modal properties of the work associated with the drinking of the coffee (for example, is it the same work if it is a different kind of coffee?). All that enters into the performance identified with the work is that the relevant manipulations of some stuff were performed in a deliberately induced state of "speediness."

7.4 Work-Constitution and Modality on the Performance Theory

As the reader may already suspect, a crucial question for the performance theorist is the appropriate level of *description* of the artist's manipulations of the vehicular medium. Before turning to this, however, we must determine whether the proposed strategy for individuating works as performances does indeed, as I have been claiming, provide us with an intuitively satisfying answer to the problem of individuation. The latter, we may recall, requires that we clarify which features of provenance are properly viewed as individuating conditions, and thus as constitutive features, of a work. The proposed individuative strategy tells us that the constitutive features of the work will include those features of provenance contained explicitly or implicitly in an adequate description of the motivated manipulations of the vehicular medium whereby the focus of appreciation is specified. In addition, however, features of provenance not obviously contained in such a description may determine properties of the specified focus. In particular, they may determine aspects of the articulated content, if, as argued in chapter 4, it is "uptake" rather than authorial semantic intentions that determines at least some of the meaning-properties rightly ascribable to an artistic vehicle. Are these features of provenance also constitutive of the work? If so, how is this to be reconciled with the proposed conception of the work as performance, which seems to exclude such features? And does this not threaten to undermine the claim, above, that the performance theory, unlike the ATH, allows for genuine disagreement as

3 *Not* itself the vehicular medium, it is crucial to note, since we are taking the manipulative action as itself the vehicle.

to what a given work achieves? What, for example, of properties of a work that depend upon the relations in which it stands to other works in the artist's oeuvre? Should we take such properties as constitutive and essential of the work, so that it can exist only in worlds in which all of the other works in the artist's oeuvre – including later works – also exist? Will a consistent application of the principles required to deal with the sorts of cases just countenanced also entail that unintended representational or expressive properties of works, deriving from events or other works unknown to the author, are constitutive of those works?

If we are to speak to these worries, we need to clarify two issues:

1 To what extent are properties of the work-focus that are at least partly determined by features of provenance constitutive, and thus essential, properties of the work?
2 How are we to construe the content of the artistic intentions which are taken to be work-constitutive in so far as they guide the manipulations of the medium whereby the work-focus is specified?

I shall address these issues in turn.

7.4.1 When are properties of the work-focus constitutive properties of the work?

It was argued in chapter 3 that all of the artistic properties that enter into the artistic statement articulated through the vehicle of a work depend in more or less subtle ways upon its history of making. Some of these properties can be viewed as constitutive and essential properties of the work because the features of provenance upon which they depend are themselves work-constitutive for independent reasons. Take, for example, any meaning-property for which actual intentionalism holds – that is to say, where such a meaning-property will be part of the artistic statement articulated in the work just in case the artist intends this to be so. If the artist's actual semantic intentions with respect to such a meaning-property guide her manipulations of the medium in a relevant manner, the performance theorist holds these intentions to be work-constitutive. Thus the meaning-properties determined by them will belong to the work in every possible world in which it exists.

The more interesting cases, however, are those meaning-properties for which actual intentionalism fails to hold. Consider, for example, the sorts of cases cited in criticism of actual intentionalism in chapter 4 – certain things that are true in a story in virtue of the shared understandings or interpretive conventions that obtain in a community of readers. In such cases, there seems prima facie to be no reason to think that the features of provenance upon which such meaning-properties depend will be implicated in an adequate characterization of the artist's generative performance. We may wonder, therefore, whether a given work could exist in circumstances where, in virtue of a difference in the historical context of reception, its work-focus would possess different meaning-properties of this kind, and would thereby articulate a different artistic statement. For example, recalling our discussion in chapter 4, imagine that Smith generates the text T in a world *w* where receivers draw upon different interpretive norms in arriving at conclusions as to what is true in a story. This difference in norms may entail a difference in the meaning-properties rightly ascribable to a work-focus with vehicle T, given an "uptake" construal of these properties. In particular, let us suppose that informed *w*-readers of T *would* take Stanley to be motivated by a fear of emotional commitment. So, in *w*, Smith *succeeds* in her intention to write a work with text T in which Stanley is so motivated. Is this, then, the same work as the one with text T composed by Smith in the actual world – call this work "*X*"? In that case, the following counterfactual would be acceptable:

> C1 Stanley in *X* might have been motivated by fear of emotional commitment rather than naked self-interest.

To begin with, we need to distinguish two different readings of C1, one of which is surely true on *any* account:

> C1a It *is* true in the story N told in *X* that Stanley *might have been* motivated by fear of emotional commitment (although he isn't).
>
> C1b It *might have been* true in the story N told in *X* (although it isn't) that Stanley *is* motivated by fear of emotional commitment.

The first of these claims is surely true, since, internal to the story N, a character's doings, motives, and appearance could have differed from what they are: internal to the Sherlock Holmes stories, for example, Holmes could have had a beard if he had chosen to grow one. It is the truth of C1b, however, that is the matter at issue. Of course, the question is *not* whether Smith could have generated a work-focus with the text T in which a character like Stanley is so motivated. Ex hypothesi, this is precisely what Smith does in *w*. The question is whether, in talking of a world in which

Smith does this, we are talking of (1) a world in which different things are true in, and therefore of, X, or of (2) a world in which Smith writes a novel X^* which resembles X in many respects. Given the centrality of the story-meaning of a novel to our sense of the novel's identity as a work, and given also the force of the anti-empiricist arguments marshalled in chapters 2 and 3 above, (2) rather than (1) seems to be the right answer to this question. But how, and at what further cost, can the performance theorist motivate such an answer?

It might be thought that the performance theorist can deal with such cases in the same way as we dealt with cases where meaning-properties of the work-focus are determined by actual authorial intention. For, it might be argued, in a world in which the norms for interpreting narratives differed in the way supposed, this is surely something that would be known by the actual author in that world, and which would inform her manipulations of the medium. But in this case, the argument might continue, since the intentions guiding her manipulations in w would differ from the intentions guiding the manipulations generative of the work-focus of X in the actual world, the generative performances, and thus the works, will differ. A moment's reflection, however, indicates that the difficulty cannot be overcome in this way, even if an artist's manipulation of a vehicular medium is standardly informed by beliefs about the norms of interpretation obtaining in the intended community of receivers. For the difference between an AI and an "uptake" construal of a meaning-property, which the Smith/Jones examples in chapter 4 are intended to illustrate, depends upon the fact that the author can *misconstrue* the interpretive norms in the community of receivers to which her work is addressed. Smith, in our original hypothetical scenario SW1, surely believes that the interpretive norms obtaining in the relevant receptive community are such that an informed reader in that community will take it to be true in the story N told in X that Stanley is motivated by fear of emotional commitment. But Smith's having that *belief* does not entail that there *are* interpretive norms having such implications in the relevant receptive community, or, indeed, that there are norms which imply that it is true in X that Stanley is motivated by unvarnished self-interest. Thus, it might seem there is no principled connection between the intentions that guide an artist's manipulations of a vehicular medium in a world, on the one hand, and the obtaining in that world of particular interpretive norms that, on an "uptake" construal of a class of meaning-properties, determine which such meaning-properties belong to the work-focus thereby specified, on the other.

Perhaps, though, we are being too hasty in rejecting a general resolution of our concerns in terms of the intentions guiding the artist's manipulation of the vehicular medium – intentions which, when bearing directly on the attempt to specify a focus of appreciation, are constitutive of the work according to the performance theory as elaborated above. For, while there may be no principled connection between an artist's manipulative intentions in a world and the interpretive norms obtaining in the intended community of receivers in that world, there is, I suggest, a principled connection between the artist's manipulative intentions in the actual world and the interpretive norms that must obtain in any possible world in which her work exists. However mistaken the artist may be about the specific interpretive norms obtaining in the community of receivers to which her work is addressed, she can be ascribed an overriding intention that her work be understood according to the norms of *that particular* community. In the context of our judging which properties are constitutive of her work, this intention, which picks out indexically a particular interpretive community, overrides the artist's specific understandings of the norms of that community. It is the norms that actually obtain in the community indexically picked out by this overriding intention on the part of the artist that are constitutive features of the context of making of the work. The overriding authorial intention will, then, make constitutive of the work all those meaning-properties that the work-focus possesses in virtue of the receptive norms actually in place. And *this* is what we require, if the sorts of provenance-grounded meaning-properties of the work-focus that enter into our intuitive sense of the identity of the work are indeed to be constitutive properties of the work. Whether or not the actual author knows *what the relevant features of provenance are*, or what the meaning-properties entailed by those features are, is not the issue.

This may also help to clarify *which* meaning-properties of a work are constitutive and essential in this way. Oeuvre-properties will be constitutive and essential properties of the work only if they are independently implicated in particular manipulative intentions on the part of the artist, for they will not fall under an analogous overriding guiding intention of the artist. Thus it is very unlikely that oeuvre-properties that stem from a given work's relation to later works will be constitutive of that work. The same will apply to the sorts of achievement-properties discussed in the previous chapter. Only if the features of the art-historical context of creation upon which such achievement-properties depend are implicated in an adequate characterization of the artist's manipulative intentions will the achievement-properties be constitutive of the work. This does *not* mean, however, that such non-constitutive oeuvre-properties or achievement-properties are irrelevant to the appreciation of the work. The performance theory is not faced with the difficulty sketched in our discussion of Currie, for whom all properties bearing on the appreciation of a work must be constitutive of the work, given the identification of the work with an action-*type*. For the performance theorist, the work is a *token* performance, which will have many non-constitutive properties in virtue of broader aspects of the context in which the performance takes place. Some of these properties may then be contingent properties of the work that nonetheless bear upon its artistic appreciation.

7.4.2 How is the content of artistic intentions to be understood?

By making the constitutive and modal status of meaning-properties of the work-focus depend upon the intentions that guide the manipulation of the vehicular medium, we reaffirm the central idea of the performance theory that works are *doings*, and that the modal properties of a work turn upon our sense of what was *done*. The overriding intention to be interpretable by the interpretive norms of a particular community of receivers rigidly picks out, as constitutive of the work, the actual interpretive norms of that community. The artist's manipulations can be guided by *this* intention only in a world in which the same interpretive norms obtain. In according such a determinative role to artistic intentions, however, we heighten the significance of the second issue raised above: How should we understand the *content* of the intentions held to be constitutive of works?

The performance theory takes the articulative intentions that guide an artist's manipulations of the vehicular medium to be constitutive properties of a work. Given the modality principle, which identifies the constitutive and essential properties of a work, a work can exist only in circumstances where such manipulations are performed with *the same articulative intentions*. But, we may now ask, under what conditions can agents be said to be acting with the same intentions? In fact, we need to answer two distinct questions: first, what is it for an agent to act with certain intentions, and, second, under what conditions are the intentions with which two agents act the same? In answer to the first question, I shall assume that an agent is rightly described as acting with certain intentions when that agent's behavior is rightly explained through the ascription to that agent of appropriate *intentionally characterized mental states*, where the latter include, but are not exhausted by, beliefs, desires, hopes, fears, and wishes. Such states, often characterized as "propositional attitudes," are themselves individuated, at least unreflectively, by reference to (1) the attitude, or generic mental state type, of the agent – belief, desire, hope, etc. – and (2) the intentional object of that attitude – for example, that the weather will be fine for the picnic. This suggests, to answer our second question, that two agents are acting with the same intentions if the same intentionally characterized mental states – that is, mental states of the same generic type with identical content – are rightly ascribed to them in explanation of their behavior.

Now, however, we must ask how the *contents* of an agent's mental states are determined. This is a matter of considerable philosophical dispute in the recent literature, often characterized in terms of "individualistic" and "non-individualistic," or of "narrow" and "broad," conceptions of content. The issue is whether the content of an agent's mental states depends only upon how the agent represents the world to herself, or whether it also depends upon facts about the way the world actually is, independently of how the agent represents it to herself. For example, when Descartes imagines that he might unknowingly be subject to massive illusion, or when we entertain the hypothesis that we might unknowingly be "brains in a vat," an individualistic or "narrow" view of content would maintain that we are hypothesizing a situation in which the contents of our mental states remain the same while the world differs. A non-individualistic or "broad" conception of content, on the other hand, would maintain that, in the hypothesized circumstance, many of our mental states would be *different in content*, even if the difference is one that we cannot recognize as obtaining. On a broad construal of mental content, the nature of the natural and linguistic environment in which we find ourselves partially determines the content of our mental states.[4]

If the contents of our mental states are taken to be "broad," then changes in the world of which we may be unaware can affect those states, and thus the intentions with which we act. And, if sameness of relevant intentions guiding the manipulations of a vehicular medium is a condition for sameness of artwork, as the performance theorist maintains, then worlds that differ in esoteric ways from the actual world may be worlds in which many of our artworks could not exist. For example, as we shall see in a minute, it might be thought that the performance theorist is committed to the following kind of claim: if mental content is "broadly" conceived, then Piero's *Baptism of Christ* could not exist in a counterfactual "Twin" world which differs from the actual world only in the respect that, while no one in either Piero's culture or the hypothetical "Twin" culture

---

4   See, for example, Burge 1979; Putnam 1975. For a broader view of these issues, see the essays collected in Stich and Warfield 1994.

is capable of telling the two substances apart, the liquid that has the phenomenal properties of water in the "Twin" world (call it "twater") is not
H_2O but XYZ.[5] For, it seems, Piero's applications of pigment to surface
were motivated by thoughts about water, whereas Piero's applications of
pigment to canvas on Twin Earth, which produced an indistinguishable
vehicle, were motivated by thoughts about twater. This consequence –
that Piero's painting could not exist in a possible world whose chemistry
differed unknowably from that of the actual world in the manner proposed – is surely very counter-intuitive. The performance theorist, then,
might try to reject a "broad" construal of the content of the mental states
that are partly constitutive of works. If, however, the performance theorist proposes a *narrow* construal of the contents of those mental states,
there is a danger that modal properties of works will not be constrained
tightly enough. Indeed, as we have already seen, there is good reason to
think that only a broad construal of the artist's intentions can account for
the constitutive role of the interpretive norms obtaining in the receptive
community to which a work is addressed.

But there is a disanalogy between the "interpretive norms" case and
the "Piero" case. In the "interpretive norms" case, the artist's manipulation of the vehicular medium is guided by her beliefs about the interpretive norms in place in the community of receivers to which her work is
addressed. Her intention is to be interpreted according to the norms of
that community, *which norms she believes to be such-and-such*. In the
"Piero" case, on the other hand, no beliefs about the fundamental nature
of the "stuff" standardly found in rivers plays any part in Piero's manipulation of the medium. All that matters are the phenomenal properties of
that stuff, which are to be rendered in interesting ways through manipulation of pigments. Thus it is reasonable to assume that Piero's manipulations would be unaffected were his beliefs about the fundamental nature
of the liquid standardly found in rivers to change. But an artist's manipulations of the vehicular medium would change quite dramatically were
her beliefs about the interpretive norms obtaining in the receptive community to change.

This suggests that not all of the mental states that guide an artist's
manipulations of the vehicular medium should be treated in the way we
have treated intentions as to how the work should be interpreted. If we

5   See Putnam 1975 for this kind of thought-experiment. In Putnam's scenario, Earth and
Twin Earth are assumed to exist in the same world. In the "Piero" example, however, where
we are interested in the modal properties of works, the "Twin" scenario represents another
possible world in which Piero exists, not a separate part of the actual world inhabited by
Piero's Twin.

do take the latter as our model in treating the contents of the guiding mental states in the "Piero" case, then we must say something like the following: (1) Piero intended to depict a river containing *whatever it is that rivers standardly contain around here*, where "around here" rigidly picks out the geographical location in which he finds himself. So (2) if rivers on Earth world standardly contain water, Piero's intention is to depict a river of water. But (3) on Twin Earth, where rivers standardly contain twater, Piero's intention to depict *whatever rivers standardly contain around here* will be an intention to depict a river of twater. So (4) the performance theorist must hold that Piero cannot produce the *Baptism of Christ* in the hypothesized "Twin" scenario. But, I suggest, the intentions guiding Piero's manipulations of the vehicular medium might be better expressed as follows: Piero intended to make marks upon a surface such that viewers would take that surface to be a representation of a river. This intention guided the manipulations of the vehicular medium in that the marked surface must be such that it is taken by viewers to represent the observable properties of the liquid found in rivers. So a change in the *observable* properties of the liquid would have been attended by different "fine-grained" depictive intentions. But, ex hypothesi, the observable properties of water and twater are identical. The underlying nature of the liquid, in the case under consideration, is quite irrelevant to Piero's intentions insofar as the latter guided his manipulations of the vehicular medium. Thus, in determining whether we can sensibly propose that an artistic performance in a possible world is an instance of a work in the actual world, we should take sameness of interpretive norms – and thus sameness of those meaning-properties that depend upon the application of those norms – to be a necessary condition for sameness of work, while allowing that at least some differences in the physico-chemical composition of the things described or depicted in the work are compatible with sameness of work.

This might be thought to be a somewhat desperate and ad hoc stratagem, clearly designed to preserve the performance theory from ruin. But, in fact, an anologous stratagem will be required by nearly every ontological theory that wants to avoid the implication that Piero could not have painted his *Baptism of Christ* in a possible world just like the actual world save that the liquid found in rivers, etc., is XYZ rather than H_2O. For, while we may resist the idea that an artist's semantic intentions generally determine the meaning-properties of the work-focus that she specifies, we surely want to hold that, for the most part, great artists (and perhaps even not-so-great artists) *succeed in realizing* their semantic intentions. So, even if Piero's intending to produce an *x*-depiction does not

determine whether the product of Piero's manipulation of pigment *is* an
x-depiction, we assume that most of the time Piero's paintings are depictions of what he intended them to depict. But suppose we adopt a view
of the content of mental states which entails that Piero cannot have the
intentions on counterfactual Twin Earth that guided him in the production of the *Baptism of Christ*. Suppose also, plausibly, that there is no
reason to think that Piero *fails* to realize his depictive intentions on counterfactual Twin Earth where he succeeds on Earth. Then, if the actual
painting and the painting on Twin Earth both successfully realize Piero's
depictive intentions, and if we have to say that the depictive intentions
differ, we must hold that the paintings differ as *depictions*. If we want to
insist, nonetheless, that Piero's *Baptism* can sensibly be supposed to exist
on Twin Earth, then, as in the case of the performance theory, we seem
forced to say either: (1) that the basic meaning-properties of a work-focus
are not essential properties of the work – surely implausible, or (2) that
the works *don't* really differ in depictive content. But (2) requires that we
revise our judgment that there is a difference in depictive intention, which,
in turn, requires a principled account of the content of an artist's manipulative intentions which permits such a revision. The account just offered
in defense of the performance theory looks like the most likely candidate
for that role. If so, then there is a need to draw the sorts of distinctions
presented in that account whether one subscribes to the performance
theory or not.

The general idea, then, is that, where some feature of the real world
that might differ in a counterfactual situation is irrelevant to the
artist's motivated manipulation of the vehicular medium, we can capture
this irrelevance in the manner in which we represent her intentions.
This doesn't commit us to denying that in many cases individuals are in
intentional states that are to be described in a fully broad fashion, but
allows us to distinguish between Piero's intentions vis-à-vis the liquid
in the rivers and the sorts of intentions I might have if I want a drink,
or that a chemist might have if he were about to perform an
experiment.

7.5 Performances, Actions, and Doings

This completes the first stage in the elaboration of the performance
theory. But a significant question remains unanswered, as to the precise
status of the event- or process-tokens with which works are to be identi-

fied. The natural answer to this question would be that, where Currie
identified works with action-*types*, the performance theory identifies works
with action-*tokens*. But, if the performance theory is so understood, it
might appear that it will not be able to accommodate the work-relativity
of the modal and constitutive properties of works for which we argued in
chapter 5. For the modal and constitutive properties of *action-tokens*
might not be thought to be relative in the appropriate sense. Let me spell
out this worry in more detail.

As we saw in chapter 5, the constitutive properties of an entity ground
our individuative practices, our judgments as to when we have the same
entity on distinct occasions. But the constitutive properties of an entity
are not defined by reference to our particular individuative practices. They
are defined, rather, by reference to (1) the *type* of thing that the entity is
and (2) the φ-properties of the entity, where it is by reference to their
specific φ-properties that things of that general type are individuated.[6] So,
for example, if gold is an entity of the type "natural kind," and if natural
kinds are individuated in terms of their microstructural properties, then
the constitutive properties of gold consist in its being the natural kind
with *this* particular microstructure.

Suppose we inquire, then, as to the general type to which particular
event-tokens belong, and the kinds of properties in terms of which
things of this type are individuated. It is a point of agreement between
otherwise conflicting theories of events that one of the properties by
reference to which event-tokens are individuated is their (absolute or
relative) *time of occurrence*. On one well-known contemporary account
(Kim 1976), an event-token is the instantiation of a property by an individual at a time. Any difference in property, individual, or time entails a
difference in event-token. On perhaps the best-known alternative view
(Davidson 1980), events are individuated in terms of the relations of cause
and effect in which they stand to other events. On this account, it is the
relative rather than the absolute time of occurrence of an event that
enters into its individuation. A third proposal (Cleland 1991), intended
to remedy problems that beset the first two, holds that an event-token
is a change in an "existential condition" occurring at a particular time.
On all three accounts, the time at which event-tokens occur is one of
the conditions by reference to which they are individuated, and thus, it
might be thought, is among what I have termed the individuating
conditions of event-tokens. Individuating conditions, in this sense, are
among an entity's constitutive properties, and therefore, according to the

6 See the discussion of this in chapter 5 above.

argument of chapter 5, among its essential properties. This suggests that, whatever their differences, all the accounts of the individuation of event-tokens just surveyed take the time of occurrence of an event-token to be a property that it must have in any counterfactual situation in which it can coherently be taken to occur. Since action-tokens are a species of event-token, what holds for the latter will also hold for the former.

If, then, the performance theory identifies artworks with action-tokens so construed, the (absolute or relative) time at which an artist specifies a focus of appreciation will be both a constitutive and an essential property of the resultant work. Thus the performance theory will be unable to allow that a work such as the naive painter's *Prairie Snowscape* could have come into existence at a different time in a counterfactual situation. However, as may be recalled, our proposed resolution of the problem posed by the work-relativity of modality, which tied our modal intuitions to our intuitions about sameness of "doing," does allow us to distinguish between works like *Prairie Snowscape*, where the time of generation of the canvas is not constitutive of the work, and works like Warhol's *Brillo Boxes*, where it is. Since the performance theory proposes to solve the problem of individuation by identifying works, as performances, with the "doings" that purportedly ground our modal intuitions about works, it appears that these performances, as "doings," cannot be action-tokens as construed above. But, if so, then what is the status of these "doings," and how can we justify the role ascribed to them by the performance theorist?

A moment's reflection on our modal discourse about events suggests that something is amiss in the inference, above, from the role that time of occurrence plays in the individuation of event-tokens to the conclusion that the actual (or relative) time of occurrence of an event-token is an essential property of the latter. For, it would seem, one of the principal uses of such discourse is in counterfactual reasoning about the implications were a particular event-token to have occurred either earlier or later than it in fact occurred. To pick up on an earlier example, we surmise that we might have had a different poem titled *Kubla Khan* if the person from Porlock had only arrived an hour later. Similarly, we reason that more people would have been saved if the sinking of the *Titanic* had occurred a couple of hours later, or that if Wilson, the centre-fielder, had started running to catch the fly ball a second earlier he would have made the game-saving catch. A natural reading of such modal claims is that we are considering a counterfactual situation in which a particular event-token – the arrival of the person from Porlock, the sinking of the

Titanic, Wilson's running to catch the fly ball – occurs at a different time from its time of occurrence in the actual world. If event-tokens always have their actual time of occurrence essentially, however, then the natural reading of the modal claims renders them incoherent. To preserve their coherence, we must reinterpret them as claims about possible worlds in which a *different* event-token occurs, an event-token which nonetheless shares many properties with what actually occurred. We are not inquiring as to what would have happened if Wilson's running for the fly ball had happened a second earlier, but as to what would have happened in a world in which the event "Wilson's running for the fly ball at t' didn't occur but in which a different event – "Wilson's running for the fly ball at t''" – did.

While some may be tempted by this analysis, I think it should be accepted only if there are no lacunae in the process of reasoning leading up to it. And, I think, there is indeed at least one such lacuna. It lies very early in the reasoning, where it was assumed that, given the place accorded to an event-token's time of occurrence in accounts of the individuation of events, time of occurrence is an "individuating condition" of event-tokens in the sense established in chapter 5. From this, it then follows, again by the argument of chapter 5, that actual time of occurrence is an essential property of event-tokens. An individuating condition, it will be recalled, is a condition that conveys what it is that is distinctive about a particular individual of a given kind – it captures our sense that, given how Xs in general are individuated, a particular X is *this* X. This is why it is reasonable to require that, if we are to entertain the thought that *this* X exists in a given counterfactual scenario, the posited existent must satisfy whatever serve as this X's individuating conditions.

But the actual time of occurrence does not, as a rule, serve as an individuating condition in this sense for an event-token.[7] It enters into the individuation of event-tokens *not* because a particular time of occurrence is part of our sense of what it is to be *this* event-token, but because we are individuating event-*tokens*, and it is a condition for something to be a *token* event that it should have a unique temporal location in a world. Thus if, in individuating event-tokens in a world, we know that e1 and e2 occur at different times, we know that they must be distinct event-tokens, however many other properties they have in common. It is a con-

---

7   It may, however, serve as an individuating condition for what are often viewed as "basic events" – see below.

dition for e's being an event-*token* that e occur at most once in a world, but it is not, in general, part of our sense of e's being *this* event-token that it occur at a particular time, nor, a fortiori, that, in any possible world in which it occurs, it should occur in that world at the particular time that it occurs in the actual world.[8]

This is not to suggest that there are no constraints on the time at which an event-token can coherently be taken to occur in counterfactual situations, or, indeed, to deny that, in some cases, it will be necessary that, in counterfactual situations, the event-token should occur at the same time as it occurs in the actual world. But such constraints come from those features of context that are built into the event-token itself, as captured in the other elements that enter into the analyses of the individuation of event-tokens canvassed above. It is these features that give the sense to talk of *this* event-token occurring in a counter-factual situation, and that indirectly constrain the temporal location of this event-token in counter-factual scenarios. For example, if we take the earlier reference to "the sinking of the *Titanic*" to be an elliptical reference to the event-token "the sinking of the *Titanic* by an iceberg on the ship's maiden voyage across the Atlantic," this event-token can only occur in counterfactual scenarios in which it follows the construction of the *Titanic*, its sailing on its maiden voyage across the Atlantic, and its entering that region of the Atlantic where icebergs are a potential threat to navigation. This, however, allows for the event-token to occur at any moment in an extended temporal interval, given that other general features of early-twentieth-century history are held constant.[9] On the other hand, given that the fly ball to which reference is made in the event-token "Wilson's running for the fly ball" is a particular fly ball struck at a particular time in a particular match,

8   It may indeed be essential, for any event-token that occurs at a time *t* in the actual world, that it should have the property "occurs at *t* in the actual world" in any possible world in which it occurs. What is *not* essential is that it should have the property "occurs at time *t*" in each such possible world.

9   Note, though, that this temporal interval will be much more tightly circumscribed if the event-token in question is the *Titanic*'s sinking as a result of hitting a *particular* iceberg. More generally, once we allow a measure of pluralism in our ontology of events, where complex events are taken to be realized or constituted by, rather than identical with, sets of more basic events, we must allow for divergence in our modal judgments about event-tokens depending upon how those event-tokens are singled out. However, this seems to be what our ordinary modal talk about events requires, independently of the requirements of the performance theory. See my further remarks about this below, although I do not claim to have offered a full analysis of these issues here.

the event-token's relative temporal location is very tightly constrained, although in a manner consistent with the coherence of the counterfactual claim entertained above. In the latter case, what tightly constrains the temporal location of the event-token in counterfactual scenarios is its being a particular instance of an event-type that has multiple instances in the actual world. Given how many times Wilson has run or might have run for a fly ball, our sense that it is *this* running, rather than any of the others, whose occurrence is being counterfactually considered requires that we take as individuating features the precise details of the context in which it occurs.

In fact, this applies more generally when we talk counterfactually about action- or event-tokens that are tokens of multiply instanced action- or event-types. Thus, ironically, an event-token may be modally tied to a particular time of occurrence not by the *richness* of the non-temporal constituents in its analysis, but by their *poverty*. If the event-token is John's drinking a cup of coffee at 9 a.m. on July 1, 2002, for example, there may be no way of giving content to the idea that it is *this* event-token that is being considered counterfactually, rather than another act of coffee-drinking on John's part, save by taking as constitutive the entire causal complex in which this particular drinking is embedded. This makes it very difficult to imagine the event-token in question occurring at a different time relative to the times of occurrence of those events making up the embedding context.

This will apply to many "simple" or "basic" actions or events by means of which other more complex actions or events are realized. For such simple or basic action- or event-tokens, actual time of occurrence, or something very close to it, may indeed be both an individuative, in our sense, and essential property. But once we understand *why* this is the case, we will not conclude that this applies to *all* action- and event-tokens. Consider, for example, non-basic actions performed by means of certain more simple or basic actions, such as my formulation of the argument expressed in the present paragraph by executing certain manipulations of the keyboard of my computer. What individuates this particular non-basic action-token is characterizable by reference to the larger intentional context in which the action takes place, a context that includes my revisions of this section of the larger manuscript I am composing. Surely there is nothing incoherent in the idea that I might have done this through a different sequence of basic actions. For example, if there had been a power-outage half an hour ago, I might have formulated this argument by writing the same sentences long-hand on a sheet of paper. Alternatively, I might have taken a brief walk around the block before returning to my computer to key these very sentences. If we take the basic actions whereby I am actually formulating this argument to have their times of occurrence essentially, for the sorts of reasons canvassed in the previous paragraph, the action of formulating the argument could nonetheless have occurred at different times and through different basic actions, as long as the conditions for performing *this* non-basic action were met. Because we characterize the latter by locating the action-token in a larger framework of intentional agency, we are able to preserve the idea that it is *this* event that is occurring at a different time as long as the framework of intentions does not itself temporally constrain the event in a manner incompatible with its so occurring.

Suppose we characterize event-tokens that permit of such different realizations by more basic actions as "*happenings*," some of which (those that implicate human agency in an appropriate manner) are "*doings*." Happenings and doings, so construed, are, I have suggested, the sorts of entities required in order to make sense of much of our counterfactual talk about events. We have no trouble understanding, and judging to be true or false, the sorts of claims canvassed earlier concerning the sinking of the *Titanic* or the arrival of the person from Porlock. We have little sympathy (outside the philosophy classroom) with one who insists that "the sinking of the *Titanic*," as an event-token, couldn't have occurred at a different time, and that what we are really considering is a different event. If it is indeed a property of event-tokens *strictu sensu* that they possess their times of occurrence essentially, then our counterfactual talk about the sinking of the *Titanic* cannot be talk about event-tokens in this sense. But this surely shouldn't lead us to desist from engaging in such counterfactual talk. Rather, we should concede that such talk is not about event-tokens *strictu sensu*, but maintain that it is about something quite objective nonetheless, namely, what I am terming happenings or doings.

We can bring these reflections to bear upon the notion of performance at play in the performance theory, and thereby clarify that theory in a number of important respects. First, as was suggested earlier in this chapter, the performance theory identifies works with doings in the sense just characterized. What individuates a particular artistic doing is given through our emerging sense, in the process of appreciatively apprehending the artwork realized through a given vehicle, of what must be included in an adequate characterization of the motivated manipulations of the vehicular medium through which the artist specified a particular focus of appreciation having this vehicle. As was seen above, such a characterization will explicitly or implicitly incorporate certain aspects of the art-historical and cultural context in which those manipulations occurred. This then allows for an artistic doing to exist in certain counterfactual art-historical and cultural contexts that differ in respects not implicated in the individuating conditions of that doing. This is why we are willing to locate the "naive" artist's *Prairie Snowscape* in possible worlds where the canvas is the product of a performance that takes place earlier or later than in the actual world. The individuating conditions for her performance do not implicate any specific features of the art-historical context in which the process occurs that would render such a counterfactual scenario incoherent.

We can also speak to another concern, as to the extent to which the specific manner in which an artist manipulates a vehicular medium is constitutive of her work, qua performance. Consider a minor difference in executing a particular abstract painting (a different order of brushstrokes), or in generating a text (writing long-hand or printing, for example). If we identified works with performances understood to be sequences of basic actions *strictu sensu*, then it might appear that any slight variation in the manipulation of the medium would result in a different work. However, applying the general strategy sketched above, what matters, in such cases, is what we take to be an adequate characterization of the motivated manipulations in question. This will determine how *fine-grained* a description of those manipulations must be to capture our sense of what was done.

The claim, then, is that artworks are *doings* of a particular kind. To appreciate a work is to appreciate what was done, and, in evaluating modal claims about works, what we are asking is whether *this* could have been done under *these* circumstances. Our sense of what *this* is is captured by what we take to be an adequate characterization of the motivated manipulations of the vehicular medium whereby the focus of appreciation was specified. It is such a characerization that identifies the individuating properties of the work. A particular doing is executed by a particular set of simpler action-tokens in the actual world, but could be realized by different simpler action-tokens in other possible worlds. In distinguishing between the modal and constitutive properties of works, as performances that are "doings," and the modal and constitutive properties of the simpler action-tokens through which those "doings" are realized in a world, I am drawing upon a distinction more familiar in the context of an object ontology of art. There has been much debate, both in the ontology of art and in more general metaphysics, as to the relationship that obtains between, for example, a particular statue and the clay of which it is composed. Against the view that a particular statue is identical to the clay of which it is composed, it has been argued that the relation is not one of identity but one of "constitution."[10] That the relation is not identity is supposedly demonstrated by the fact that the statue and the lump of clay differ in both their modal properties and their persistence conditions. Certain properties that are essential to something's being a particular lump of clay are not essential to something's being a particular statue, and vice versa. Also, the statue can survive a degree of division and dispersal of the elements that make up the lump of clay. While I cannot further evaluate the "statue" debates in this context, I am assuming that, to the extent that the argument for a constitutive rather than an identity relation in an object ontology of art is good, a similar argument can be constructed in the event ontology of art defended here.

In conclusion, it is important to stress that, in endorsing this conception of a work as a "doing," I am in no sense reinstating by the back door Currie's claim that works are action- or event-*types*. Doings are token events concerning which we can sensibly entertain certain counterfactual claims. A particular doing might have occurred at a different time, or have been executed through a different set of more basic actions, or have occurred in an art-historical or cultural context that differs in certain respects from the actual world. It possesses these modal properties because its individuative properties – which specify our sense of what makes a given event *this* doing – permit such variation across possible worlds. But these modal properties of doings in no way impugn their status as event-tokens which can, as tokens, occur at most once in a world. The difference between doings and more basic action-tokens is a modal one, not a matter of in principle multiple instantiability in a world. However, works, as doings, do involve an abstraction from the overall context of agency of the sort that is required in the bringing of action-tokens under types. Our sense of a work as a particular doing makes explicit, through the individuating conditions of the action-token, those features of what was done that we might conjoin to arrive at a conception of the type of thing we are appreciating in appreciating the token action in question. But these action-types are not Currie's action-types – they do not contain Currian heuristic paths or structures for the reasons spelled out earlier in this chapter – and the action-types are not themselves the works: they simply capture what it is about the artist's overall performance, qua token action, that bears upon our

10   See in particular Rudder Baker 1997; Thompson 1998.

appreciation of the artist's performance. If there is any residual temptation to infer from this that the works themselves are action-types, I hope
it is clear from the discussion of the last two chapters why we should resist
such a temptation.

Revisionism and Modernism Revisited

8.1 Revisionism Revisited

In the preceding chapters, I have offered a number of related arguments in support of the performance theory. The latter, so I have claimed, is better able to deal with significant aspects of our critical and appreciative practice than alternative ontologies of art – structuralism, contextualist ontologies such as Levinson's "indicated-structure" theory, and Currie's "action-type hypothesis." Unlike these ontologies, the performance theory provides a principled account of the individuation of artworks that accords with the modal intuitions embodied in our critical practice, and a principled account of the contribution, to our appreciation of a work, of features of provenance that do not determine non-relational properties of its work-focus. As I have noted, other non-structuralist theories can be reformulated to take account of those features of the performance theory that furnish such principled answers to questions arising out of our artistic practice. However, the performance theory is preferable to such reformulations because any explanatory and illuminatory virtues ascribable to the latter are inherited from the former, and because such reformulations mask the crucial role that the notion of artistic performance plays in our commerce with artworks. Furthermore, as I shall argue in the later sections of this chapter, the performance theory is better able than its competitors to make sense of continuities and discontinuities between late modern and traditional art, and also offers a better resolution of other puzzling features of artistic practice with which we began this study.

But such arguments can have suasive force only if the performance theory is an otherwise credible ontology of art. Only then can one hope, by such means, to wean the reader away from whichever of the currently

dominant ontologies of art she favors and bring her to look more posi-
tively upon the performance theory. As we saw in chapter 6, however, it
is commonly assumed that, whatever their proposed explanatory advan-
tages, theories that identify works with processes or events rather than
with their products or outcomes are unacceptable because they entail
major revisions in the way we talk about artworks. To put the point more
forcefully, they entail that much of our ordinary discourse about art is
either false or hopelessly imprecise. This "revisionism" objection, it will
be recalled, rests on two related claims: (1) we say all manner of things
about artworks that cannot sensibly be said about generative artistic performances, or about discoverings of structures via heuristic paths; and (2)
the performance theory and the ATH commit us to the coherence and
possible truth of claims about works of art that violate standards of
accepted linguistic usage.

Most of those who bring the revisionism objection against the idea that
artworks are process-like entities have type-(1) cases in mind. This may
be because the quarry of such critics has generally been the ATH, and
because it is more difficult to develop type-(2) cases that intuitively
count against the latter. Let me begin, however, with type-(2) cases. Recall
how such cases were presented as a challenge to the performance theory
in chapter 6 above. A token performance, it was claimed, takes place at
a particular time in a particular place, lasts for a certain amount of
time, and may be subject to various kinds of interruptions. Thus, if *Le
malade imaginaire* is identified with a particular generative performance,
then it can both coherently and perhaps truly be claimed that *Le malade
imaginaire* occurred in 1673, in France, took a number of months, and
was interrupted by bouts of tuberculosis. I think the performance
theorist should respond that this runs together properties of the work
bearing on its artistic appreciation, properties of the work that have no
bearing on its artistic appreciation, and properties that do not belong to
the work at all, qua doing, but only to what the artist did understood in
different terms. Thus the bouts of tuberculosis will not enter into the
identity of the work, qua doing, although, like the artist's consumption
of opium, they may enter a causal explanation of how the work
came into existence – a role such things may also play on standard
contextualist conceptions of the work. On the other hand, the precise
temporal location of the work is among its properties, and may even be
among its constitutive properties, qua doing, if such a temporal location
is entailed by the nature of the doing in question. Otherwise, it is a
contingent property of the work having no bearing on its proper

appreciation. Similarly, the spatial location will be relevant to the artistic appreciation of the work only insofar as it is entailed by features of the cultural context that enter into the identity of the work, qua doing.

It should not be forgotten, in this context, that even in the case of an ontology that identifies a painting with a physical object, there will be many statements about the work that strike one as counter-intuitive, but that are nonetheless true although without artistic significance. For example, if Turner's *Snowstorm* is a physical object, then it has a certain temperature at the moment of writing, is a determinate number of miles from Kuala Lumpur, weighs a certain number of grams, and would displace a determinate amount of water if dropped into my neighbor's swimming pool. If paintings are physical objects, then the work has all these properties. But, of course, none of these properties has any bearing upon the appreciation of the work, and their existence is not in itself an objection to the physical object hypothesis concerning such works. Type-(2) objections are, I think, no more of a problem for the performance theory, for the reasons just sketched.

I shall therefore focus on type-(1) cases. I shall not rehearse the various examples of type-(1) cases presented in chapter 6, but only remind the reader of how a proponent of the ATH or the performance theory should try to answer this kind of objection. The strategy of choice is to argue that features of our discourse about artworks that, taken at face value, are incompatible with the idea that works are process-like rather than product-like entities are best reinterpreted, on reflection, as discourse about (Currian) *instances* of works, or as discourse about the elements that make up the work-focus, rather than as discourse about works themselves. It is, for example, not Turner's *Snowstorm* that hangs in the Tate Gallery in London, has lost some of the brightness of its original color, is protected against acts of vandalism by an elaborate security system, and is distinguishable from forgeries by suitably trained experts. Rather, for the performance theorist, these are properties of the vehicle through which Turner articulated a particular artistic statement in carrying out the performance which is the work. But, as I also noted, the almost canonical role that ascriptions of these sorts of properties play in our discourse about art places a further burden upon anyone who offers this kind of response to the revisionism objection. If the performance theorist is to counter the charge that her account entails unacceptable revisions in our discourse about art, she must provide some reason, other than its congeniality to her ontology of art, for accepting the distinction, central to her analysis, between talk about works and talk about work-focuses.

In this section, I shall try to discharge this burden. I shall defend the following conditional claim: *if* certain features of provenance, over and above those that determine category of art, are constitutive of works, then the performance theorist can provide a principled basis for the distinction between talk of works and talk of work-focuses. Given our earlier discussions, it will be apparent that the antecedent of this conditional holds if the sorts of arguments levied against structuralist ontologies of art prove decisive. I have argued that these arguments are indeed decisive, and I shall therefore assume that, if I can establish the foregoing conditional, I shall have demonstrated that the revisionism objection is not conclusive against the performance theory. Indeed, so I shall argue, the performance theory may be better placed than contextualist accounts in this respect. For contextualist theories are vulnerable to a similar objection, and must have recourse to a similar distinction between talk of works and talk of something else, but it is not obvious that the contextualist can give a principled account of this distinction like the one I shall propose in the case of the performance theory.

As we have seen, ontologies of art that factor provenance into the individuation and constitution of artworks fall into two broad categories: those that identify the work with a particular product or outcome as produced by a particular process, and those that identify the work with a particular process (type or token) generative of a particular product or outcome. The first category – what we have termed "contextualist" ontologies – includes Levinson's "indicated-structure" theory, Binkley's account in terms of pieces specified within artistic indexing conventions, and Margolis' theory that identifies works with culturally emergent but physically embodied entities. The second category – what we may term "process-centered" ontologies – comprises the performance theory and Currie's ATH.

Consistency requires that anyone impressed by the revisionism objection against process-centered ontologies endorse a similar objection against any contextualist ontology that has to avail itself of a distinction between talk about works and talk about some component of works in order to accommodate the sorts of things we say about "works" in our ordinary critical and appreciative practice. Thus any consistent advocate of the revisionism objection should also reject Margolis' "emergentist" conception of what artworks are. Many of the problematic "type-(1)" properties are no more plausibly ascribed to the culturally emergent entities with which artworks are to be identified, on such a conception, than they are to performances or action-types. For example, it is surely the entities which supposedly physically embody such emergent entities that hang on gallery walls, or undergo cleaning, or require elaborate security precautions, rather than the emergent but physically embodied entities themselves. Similar reasoning would show that these sorts of properties cannot coherently be ascribed to Binkley's intensionally individuated "pieces."[1]

If the revisionism objection is to rule in favor of a contextualist ontology rather than a process-centered ontology, therefore, there must be some contextualist ontologies to which the objection does not apply. Rather than rehearse proposed contextualist ontologies, I shall focus on Levinson's characterization of musical and literary works as indicated structures, which is the best-known and most-discussed ontology of this kind. I shall examine whether the indicated-structure theory offers us a non-structuralist option that *doesn't* require that we distinguish, within our discourse about "artworks," between talk that is genuinely about works and talk that is about something else that is involved in works. I shall assume, although I cannot argue for this here, that, mutatis mutandis, analogous reasoning would apply to other contextualist ontologies.[2]

Is it, therefore, the case that Levinson's account is *not* revisionist in the relevant sense? That is, can indicated structures bear the sorts of properties whose apparent ascription to musical or literary works in our ordinary discourse about art is brought against process-centered ontologies? Fairly obviously, we can listen to an instance of a musical structure, but can we listen to an instance of a structure-as-indicated-by-X-at-t? If so, would the latter differ from simply listening to the structure *in the knowledge that* such a structure was indicated by X at t? How would this differ, as a listening, from listening to the structure in the knowledge

---

1 Similar difficulties beset Wolterstorff's sophisticated structuralist account of musical and literary works as "norm kinds," although, interestingly, he brings the revisionism objection to bear on the ATH in his 1991. For, as he acknowledges (1975), it is a consequence of his account that musical and literary works do not possess many of the properties we regularly seem to ascribe to them – for example, containing a C# in the seventh measure, or beginning with the words "April is the cruelest month" – but, rather, such properties as "being such that every correct performance contains a C# in the seventh measure" or "being such that every correct instance begins with 'April is the cruelest month.'"

2 If we extend the following line of reasoning to the visual arts, for example, the issue will be whether something like Danto's "objects under an interpretation" can sensibly be ascribed the sorts of properties that are unproblematically ascribed to physical objects simpliciter.

that the same structure was indicated by Υ at t', as in the sorts of examples offered by Levinson in arguing for the fine individuation of musical works?

If we are to answer such questions, we must first be clear just what an indicated structure is, ontologically speaking. Currie, as noted earlier, charges that the notion of an indicated structure is "metaphysically obscure" (1989: 58), further maintaining that if we admit such things into our overall ontology, we must also admit such entities as America-as-discovered-by-Columbus-in-1592. According to Currie, the ATH is to be preferred to the "indicated-structure" theory on the grounds that the former assigns artworks to an ontological category for which we have need in many other contexts, and doesn't require that we embrace a novel ontological category of dubious intelligibility.

As noted when this charge was mentioned earlier, recent work in the philosophy of mind suggests a possible answer to Currie. What is being proposed, it might be argued, is no more metaphysically obscure than such conditions as sunburn or such entities as footprints.[3] The ontological status of the latter is addressed by Davidson in arguing that "token physicalism" concerning the mental can meet a challenge posed by "externalist" views of the individuation of mental states.[4] The token physicalist holds that each token mental state is identical to some token physical state. The externalist asks how this can be so if, as externalism maintains, individuals who are molecule-for-molecule duplicates of one another can be in different mental states. Davidson suggests some homely analogies: John's sunburn is a (local) token physical state of John, but John could be in a molecule-for-molecule identical physical state yet *not* be sunburned. Again, a footprint in the sand is a token physical state of the relevant area of the beach, yet a molecule-for-molecule identical state of affairs could exist yet not be a footprint. In each case, Davidson argues, there is the appearance of mystery only if we conflate (1) the ontological status of the entities in question with (2) the manner in which such entities are individuated. Sunburn and footprints are physical states that are so classified because of their causal histories. Similarly, Davidson holds, beliefs are token physical events in cognitive agents that are individuated as particular mental events by reference to the social and environmental context in which those physical events occur and the principles that govern the ascription of intentional states.

---

3   See Davidson 1987 for this argument.
4   For a characterization of externalism, see, for example, Burge 1979.

It might be thought that an analogous strategy can rescue the thesis that musical and literary works are "indicated structures" from Currie's charge of metaphysical obscurity. But care is necessary in extending the Davidsonian analysis to artworks. The most obvious option might be to argue that, in place of the structuralist idea that works are *types* of structures, we should hold that works are *tokens* of those structures which are individuated as particular artworks in virtue of the art-historical context in which the structure is tokened. There is nothing ontologically mysterious about artworks, so conceived, nor, in construing artworks in this way, do we commit ourselves to bizarre additions to our overall ontology. America is not plausibly viewed as something tokened by Columbus, for example. But this line of reasoning is unlikely to appeal to proponents of the "indicated-structure" view. For, on the proposed analysis, it is not a *token* of a structure that is plausibly identified with the artwork, but a *tokening* of that structure. The token of the structure, after all, is the physical pattern generated by the composer or writer, and this particular pattern can be destroyed or otherwise damaged without in any way harming the work. To identify the work with the tokening of the structure, however, is to embrace the "process-centered" view that the work is a process token enacted by the artist.[5]

The indicated-structure theorist must therefore maintain that works are structure-*types* individuated as works by reference to the provenance of their instances. Here, however, we face a second problem in extending the Davidsonian analysis. In the case of sunburn, footprints, or corrosion, a physical state qualifies as an instance of the phenomenon in question in virtue of having been caused or produced by a distinctive kind of process. In the case of particular beliefs, according to Davidson, a physical state qualifies as the belief that p in virtue of the causal relations in which it stands to specific features of its environment and the principles that govern right interpretation. But how are we to characterize the relationship in which a structure-type must stand to something else in order to be an artwork, or in order to be a particular artwork? It might be argued that we cannot give a coherent and unified account of the kind of process that is implicated in the *individuation* of those structures that are artworks.

5 This argument will not apply to works of fine art, however, to the extent that one agrees with Levinson in identifying such works not with structures, but with particular physical objects. But see Danto 1981; Binkley 1976, 1977, for arguments against such an identification.

Levinson's original formulation of the "indicated-structure" theory actually says very little about how the notion of "indication" is itself to be understood, but, as noted earlier, he later endorses an interpretation in terms of Wolterstorff's notion of "norm-kinds," kinds that incorporate a norm or standard that determines whether something qualifies as a correct instance of that kind. Levinson suggests that we think of indication as a matter of making a particular structure-type "normative" in this sense. A work is then a structure-type as made normative by an individual at a time. The relation which must obtain between a structure-type and features of a context in order for there to be an artwork is *intentional* in nature. What is required is that an individual intend, in a particular context, that the structure-type be normative for a class of performances, and that she communicate that intention through a score or script or some other sanctioned means. While artistic creation in the literary and musical arts will usually involve producing a token of the relevant structure-type, it is the type itself that is thereby "indicated" in the relevant sense.

A Davidsonian defense of the "indicated-structure" view against Currie's charge of metaphysical obscurity, then, must take a musical or literary work to be a structure-type *individuated* as the work that it is through an act of "indication," in the above sense, performed by an individual at a time. Indicated structures, so construed, would be no more metaphysically obscure than sunburn or footprints. In the latter cases, we have a physical state of affairs that is individuated as a state of a particular kind in virtue of its provenance – the kind of process that brought about that physical state of affairs. Analogously, artworks are structure-types individuated as works in virtue of *their* provenance – their having been "indicated" in the right kind of way in a given context.

As may be apparent, however, this "defense" fails to do the trick. A difficulty emerges as soon as we entertain the sorts of hypothetical cases sketched by Levinson, where the same structure-type is indicated, in the sense specified, by more than one individual in a world – for example, where the structure-type indicated by Brahms in his Piano Sonata op. 2 is independently indicated by Beethoven. Consider a "footprint" analogue for this kind of circumstance. Suppose that John and Jane are wearing identical shoes, and Jane steps precisely into the indentation in the sand left by John's shoe. Then, we might say, we have two causings of a given physical state of affairs, resulting in a male footprint and a female footprint. But, crucially for Davidson's analysis, there is only *one* physical state of affairs which is correctly describable as *both* a male footprint and a female footprint in virtue of its causal history. Ontologically speaking, the male footprint just is that physical state of affairs, and the female foot-print just is the *same* physical state of affairs. The two causal histories enter into how that state of affairs is properly characterized or individuated, but do not change its ontological status. But if we apply this same way of thinking to musical works conceived as indicated structures, we must say that, where we have two indicatings of the same musical structure-type, there is a single structure-type that is correctly describable as both a work by Brahms and a work by Beethoven. Ontologically speaking, it would seem, we have a single entity that can be correctly classified in two distinct ways. What we *don't* seem to have is what Levinson requires, namely, an ontological distinction between two different works. In other words, Levinson requires the very thing that Davidson is at pains to deny, namely, that what enters into the individuation of things as artworks effects or reflects an ontological difference in the status of the things thereby individuated.

The Davidsonian strategy, then, seems better suited to a structuralist than to a contextualist like Levinson. For it offers a way in which the former could accommodate the possibility of multiple composition of the same work. The strategy preserves the structuralist idea that the work is the structure-type, assigning to indication a role in individuating structure-types *as* works, but not in individuating works themselves. If indication by an individual at a time is to enter into the ontological status of the work, then indicated structures cannot be ontologically "tamed" by Davidsonian means. The Davidsonian strategy would indeed allow us to say that musical or literary works have the properties ascribed to "works" in our ordinary discourse, thereby avoiding the revisionism objection. But the strategy fails to clarify the ontological status of Levinson's indicated structures because it fails to build the event of indication into the identity of the work. It remains unclear, therefore, how Levinsonian musical and literary works can be understood so as to have the sorts of properties cited in the revisionism objection, and thus how the indicated structure theory can avoid making a distinction between talk about structures per se and talk about works, as indicated structures.

This point can be made in a slightly different way if we draw upon Julian Dodd's recent critical discussion of Levinson's claim that an adequate ontology of musical works must render the latter *creatable* by their composers (Dodd 2000). Dodd argues that Levinson's own account of musical works fails to meet this requirement. Levinson contends that indicated structures are themselves *types*, but types that are "initiated" by a composer and therefore creatable. Dodd objects that no types are creatable, since a type exists as long as the property associated with that type is instantiated at some time, past, present, or future. We need not assess this claim. What is interesting in the present context is Dodd's further observation that Levinson treats the *time* at which a structure is indicated as a *constituent* element of the work. Dodd objects that the only things that can have times as *constituents* are events, and he summarily dismisses the idea that musical works can themselves be events. He concludes that we should reinstate the structuralist conception of the work.

Dodd's contention that events are the only things that can have times as constituents might be challenged on the grounds that one can coherently propose that a particular physical object has its rough time of creation as a constitutive and essential property. But the Davidsonian distinction between matters of ontology and matters of individuation is crucial here. While we might individuate artifacts of some kind – for example, 1997 Canadian dimes – by reference to their date of origin, their ontological status remains that of being physical objects. But Levinson requires that times be *constituents* of works, and this is a matter of ontological status, not of individuation. If we grant Dodd's claim about events, however, this sets up the following dilemma for Levinson, and, by extension, for any contextualist ontology of art. If either time or historical context is taken to be a constituent feature of a work, does this not force us to adopt an "event" ontology of art? If, on the other hand, reference to a time or historical context is not a constituent feature of a work but enters into the individuation of structure-types in a Davidsonian fashion, does this not amount to a tacit reinstatement of structuralism? The first horn of the dilemma seems to entail that we must avail ourselves of a distinction between work and work-product in order to avoid the revisionism objection. The second horn of the dilemma means we would have to counter the objections to structuralism so well expounded by contextualist critics like Levinson. If structuralism is rejected, only the first horn of the dilemma remains as an option.

However, the Davidsonian analysis of such things as sunburn may also help the performance theorist in another way. Characteristically, where we have a term that refers to entities that are the products of a particular kind of process, the term has an alternative use to refer to the process generative of such products. For example, "sunburn" is sometimes used to refer to a particular physical state and sometimes to the process that causes that state. Similarly, "corrosion" may refer to the physical state of an object or to the process whereby the object came to be in that physical state. It was suggested above that one who attempts to answer the revisionism objection by appealing to a distinction between talk of works, as process-like entities, and talk of work-instances or work-focuses, as product-like entities, owes us a principled account of this distinction. We might hope to develop such an account if we can find a principle underlying the different uses of terms like "sunburn" and "corrosion," where there clearly is a distinction between process-talk and product-talk.

Here is one such principle bearing on present concerns. When we talk of *studying, understanding,* or *investigating* X, where "X" is one of the terms in question, it is characteristically *the process generative of the product,* not the product as so generated, that is the subject of study, understanding, or investigation. Alternatively, when we speak of physical operations in respect of X, it is characteristically the product that is at issue. For example, when I treat John's sunburn, I treat the product of a particular process, but when I study sunburn, it is the process that concerns me. Similarly, the corrosion that is remedied by the auto-mechanic is the product of a particular process, but what scientists study is the process generative of that product. Interestingly, the same applies even where we use different locutions to refer to the process and its product, as in the case of "footprint." If I investigate footprints in the garden, it is the process generative of those footprints that is of interest, but that which the criminal left and of which the police take a plaster-cast is the product of that process.

If the performance theory is correct, we might expect a similar process–product ambiguity in our discourse about artworks, such that the latter comprises both talk about generative processes and talk about the generated products. More important in the present context, we might expect that the object of discourse would be determined by the following principle: if "*X*" is the name of a work, then, when we speak of physical operations in respect of *X* or of an instance of *X*, the object of our discourse is the generated product, whereas when we speak of studying or understanding *X*, the object of discourse is the generative process. If criticism and appreciation are the proper analogues, in the case of artworks, for understanding or studying in the case of sunburn and corrosion, then the object of discourse in talk about criticizing or appreciating an artwork is the *process*, not the product as generated by that process. And if our interest in artworks, in the philosophy of art, is an interest in them as the units of criticism and appreciation, then, as philosophers, we should identify works with generative processes rather than with their generated products, while acknowledging the legitimacy of those idioms in which the term "artwork" is used to refer to the latter rather than the former. Of course, our scientific interest in sunburn or corrosion, as processes, requires that we take careful account of the product of these processes. Analogously, our appreciative interest in an artwork, as performance, requires that we take careful account of the focus of appreciation that completes that performance: as noted earlier, the performance theory in no way denies the importance, for an appreciative understanding of any artwork, of the closest attention to the details of the work-focus.

There are two premisses in the foregoing argument that call for comment. First, it is claimed that, for the purposes of the philosophy of art, an artwork is whatever functions as the unit of criticism and appreciation. I take this premiss – which is part of the pragmatic constraint – to be common ground for the philosophers whose views are currently under review. Second, it is claimed that talk of appreciating works is properly analogous to talk of studying or understanding natural phenomena, and to be contrasted with talk about physically interacting with such phenomena. This is more controversial in abstract, but less so in the present context, where we are assuming that provenance features essentially in the individuation of works.

We might appeal, here, to Michael Baxandall's characterization (1985) of the task of inferential criticism in the visual arts. The inferential critic, according to Baxandall, seeks to appropriate and appreciate a particular painting as a solution to a problem or set of problems in a situation. Translated into the terms of our current discussion, the claim is that appreciating the work (process) is a matter of historically explaining the work-focus (product), just as understanding sunburn (process) is a matter of causally explaining sunburn (product). Currie, we may note, clearly regards Baxandall's work as supporting his process-centered ontology of art. But this might be thought to conflict with Baxandall's own insistence that what is subject to historical ("inferential") criticism in the fine arts is the *object* produced and not the action of producing it (1985: 12ff). However, there is only the appearance of conflict here. While what we seek to explain in history is an action, what we seek to *explain* in the inferential criticism of an artwork is indeed the *product* of a generative process – what I am terming the work-focus – and our explanation is a reconstruction of the process completed by the work-focus. Our goal in the inferential criticism of artworks differs from our goal in the historical explanation of actions, in that the former goal is to arrive at a better *appreciation* of the work, but not to *explain* the work. If the work is a generative performance, an explanation of the work presumably falls within the ambit of the social scientist, or the psychologist. But this is distinct from the kind of inferential explanation that falls within the ambit of the critic, where such explanation is *interior* to the activity of appreciation. Explaining the work-focus, by locating it in the work, is crucial to appreciating the work.

8.2 Performance and the Challenge of the Modern

As we saw in chapter 1, much of the discomfort that receivers experience in their attempts to appreciate the art of the "late modern" period, and much of the hostility directed at that art, stems from uncertainty as to what one is supposed to *do* in order to appreciate a late modern work. Receivers who are experienced in looking at and appreciating traditional representational painting learn, without too much difficulty, how to look appreciatively at Impressionist and Post-Impressionist painting, comprehend Cubist modes of representation, and respond to the painterly qualities of Abstract Expressionist works. But what begins as a sense of frustration in peering at the large minimalist canvases of painters like Rothko, Newman, and Stella becomes puzzlement when confronted with Readymades, Brillo boxes, and the creations of artists such as Damien Hirst, and turns into utter bewilderment in the face of much conceptual art, found art, and installation art.

I suggested in chapter 1 that a primary reason for the inaccessibility of much late modern art to receivers who obtain great satisfaction from engagement with the art of earlier periods is that such receivers bring a set of largely implicit assumptions to their encounter with a work of fine art, and, indeed, with a work of art in general. According to what I termed our "common-sense theory" of art, works of visual art are objects of the sort exhibited in galleries, objects which were created with the intention that value be found in experiences elicited in a direct perceptual encounter with them. The receiver, armed with the common-sense theory, stands before the objects exhibited in galleries dedicated to late modern art and wonders why the experience elicited in a perceptual encounter with these objects is featureless, aesthetically speaking. There is this object – a urinal, a stack of Brillo boxes, a pile of felt stacked with no apparent order, a piece of ugly twisted metal, a canvas smeared with industrial-colored paint, a collection of photographs of a performance – which one is presumably intended to appreciate, and whose presence in the gallery suggests that it is deemed by the curators and critics to be a valuable work of art. But what is one supposed to *do* with the object to realize its value as a work? Is one supposed to admire its aesthetic qualities, as some philosophers have seemed to suggest? Certainly, if "aesthetic attitude" theories of aesthetic experience are to be believed, one can admire *anything* aesthetically. But the common-sense theory suggests that the objects exhibited in galleries are there because they particularly reward the adoption of an aesthetic attitude toward them. Yet many late modern art-objects seem designed to repel rather than seduce one who approaches them with such an aesthetic intent.

Given this sense of not knowing what to *do* with late modern works, one may respond with a resigned admission of one's own lack of sensitivity, or, echoing Tom Wolfe, dismiss much of what passes for late modern art as a triumph of art theory over art, marking a sharp discontinuity in the history and epistemology of the arts. I suggested in chapter 1, however, that the problem lies deeper, in a misconception of what artworks in general are and of what is involved in their appreciation – a misconception hidden from view because the common-sense theory seems to account fairly well for our appreciative engagement with earlier art. We also saw in chapter 1 that the common-sense theory faces difficulties in accounting for aspects of our appreciation even of more traditional works of fine art. Art appreciation depends upon a sensitivity not just to the manifest properties of an art-object, but also to the provenance of that object. One might hope that a clearer recognition of the place of provenance in the being and being appreciated of artworks would help to clarify features of our practice that are barely comprehensible when viewed through the lens of the common-sense theory.

But making a place for provenance is not sufficient to dispel our artistic puzzlement. For example, the urinal exhibited by Duchamp, or the pile of Brillo boxes exhibited by Warhol, certainly differ in their provenance from an identically designed urinal in a Paris *pissoir* or an indistinguishable stack of Brillo boxes in the store room of a hardware store in a small town in mid-West America. But in what ways do such differences in provenance *matter* as far as the appreciation of the respective artworks is concerned? Does a urinal's being exhibited in a gallery somehow confer upon it appreciable properties that it failed to possess when in its natural habitat? Some have made a direct appeal to provenance in an attempt to resolve the aesthetic puzzles engendered by the common-sense theory, holding that arthood *just is* a matter of provenance – of being generated or presented in the right sort of institutional context – rather than requiring the possession of "aesthetic" qualities. Proponents of such simple "institutional" theories of art[6] tacitly assume that no resolution to our

6   See, for example, Dickie 1974, which I discuss in chapter 10 below.

artistic puzzlement concerning late modern art is forthcoming at the level of *ontology*. The difference between works and non-works, in the puzzling cases – between *Fountain* and a perceptually indistinguishable urinal of the same manufacture – is not a difference in kind of *entity*, but a difference in the place or role an entity of a given kind has acquired in an institutional context. Given our ontological investigations thus far, however, we may hope to throw a somewhat different light on these matters.

Let me distinguish two ways in which, accepting the force of the anti-structuralist arguments discussed and developed earlier, and acknowledging the various ways in which provenance enters into the being and the being appreciated of the artwork, we might try to accommodate late modern works of fine art by reconceiving the ontological status of the work.

8.2.1 Works as contextualized entities

The standard ontological strategy for accommodating late modern art is to adopt some form of contextualism. The contextualist, as we have seen, preserves the idea that the work is the *product* of the artist's creative endeavors, but reconceives that product so that it somehow incorporates elements of provenance. This then explains why the appreciation of works – both traditional and modern – involves attention not simply to the manifest properties of exhibited objects or structure-tokens, but also to "invisible" properties that depend upon the relations in which these entities stand to their art-historical contexts of generation. This is essentially Danto's strategy, in *Transfiguration of the Commonplace* (1981), where it is argued that a visual artwork is tantamount to an object under an interpretation, the relevant interpretation being determined by the art-historical context in which the artist is operating – the "artworld" in Danto's sense – in which we must locate the object if we are to see it and appreciate it as a particular artwork. It is the artistic properties conferred upon an object through the artist's acting in an artworld that distinguish, for example, the work *Fountain* from an indistinguishable object encountered on the streets of Paris, or the paintings in the gallery of red rectangles both from one another and from non-works that share with them all manifest properties. Binkley's strategy for accommodating late modern works is also of this kind. Works, for Binkley, are intensionally individuated "pieces" which, while traditionally specified by manipulating objects to bring into being aesthetic properties, are specifiable in more imaginative ways in late modern contexts. This strategy is also to be found in Margolis' talk of works as "culturally emergent" from the physical objects that embody them, and is the strategy that Levinson might use to accommodate, as indicated structures, late modern musical and literary works.

If we think of works as contextualized entities in any of these ways, it clearly *does* help to explain what is going on in much late modern art, and to dispel the sort of artistic puzzlement generated by such art if one endorses the common-sense theory. By elucidating the particular manner in which aspects of provenance not determinable from an "innocent" perceptual scrutiny of an art-object are partly constitutive of the work somehow represented by that art-object, we can help the puzzled receiver understand what to *do* with the art-object in order to appreciate the work. We can also explain how perceptually indistinguishable objects or structures can "represent," in some sense, very different works. In such cases, we might say, manipulations of a vehicular medium that result in indistinguishable objects or structures serve to articulate different artistic statements, because those manipulations are conducted in different art-historical contexts and are differently motivated.

This approach seems inadequate to account for at least some late modern works, however. In such cases, it seems wrong to think of the vehicle, through which an artistic statement is being articulated, as an *object* or even a *structure* that is the end-product of a sequence of motivated manipulations of a medium. It is tempting, for example, to say that, in the case of a Readymade like *Fountain*, the vehicle whereby an artistic statement is being articulated is not the *object* exhibited – the inscribed urinal – but, rather, the complex *act or gesture* involved in proposing such an object for exhibition in a given art-historical context. Even if the reader resists such a reading of Duchamp's work, this sort of analysis is arguably necessary to make sense of those late modern artworks where it seems to be an action or gesture, rather than an object entering into an action or gesture, that articulates the content of the work. Consider, for example, Christo's wrappings of natural objects such as the Grand Canyon, Claes Oldenburg's infamous "grave" (a grave-shaped hole dug and then filled in again in Central Park, New York), much "installation art," and many of the conceptual pieces catalogued by Lippard in *Six Years* (1973).

To accommodate such works, a contextualist might advance the following revised position. The work, she might insist, is indeed the contextualized product of the artist's creative endeavors, and, in the case of traditional works, works are contextualized objects or structures as originally proposed. But, in the case of many puzzling late modern works, the product of the artist's endeavors is not an object-like entity but an *action* or *gesture*. On such an account, Wolfe's discontinuity thesis, discussed in chapter 1, is at least partly right. The ontological status of the artwork, as product, changes dramatically in the late modern period. While traditional works in the visual arts and some late modern works are contextualized physical objects, those late modern works not plausibly identified with physical objects are contextualized action-tokens. Note that this revised contextualist account does *not* identify certain late modern works with performances in the sense proposed by the performance theorist. The action-token with which such a revised contextualism would identify Oldenburg's "grave," for example, is the *vehicle* through which Oldenburg articulates a certain artistic statement: it is not the performance whereby a focus of appreciation having such a vehicle was specified.

The "late modern work as performance art" thesis *does* assist in making sense of some kinds of late modern works. Consider, for example, installation art. There is a collection of objects, and we seem to view the appreciation of installational artworks as requiring that one *visit* the installation and *attend to* the disposition of objects, at least if critical reviews of such works are to be our guide. On the other hand, the collection is disassembled at the end of the installation, and this prompts those who think of such works in "object"-terms to say that the works "go out of existence" after a limited time, and that this is a radical challenge to the idea of the enduring work of fine art. If we think of installation art as a form of performance, on the other hand, so that the work is the setting up and eventual dismantling of a given installation, then we are less troubled by the supposed transience of the work. For we are used to the idea that performances always take place at a particular time, but this does not lead us to say that works of performance art somehow come into and go out of existence.

One problem for this sort of account, however, is that it lacks a persuasive story as to how the *constitutive* properties of late modern works so conceived are determined, and how such works differ from more straightforward cases of so-called "performance art," such as that associated with artists like Eric Bogosian and Laurie Anderson. We might think of performance art as a form of improvised or semi-improvised theater,[7]

---

7   As we shall see in chapter 9, finer distinctions need to be drawn here.

to the appreciation of which we bring a lot of the same skills and expectations as we bring to the appreciation of theatrical performances. It seems, furthermore, that one cannot adequately appreciate a work of performance art without *viewing* it, whether in person or on film, and that we take visible aspects of the performance-event to be relevant to the aesthetic and critical appreciation of the work, even if we also think that a proper appreciation of a performance piece requires that the performance be viewed in its art-historical context. If late modern works of fine art are viewed as gestures or action-tokens, however, their appreciation seems to differ dramatically from the appreciation of performance art. For one thing, it is almost never the case that, in attempting to appreciate such a work, we are in a position to view the action-token identified with the work, or even a filmed representation of this action. Second, it seems that, in the cases at hand, many and perhaps all properties of the action that would be manifest in such a viewing would be irrelevant to the appreciation of the work. If a work such as *Fountain* is an action-token, in the proposed sense, rather than an object, then surely the properties relevant to its appreciation are *relational* properties of that action-token, rather than manifest properties that we could only have observed had we been contemporaries of Duchamp somehow involved in the complex sequence of events that led to the acknowledgment of *Fountain* as an artwork.[8] In fact, we are presumably willing to countenance *Fountain* existing in a possible world where the "performance" was accomplished by a completely different set of actions, as long as these actions "made the same point." Thus, if the work is an action or performance in the sense under consideration, it seems to be as *a particular making of a point*, rather than as the specific actions employed to make that point, that the work is appreciable.

The revised contextualist view is also unconvincing as an account of what is going on in much conceptual art. In the case of Barry's *All the things I know . . .* , for example, such a view will presumably entail that the work consists in Barry's action or gesture of specifying the piece in the given circumstances. But if "specification," here, is a matter of making specific and making public, how does this act of specification differ, in principle, from the "specification" of traditional pieces through the manipulation of a vehicular medium? If, in traditional cases, the work is identified not with the act of specification but with the object specified, what justifies the contrary way of proceeding in the case of conceptual works?

8   See de Duve 1996: ch. 2.

8.2.2 Locating performance in the work: an example

An example may help to bring out more clearly what is unsatisfactory in the revised contextualist's selective identification of late modern works with actions or gestures. Many so-called "conceptual" artists photograph or film some of their activities and often provide the resulting images as "documentation" of the pieces in question. One such artist, mentioned in chapter 1, is Vito Acconci, whose works include photographically documented performances, videos of live performances of a public nature, and videos of various bodily transformations performed by the artist on himself, and sometimes video-taped by the artist in the course of executing the transformations. As examples of each of these types dating from a two-year period, we may take:

1 *Following Piece* (1969): "Activity, 23 days, varying durations. New York City. Choosing a person at random, in the street, any location, each day. Following him wherever he goes, however long or far he travels. (The activity ends when he enters a private place – his home, office, etc.)"

    The "execution" of this piece by Acconci in 1969 is documented by photographs that accompany the description of the piece.[9] The photographs were reportedly "staged" later (Poggi 1999: 259), something to which I shall return.

2 *Adaptation Studies* (June 1970), three studies one of which involves repeated attempts by the blindfolded artist to catch a rubber ball thrown at him by an unseen collaborator. Each "study" was recorded by an "accomplice" on silent super-8 film.

3 *Conversions I, II, and III* (1971), described in a recent exhibition catalog as follows: "Acconci attempts to alter his sexual boundaries and, by implication, his sexual identity by turning himself into the image of a woman,"[10] where one of these attempts involves using a candle to burn the hair off his chest. This was again recorded without sound on super-8 film. Acconci himself filmed the segment with the candle, holding the camera in one hand while moving the candle over his body with the other.

Each of these works incorporates in some way performance-events, enacted by the artist, that realize a specifiable set of performative con-

9 See Lippard 1973: 117 for a description of the piece and reproductions of some of the "documentation."
10 Catalogue for Vito Acconci exhibition, May 29 to July 14, 2001, 11 Duke Street Gallery, London.

straints. Furthermore, in each case there is a single performance-event that roughly satisfies those constraints. But the performance-event enters in very different ways into the identity of the work in Acconci's pieces. I shall have more to say about such matters in the following chapter, where I look in much greater detail at the ways in which performance-events enter into the being and the being-appreciated of works. For the present, however, I shall offer a brief analysis of the three pieces by Acconci that anticipates the fuller treatment to follow.

Take, first, *Following Piece*. Here there is a performance-event, but it enters into the identity of the work only by instantiating the *type* of performance characterized in the performative constraints set out by Acconci. The photographic record serves only to imaginatively enliven the performance for the receiver, to help her to imagine what the performance was like in virtue of satisfying those constraints. The use of photography in such a minimal documentary role is understood by the receiver as indicating that visible features of the actual performance not preserved on film are not important for the appreciation of the work. The photographs serve to isolate those features of the performance-event, as vehicle, which bear upon the articulation of an artistic statement. This analysis of *Following Piece* usefully extends to such works as Duchamp's *Fountain*, if, as suggested above, we take the performance of exhibiting the urinal, rather than the urinal itself, to be the vehicle whereby an artistic statement is articulated. For, while Duchamp ensured that there was photographic and other documentary evidence of his performance,[11] our appreciation of the work is not impaired by our inability to view that performance either directly or indirectly.

In the case of both the *Adaptation Studies* and *Conversions*, a super-8 recording of the performance-events was made, and this might lead us to think that, in these cases, appreciation of the work does require taking full account of the perceptible features of the performance as "preserved" in the documentation. This then suggests that in both cases we have something analogous to those performance-events that are themselves the vehicles of works in improvised musical or theatrical presentations and in works of performance art. This is true to some extent in the case of the *Adaptation Studies*, in that the artistic statement articulated in the work clearly depends upon features of the performances preserved on film. But the performance, as vehicle, still operates in a more attenuated way than

---

11　See, again, the extended account of the process whereby the art-object in *Fountain* was accepted as art in chapter 2 of de Duve 1996.

do the performance-events in such performance works as jazz improvisations. It is not the cinematically preserved details of Acconci's "adaptive" behaviors that serve to articulate an artistic statement here. Rather, the vehicle is the performance-event conceived as the enactment of a set of specifications, where the content of those specifications is deepened by the details revealed in the recording of that event. The recording again enlivens our conception of what it is to act is such a way as to satisfy those specifications. The difference between this work and *Following Piece* in respect of the place of the performance-event in the work is one of degree, not one of kind.

Conversions, however, is significantly different in two respects. First, whether this was Acconci's intention or not, the cinematic record not only serves to make accessible to receivers manifest properties of the performance-event, but also enters into the identity of the work in its own right in its celebration of the opacity of the photographic medium. In its graininess and its play of light and dark as the candle throws its shadows over Acconci's body, the visual image is arresting in a way that is completely absent in the other works. Thus the cinematic record itself functions as a vehicle through which elements in an artistic statement may be articulated. But, more important, the very fact that the camera is recording the very "private" activities carried out by Acconci is itself an integral part of the performance that serves as vehicle in the piece, and crucial to the artistic statement articulated through that vehicle. For, as Kate Linker stresses in her monograph on Acconci (Linker 1994), one of the central themes in his work of this period is the breaking down of the barriers that traditionally separate artist from receiver, and the attempt to integrate the receiver into the work itself – something most notoriously celebrated in his *Seedbed*. In *Conversions*, the observing camera for whom the regendering of the self is staged represents the receiver herself. Further, as noted, in one part of the performance it is Acconci himself who directs the "vision" of the camera, thereby simultaneously realizing both the performer's and the receiver's roles. Thus, rather than being a documentation of the performance which serves as artistic vehicle for the work, the filming of Acconci's self-manipulations is itself a crucial *part* of that performance. The specifications for the performance itself include the intrusive and collusive eye of the camera.

This inclusion of the photographic presence within the performance that serves as artistic vehicle also figures in the articulation of another important theme in Acconci's work of this period – the mediation between personal and private spheres. Linker writes that "in its capacity as a record, the photograph has the capacity to re-present and make public an activity that would otherwise go unremarked: it provides a means of transforming private acts into public information, accessible to multiple channels of distribution" (1994: 18). One might argue for an analogous reading of the three *Adaptation Studies*. Linker tantalizingly remarks, of these pieces, that they are "importantly titled *Adaptation Studies* (and, as important, recorded on film)" (1994: 26). The presence of the camera might again signify in virtue of its capacity to make public the "private" accommodation of the body to stress – the theme of the three studies. Note, however, that no such account is forthcoming in the case of *Following Piece*. If the images were indeed taken later, the process of photographing cannot enter into the performance itself, or, at least, not into the performance as specified in the description of the piece.

8.2.3 Works as performances

This sort of example brings out very well, I think, the problems that confront the revised contextualist claim that late modern works are to be identified with performances whereas other works are to be identified with either objects or (contextualized) structures. For, as we have seen, the performance enters in very different ways into the identity of the work in Acconci's pieces. In bringing out the different roles that performance-events can play, we have tacitly appealed to narratives that contextualize those performance events, locating them in the context of generative activity on the part of the artist who ascribes such different roles to these events. Without the embedding of the performance-events in the different kinds of narratives surveyed, the artistic statements articulated in the respective works would be inaccessible to us.

This exemplifies the more central role of artistic performance in the epistemology and ontology of art for which I have argued in this study. As I have maintained, one kind of legitimate interest in *any* artwork takes the work to be, or be representative of, a performance which constitutes some kind of achievement. While this is not the only legitimate interest in an artwork, it is an interest that grounds much of our discourse about art, and is central to discourse about the self-referential and self-reflexive art of the late twentieth century. Attention to an artistic vehicle – a painted canvas, a shaped pieced of marble, a text, a sound structure as produced by certain instruments – refers us to an artistic performance generative of that vehicle. This holds equally for quintessentially "modern" expressivist works like Pollock's "Action Paintings," and for postmodernist reactions to such expressivism – such as Lichtenstein's *Brushstroke*.[12] Much of what we value in works, traditional and contemporary, is a matter of artistic performance which requires the contextualization of the artistic vehicle – whether it be Turner's radical use of the medium of oil paint in the treatment of light in his later seascapes, or the elision of the epsilon in Perec's *La Disparition*. What is brought out by the examples from Acconci is that determining what the vehicle itself is, in the case of works that somehow incorporate performance-events, requires that we refer those events to a history of making. Our appreciative interest in art is an interest in a generative performance whereby a focus of appreciation is specified, a focus that may itself incorporate other performances in different ways.

In order to bring out these sorts of differences, then, we need to locate a performance like that of Acconci *within* a broader performance on the part of the artist, whereby the former performance is used as a *vehicle* in the specification of a focus of appreciation. This motivates an alternative strategy for accommodating late modernist works, which identifies works in general with generative performances, and takes the distinguishing feature of late modern works to be the nature of the work-focus specified. This approach rejects the idea that the work is the product of the artist's creative activity, and identifies it, rather, with the *process completed by that product*. The sorts of differences between traditional and late modern artworks, and between different late modern artworks themselves, as discussed in the preceding paragraphs, are *not* to be explained in terms of a discontinuity concerning the ontological status of the work. Rather, these differences are explicable in terms of the different kinds of resources that can serve as vehicles whereby an artistic statement is articulated through an artistic medium, or in terms of different artistic media that can be employed with the same vehicles. Whereas the artistic tradition in which late modern visual art is grounded employs such materials as canvas, stone, wood, and pigment of various kinds as its vehicular media, the vehicle in some late modern art can be viewed as itself an action-token, or as some composite entity that comprises both action-like and object-like entities, as in Acconci's *Conversions*.

---

12 As noted in chapter 3, Roy Lichtenstein's *Brushstroke* involved the application of tiny dots of acrylic paint to canvas (manipulation of the vehicular medium), whereby he articulated an artistic statement whose base-order "meanings" include being a representation of a single brushstroke and being in a pseudo-pointilliste style, and whose higher-order "meanings" include being a parody of the fetishism of the brushstroke in Abstract Expressionist painting of the preceding 20-odd years.

In determining the nature of the vehicle, we also clarify what kind of activity is required on the part of the receiver if she is to properly appreciate the work. In particular, we help to resolve the receiver's puzzlement as to *what she is supposed to do* with whatever confronts her in a gallery that catalogs or exhibits late modern works – whether, for example, proper appreciation requires a direct perceptual engagement with one of the entities on display, or whether it requires an exercise of the imagination or of conceptualization guided or directed by what is on display. More importantly, perhaps, we provide the receiver with some direction in deciding for herself what kind of activity might be appropriate if she wishes to further her appreciation of a work. I shall say more on this in the following chapter, when I consider in more detail the role that performances can play *internal to* works which are themselves taken to be performances.

The *transience* of some art-objects does not introduce a radical gap between traditional and modern art, on the performance theory, because the work is *always* a generative process, and therefore always exists as a work insofar as the process has occurred. What may be transient is some part of the work-focus, and, if it is, and if there are appreciable properties of the work-focus that depend upon a direct perceptual encounter with what is no longer available to the receiver, then the work cannot be *fully* appreciated once that element in the work-focus is gone. But this should not disturb us – it is, after all, what we say about works whose transience is less planned – works whose vehicles are lost, or damaged, or lose their lustre, etc.

8.3 More on Forgeries

To conclude this chapter, I want to return to another of the problems discussed in chapter 1, that of accounting for our treatment of forgeries. Forgeries, it will be recalled, are of two kinds. Sometimes we have two objects which it is very difficult to tell apart, each of which is put forward as the "original" work but one of which is a later copy. In other, more interesting, cases, we have a single object which is presented as being by an artist of some note, when it has actually been fabricated at a later date with the intention of deceiving spectators. Here, once again, I shall maintain that the performance theory provides a more satisfactory account of the issues than do contextualist alternatives.

The difference between a forgery of an existing work and the original of which it is a forgery is, fairly obviously, at least in part a difference in provenance. The same applies to forgeries that, while not copies of an existing work, are "in the style" of an artist other than the one responsible for their existence, but are misrepresented as being by the former rather than the latter. This much is common territory for those who have argued about our artistic practice in respect of forgeries. The question at issue is whether differences in provenance of this sort provide any sort of *justification* for that practice, and, if so, what *kind* of justification they provide. As we saw in chapter 1, if one argues from "common-sense" assumptions about art and artistic appreciation, then the differences in provenance that distinguish forgeries of either kind from "genuine works" do not disenfranchise the former either as aesthetic objects or as objects of artistic appreciation. Our treatment of forgeries may then be seen as having at best a socio-economic justification, given the non-artistic values ascribed to works in the market place.

As we saw in chapters 2 and 3, there are good reasons to reject the empiricist view of artistic appreciation upon which such an argument rests. Appreciating a painting is not reducible to the appreciation of those properties given in an immediate perceptual encounter with a painted object uninformed by knowledge of provenance. Rather, appreciating such an entity *as an artwork* requires an awareness of properties that depend, at least in part, on aspects of provenance over and above those that determine category of art. However, recognizing that provenance has a crucial bearing on artistic appreciation is not by itself sufficient to artistically justify our treatment of forgeries. We must also argue that, among the features of provenance that do bear upon artistic appreciation, there are features that bear in such a way as to explain our treatment of forgeries.

For the contextualist, as we have seen, provenance bears upon the appreciation of a work to the extent that it determines artistically relevant properties of the product of artistic activity. In the terms used in this study, it is through determining properties of the focus of appreciation specified by the artist that provenance enters essentially into the appreciation of works, for the contextualist. So when, as in the case of Danto's red rectangles, provenance is partly determinative of the different artistic statements articulated through manipulation of the vehicular medium productive of indistinguishable objects, the contextualist has no problem accounting for the intuitive differences between works. Again, if knowledge of provenance is necessary in order to determine properties of the vehicle through which an artistic statement has been articulated, this is something for which the contextualist can account.

But the bearing of provenance on our treatment of forgeries does not obviously fall under either of these heads. Take the van Meegeren example. It is not obvious that learning that van Meegeren rather than Vermeer was the painter of the *Disciples at Emmaeus* leads us to revise our assessment as to the artistic statement articulated by the picture, unless we hold that the artistic medium differs. Certainly, it is far from clear that any of the first-order meaning-properties have changed. Knowledge of provenance will affect our understanding of the vehicle through which an artistic statement was articulated, in that we will learn of the special pigments and other chemicals which van Meegeren employed to give the impression of aging in a newly painted canvas. But it is not clear that this difference affects the focus of appreciation in such a way as to explain how our treatment of the painting is affected by our learning its true origins.

The problem for the contextualist is that the real change is *not* in our assessment of the specified focus, but in our assessment of the kind of achievement involved in specifying such a focus. While the contextualist may think she is perfectly entitled to count such "achievement-properties" among a work's artistic properties, these are features of what was done, as a performance, rather than of what was brought about through that doing. Thus the most straightforward way in which to make a case for the artistically flawed nature of forgeries is to hold that artistic appreciation is centrally concerned with what is *achieved* in a work. One can then maintain that the artistic inferiority of a forgery consists in its being an inferior *achievement* relative to the "genuine" work for which it was mistaken – either the genuine work of another artist of which it is a copy, or the genuine work of another artist who turns out to have produced no such work.

This is precisely the strategy adopted by Denis Dutton (1979) in a very interesting paper on forgeries already cited in chapter 2. Dutton argues that every artwork, whatever its medium, "involves an element of performance," where this implies "some sense of accomplishment, of achievement." Artworks, he maintains, are artifacts that are the products of human agency, and that stand in testimony to the performances that have produced them: "As performances, works of art represent the ways in which artists solve problems, overcome obstacles, make do with available materials" (1979: 24). The fundamental question we must ask, in our attempts to appreciate a work, is: "What has the artist done, what has he achieved?" We can answer this question only if we have "some idea of the limitations, technical and conventional, within which he has worked" (1979: 26). The connection between an artwork and the performance that produces the art-object is a *conceptual* one, Dutton maintains, and "grasping what sort of achievement the work itself represents" is therefore part of what it is to understand something *as* a work of art. For this reason, it *must* make a difference to our appreciation of an art-object if we learn that it is a forgery, whether of another work or of another artist's style. For the forgery, by its very nature, involves a *misrepresentation* of what has been achieved, and our appreciation of the art-object, when we were unaware of its status *as* a forgery, was predicated upon that misrepresentation. When its status is revealed, we can no longer appreciate it as before because it does not represent the achievement we took it to represent.

This provides us with an elegant solution to our puzzlement concerning forgeries of both types, if we accept that artistic appreciation requires the appreciation of what has been achieved. And we have already seen in chapters 2 and 3 more general arguments that can be given in support of this thesis. Currie, we will recall (chapter 6), thinks that one can infer the ATH from the fact that works are appreciated for their achievement-properties, since it is action-types that possess such properties. The performance theory, as we have also seen, draws an analogous conclusion, that insofar as the object of critical and appreciative attention is *what has been done*, works are to be identified with particular generative performances. But Dutton seems committed to the idea that works themselves are the *products* of artistic performances, even if our interest in those products is to a large extent an interest in the properties of the performances that brought them into being. As we have just seen, he talks of the work "*representing*" a particular kind of achievement, where this is *not* to be understood as (1) the identification of the work with the achievement, qua performance, but as (2) the claim that the work, as art-object, somehow "stands for" the performance that produced it. Works of art, he maintains, are "the end-products of human activities," which "can be seen under the aspect of performance." The work of art "[has] implicit in it the possibility of achievement of some kind" (1979: 29).

These somewhat slippery characterizations should be familiar to us by now. They are the sorts of things one finds oneself saying when one acknowledges our appreciative interest in process yet wishes to cling to the identification of work with product. But why does Dutton resist the temptation (irresistible to some!) to *identify* the work with the performance, rather than postulate some shadowy relation of "representation" or "implicit embodiment" between the two? His concern seems to be to do justice not only to our interest in works as achievements, but also to the sort of concern that motivates empiricist aesthetics – "our interest in the work of art as visual, verbal, or aural surface" (1979: 29). A work has to be something in which we can have such a dual interest – an interest in artistic performance and an interest in aesthetic features of the product of that performance. Of Schubert's *Erlkonig*, Dutton writes:

> It is this pretty sonic experience, certain words strung together and sung in certain tones to piano accompaniment, and we can talk endlessly about the beauties of that aural surface just as we could talk of the appealing proper- ties of the piece of driftwood. It is also a profound human achievement, something done by someone; it is precisely a *setting* of Goethe's poem, one of perhaps fifty other such settings produced in the nineteenth century. What is understood and appreciated about Schubert's *Erlkonig* is neither of these to the exclusion of the other: both are part of our understanding of this great work of art. (1979: 25–6)

Dutton thinks that the work, as something in which we can have this dual interest, must be identified with the *product* of the performance, because only the product possesses the *aesthetic* properties as well as the achievement-properties. But there is a certain equivocation in this passage, in talk of the work, conceived as the *product*, as "a profound human achievement, something done by someone." The term "achievement" has a process–product ambiguity. If it is to apply to the thing that has the "aural surface" and its attendant aesthetic properties, it must refer to the *product*. But, as "something done by someone," the achievement is a *process* productive of that product. We see the same ambiguity in Dutton's characterization of Schubert's work as a "setting" of Goethe's poem. Our interest in the work as performance is an interest in the process whereby the poem is *set* to music, the product of this performance being a *setting* to music of Goethe's poem. It is therefore *not* the case that, by equating the work with the product, we account for our dual interest in works. Rather, we trade on the process–product ambiguity of talk of "achieve- ments" or "settings," such that we have one interest in the *process* and the other in the *product*.

The performance theory also acknowledges our "dual interest" in art- works, but accommodates this by identifying the work with the genera- tive performance *completed by* the work-focus. Our interest in the aesthetic properties of the work-focus is an essential element in our appreciation of the work, so construed, because we can only understand the generative process through understanding the product that completes it. Our inter- est in the artistic performance generative of the work-focus is also an

essential part of our appreciation of the work, of course. Thus, by explicitly recognizing the distinction between work and work-focus, and by
building the work-focus into the conception of the work, the performance theory is able to provide the ontological foundation required for
Dutton's insightful analysis of our treatment of forgeries.

Performance as Art

9.1 Performance as Art

In the final section of chapter 8, we considered Denis Dutton's claim that our interest in something as an artwork of any kind is an interest in a particular performance. In making such a claim, Dutton is challenging an established distinction between what might be termed the "creative" and the "performing" arts. According to this distinction,[1] those working in the "creative" arts bring into being artworks, while those in the "performing" arts for the most part "realize" certain of those artworks for the benefit of receivers. The creative artist writes the play, or composes the symphony, or conceives the dance, and these works are then *performed* through the combined agency of individuals who serve as directors, conductors, actors, musicians, and dancers. It is commonly assumed that the activities of those in the performing arts complement the creative endeavors of playwrights and composers, realizing through their particular performances the aesthetic and artistic values that the latter's conceptions make possible. Thus, when we watch a performance of a play, or attend a concert, we appreciate two different kinds of thing: the qualities of the performance, attributable to the *skill, sensitivity, and artistry* of the performers, and the qualities of the work performed, attributable to the *creative powers and imagination* of the artist. As Dutton notes (1979: 23), to maintain that the appreciation of a work is always the appreciation of a performance is to break down this distinction between "creative" and "performing" arts, with its implicit valorizing of the former over the latter, and to acknowledge that "in certain respects all arts are creative, and correlatively, all arts are performing." Why Dutton believes that there is a

---

1   See, for example, Lessing 1995, to which Dutton is responding.

performative dimension in the so-called "creative" arts should by now be clear, but he says nothing in this context concerning the creative dimension of the "performing" arts. Some of my remarks below will speak to this issue.

My principal concern in this chapter, however, is to consider how the performance theory applies to those art forms that, traditionally conceived, incorporate distinct "creative" and "performative" moments – the dramatic arts, music, and dance being the most obvious examples. For convenience I shall term such art forms *performance arts*, as distinct from the so-called "performing arts" that constitute one moment of such arts. Thus music is a performance art which comprises musical composition, on the one hand, and the performances of the conductor and assembled musicians, on the other. I shall tentatively define[2] the performance arts as those art forms in which, as we would normally put it, our access to, and appreciation of, *works* (as receivers) is at least in part mediated by *performances of those works*.

Intuitively, our access to works in the performance arts is at least in part *mediated* by performances because certain qualities of works, relevant to their appropriation and proper appreciation *as* the particular works that they are, are only realizable, and therefore made apparent to receivers, in performances. The need to experience a performance of a musical or theatrical work in order properly to appreciate that work is the analogue, in the performance arts, of the need to engage in an unmediated experiential encounter with a canvas or projected copy of a film in order to properly appreciate a work in the visual or cinematic arts. There may be individuals who are able to *imaginatively* realize the relevant qualities of at least some works in the performance arts in the absence of a *public* performance – for example, individuals who can "hear" a piece of music when reading a score. To the extent that such mental "acts" are exercises of individual capacities, we may regard them as "private performances," instantiations of the relevant properties of the work *by* the individual in question *in foro interno*.

I shall argue that, if we accept the performance theorist's claim that the appreciation of *every* work requires that we relate a work-focus to a particular performance through which that focus was specified, the appreciation of performable works in the performance arts requires that we take account of sometimes very complex relationships between different

---

2   This definition is "tentative" because, we shall see, it stands in need of slight modification. The performances through which our appreciation of a work is mediated need not be performances *of that work*, although they nearly always are.

performances and performance-types. Let me begin with some examples that are either clearly works and/or performances in the performance arts, or sufficiently resemble such works and/or performances to be puzzling cases:

1 Elgar's cello concerto may serve as a paradigm example of a *performable work* in the performance arts. A paradigm example of a performance of such a work is the August 1965 recorded performance of Elgar's cello concerto by the LSO, conducted by John Barbirolli and with Jacqueline du Pré on cello (EMI CDC 5-55527-2).

2 Consider, next, the "standard" "My Favourite Things," and the performance of this by the John Coltrane Quartet at the Newport Jazz Festival on 7 July, 1963 (Impulse AS9161). This is one of many sonically very different performances of this piece by Coltrane ensembles.

3 Consider, now, four works, as characterized by the following descriptions:

a "A series of five scales, each to be played as long as the soloist wishes until he has completed the series." This description, by Bill Evans,[3] of Miles Davis' piece *All Blues*, would obviously require further elaboration (*which* series of five scales?) in order to fully identify the piece. A canonical recorded *performance* of this piece by the Miles Davis Quintet is on the album *Kind of Blue*.

b "On a wall, using a hard pencil, parallel lines about 1/8″ apart and 12″ long are drawn for one minute. Under this row of lines, another row of lines are [sic] drawn for 10 minutes. Under this row of lines, another row of lines are drawn for one hour." This description identifies a piece by Sol LeWitt, included in the *557,087* show at the Seattle Art Museum in September–October 1969. This piece was not "completed" for the show due to "bad carpentry and weather conditions," but was "executed" in Vancouver by Glenn Lewis.[4]

c "Activity, 23 days, varying durations. New York City. Choosing a person at random, in the street, any location, each day. Following him wherever he goes, however long or far he travels. (The activity ends when he enters a private place – his home, office, etc.)" This description, familiar from the discussion of the previous chapter, identifies *Following Piece* by Vito Acconci. As noted earlier, the "execution" of this piece by Acconci in 1969 is docu-

---

3   See the liner notes to Miles Davis' *Kind of Blue* (Columbia WPC-8163).
4   See Lippard 1973: 110–13 passim.

mented by photographs that accompany the description of the piece.

d "Drill a hole into the heart of a large tree and insert a microphone. Mount the amplifier and speaker in an empty room and adjust the volume to make audible any sound that might come from the tree." This description identifies a September 1969 piece by Bruce Naumann, which featured in a 1970 exhibition entitled *Art in the Mind*. The described action was not, as far as I know, actually performed, by Naumann or anyone else.[5]

In each of these cases, the description identifies a recognized artwork, and does so by offering what appears to be a prescription for a particular performance, or for a class of performances.

5 Consider, finally, a piece of *freely improvised music*, for example, the series of improvisations by Keith Jarrett known as the *Koln Concerts*. In such a case, let us assume, there is no pre-existing or repeatable "work" that is being performed, and the performance fails to qualify as an event in the performance arts in the sense specified above.

My aim, in what follows, is to set out a framework in terms of which we may understand the performance-events to which reference is made in the foregoing examples, and their bearing upon the appreciation of particular artworks. I shall try to clarify what is surely our sense that there are important differences between these examples as to what the work *is*, and how our attention to an artistic performance bears upon the *appreciation* of that work. More generally, I hope to illuminate the following issues:

1 How can we best conceptualize the relationship between "works" and "performances of works" in the performance arts, either in terms of what they *are* or in terms of *what is involved in their appreciation*?
2 If what we value in performances of works is often the *interpretation* they provide of the performed works, what is it for something to be an *interpretation* of a work?
3 More crucially, how can the qualities realized in a performance which *interprets* a work bear upon the appreciation of the *work* interpreted?
4 Finally, how do *works* in the performance arts differ from *works* in the non-performance arts, such that the former works are properly appreciable only through their performances?

5 See Lippard 1973:162–3.

9.2 Performed Works and Work-Performances

The task in this section is to clarify the status of, and the relations between, what we normally characterize as works in the performance arts and those performance-events whereby such works are presented to receivers. The former – such things as *Hamlet*, *Swan Lake*, and Elgar's Cello Concerto – may be termed *performed works*. The latter I shall term *work-performances*. According to the performance theory, a performed work, like any other artwork, is itself a generative performance whereby a focus of appreciation is specified. We may begin by asking how we should construe the focus of appreciation in the case of performed works, such that appreciating a generative performance completed by such a focus of appreciation is plausibly identified with appreciating a performed work. We can then enquire how work-performances are to be understood, what their appreciation involves, and how this bears upon the appreciation of performed works.

The focus of appreciation was defined (chapter 2) as that which, as the outcome or product of a generative performance on the part of one or more individuals, is relevant to the appreciation of the artwork brought into existence through that performance. For contextualists and other ontologists who identify the work with the focus of appreciation, to ask about the nature of the focus specified through a playwright's or a composer's creative activity is just to ask about the nature of the dramatic or musical work of art itself. Given that many of the properties of a dramatic or musical work relevant to its appreciation are properties only realized through *performances* of the work, what the artist produces must bear in some essential way on these performances. Two alternative accounts of this relationship have found favor amongst theorists. Some have held that the product of the artist's generative activity is a set of constraints upon the class of legitimate performances of the work. Wolterstorff, as we have seen, thinks of a musical work as a "norm-kind," which mandates certain properties in anything that is to count as a correct performance of the work. As we have also seen, Levinson avails himself of a similar notion in elucidating his conception of what it is to "indicate" a sound/performance means-structure. The alternative account, most famously endorsed by Goodman, identifies the work not with something that establishes a set of constraints on right performances, but, rather, with the class of performances satisfying that set of constraints.

Given our analysis of the structure of the focus of appreciation in chapter 3, we will want to build some reference to the articulation of a particular artistic statement into our account of the focus specified in the performance arts. The two ontological proposals in the preceding paragraph can be seen as alternative ways of characterizing the other components in the focus through which such articulation occurs. Only one of these ontological proposals seems compatible with the performance theorist's conception of the focus of a performed work, however. For the performance theorist, the work-focus is that which completes the artist's motivated manipulations of the vehicular medium. Given that those manipulations so completed are to be conceived as a "doing," usually by a single agent, the work-focus must be something that can plausibly be said to complete such a doing. The class of performances that complies with a set of constraints, however, is rarely if ever the completion of a doing by a single agent, and will usually itself be incomplete at any given time, since there will still be future performances belonging to that class. Thus, for the performance theorist, the work-focus in the performance arts is most plausibly viewed as including a set of constraints that is normative for the class of performances of the work, and that therefore indirectly serves to articulate an artistic statement through those performances.

This raises a crucial question, however. What form do the constraints on right performance specified by the composer or playwright take, and how are they *realized* in the focus of appreciation, such that they can guide the activities of those wishing to present a performance of a work? The simplest and most obvious answer to this question locates the constraints on right performance in the most tangible product of an artist's generative activity in standard cases of composition, namely, a script or score in which certain instructions for performing the work are explicitly set forth. However, such an answer threatens to admit, as right performances of a work, performance-events that, while observing the letter of a script or score, wantonly disregard the presumed intentions of the artist as to how the prescribed features of the work in question should be realized in a performance. A willingness to embrace such consequences is manifest in Nelson Goodman's notorious insistence (1976: 179ff) that the class of legitimate performances of a musical work comprises all and only those performance-events that comply with *notational* features of the score generated by the composer. Since natural languages are not notational, legitimate performances of a work the score of which incorporates only verbal indications of tempo will be temporally unconstrained. Thus a work whose performances normally last in the region of 30 minutes will have legitimate performances that last 12 hours and legitimate performances that last 12 minutes, as long as there are performances of those durations that satisfy all of the notationally represented constraints in the score.

Goodman's position is particularly counter-intuitive because, in addition to limiting constraints on legitimate performance of a musical work to what is explicitly represented in the score, it allows only certain features of the score to function as such constraints. However, a little imagination can conjure up similarly counter-intuitive examples even if all explicit features of a score or script are counted as prescriptive for legitimate performance of a work. For example, it is nowhere made explicit in a standard musical score that all of the musical parts are to be performed in a single acoustic space. Thus there will be performance-events, conforming to all the explicit requirements of a score of a musical work, that involve musicians geographically and acoustically isolated from one another, whose actions are regulated by the cinematically transmitted images of a single conductor and whose rendering of the notes is not itself transmitted to any common point of audition. Even on the proposed liberalization of Goodman's account, these will count as legitimate performances of the work. Less esoterically, consider a score by Bach employing the notational device of figured bass.[6] A Goodmanian must say that any performance that strictly complies with what the score requires is a legitimate performance, however much it departs from the manner in which the device in question would have been understood by Bach and those performers to whom his score was addressed. The problem with any view that identifies the constraints comprised by the work-focus of a work in the performance arts with the set of constraints explicitly furnished by a script or score, however, is not *just* that it lends itself to such bizarre examples. More seriously, for reasons that will become apparent, it yields a conception of "legitimate performance" that cannot help to answer our question about the manner in which appreciation of performances of works bears upon appreciation of works. How the notion of "legitimate performance" *can* help to answer this question will become clearer in the sequel.

A more plausible construal of the constraints determining the class of legitimate performances of a work will include in those constraints not merely what is *explicitly* represented in a script or score, but also certain non-explicit understandings as to how the script or score is to be *interpreted* for the purposes of performance of the work.[7] There are two possible sources for such constraints. One would be the *composer's*

6   My thanks to Paul Pietroski for this example.
7   See, for example, Wolterstorff 1975.

understandings as to how the work is to be performed, given the score. The other would be the understandings obtaining in a given *community of performers*. For reasons that parallel those adduced earlier in considering other properties of work-focuses in the non-performance arts, the second option is clearly preferable. The specification of a work-focus serves to make a work accessible for appreciation, and, in the performance arts, for performances through which appreciation is mediated. The composer or playwright, in specifying a work-focus, recognizes that the product of her generative activity will be appropriated first by performers, and then by receivers, who will, in their different ways, seek to realize and appreciate that product by applying interpretive norms in place in the interpretive communities to which they belong. In the performance arts, the artist must take account of two sets of interpretive norms: "semantic norms," determining, as in the non-performance arts, the artistic statement articulated through a vehicle, and "performative norms," determining which performance-events are acceptable realizations of a set of constraints on performance. As was seen to be the case with semantic interpretive norms, the artist's creative activity is governed by an overriding intention that she be understood according to the performative norms of *this* interpretive community. This intention, as we saw in the previous chapter, picks out indexically a given community whose specific norms may be misunderstood by the artist in various ways. This allows us to accommodate in an intuitively acceptable manner the sorts of examples that plague the Goodmanian account. For example, we can rule out, as not legitimate, performances of Bach's work that ignore the performative conventions concerning figured bass notation a knowledge of which Bach was assuming in the performing community to whose members his score was addressed. Only some features of the constraints on right performance comprised by the work-focus are explicit in a score or script, because, in any performance art, artists prescribing for a class of performances assume that some things *don't need to be said*, given the performative norms in place in the community of performers to whom the work is addressed.

The work-focus in the performance arts, then, comprises a set of constraints on legitimate performance of the work which takes account not only of what is explicitly represented in a score or script, but also of the manner in which that score or script is to be taken, given the interpretive conventions of the performing community to whom it is addressed. The relevant set of interpretive conventions is picked out by the overriding intention of the playwright or composer that her constraints be interpreted in the way *this* community would interpret them. To express this in terms of our earlier analysis of the structure of the focus of appreciation, we can view an established system of musical notation – where symbols are interpreted as prescribing the production of certain sonic events in certain ways – together with the acoustic potentialities of the range of instruments available to the composer, as the vehicular medium which she works. The shared understandings within a performative community as to how working this vehicular medium permits one to establish certain determinate constraints on performance will then be part of the artistic medium in which the composer works. We can say the same, mutatis mutandis, for performed works in the other performance arts.

The constraints on right performance specified by a composer or playwright are, as noted above, only part of the focus of appreciation specified by the latter. The purpose of the act of specification, as in the non-performance arts, is to articulate an artistic statement in a vehicle. But, in the performance arts, the nature of the artistic statement articulated is determined by the qualities realizable in those performance-events that stand in an appropriate relation to the constraints specified by the artist. Here, again, the artist must draw upon shared understandings as to the representational, expressive, and exemplificational import of such performance-events – this is a further element in the artistic medium within which the artist works. This is why the proper appreciation of performed works is necessarily mediated by their work-performances, the experiences of which play a role in the performance arts analogous to that played by direct experiential encounters with canvases or lumps of stone in the non-performance arts.

There is an added complication in the case of the performance arts, however. In the case of the visual arts, our grasping of the artistic medium in which the creator of a given pigmented canvas worked enables us to determine the first-order meaning-properties that enter into the artistic statement articulated by the artist. Furthermore, in referring the focus of appreciation to the act whereby it was specified, we can ascribe higher-order "meaning"-properties to the work and assess what has been achieved in articulating a particular artistic statement in a given vehicle through a given artistic medium. Appreciation, so conceived, can take place through the encounter with the artistic vehicle, given the knowledge of artistic medium and of other features of provenance that we bring to that encounter. There is no further problem, in the case of the visual arts, as to whether the "meanings" ascribed to the pigmented canvas in such an informed encounter are properly referable to the *work*.

But things are not so clear in the appreciation of performed works. For we have not yet determined under what circumstances a performance-event is to count as a performance *of a particular work*, and how we answer this question will, as we shall see, bear directly on when a quality rightly ascribable to a performance of a work can be reasonably ascribed to the performed work. We must at least touch here on issues that have been hotly contested in the recent literature in the philosophy of music, and it is obviously not possible in the present context to do full justice to these matters. I shall merely sketch what I take to be the relevant alternatives, and the sorts of broad reasons that lead me to favor one of these alternatives. My more immediate concern is to draw out the implications of the view I favor for the appreciation of performed works in the performance arts.

There are two conceptually distinguishable questions that arise when we ask about the relation between performed works and performance-events that are possible performances of those works. First, we may ask when a performance-event counts as a performance of a work *W*. Second, we may ask when a performance-event is a *correct* performance of *W*, where the correctness of a performance of *W* is a matter of that performance's *fully* satisfying the constraints specified in the work-focus of *W*. Some, such as Goodman (1976: 186–7), have elided the distinction between performance and correct performance by making full satisfaction of the constraints specified in the work-focus of *W* a necessary condition for being a *performance* of *W*. Goodman, who, as already noted, identifies a musical performed work *W* with the class of performance-events that fully satisfy the notationally characterizable constraints in the score for *W*, is thereby committed to a view that is both counter-intuitively broad (it admits as genuine performances performance-events that violate non-notational constraints) and counter-intuitively narrow (it excludes performance-events containing even one violation of what is required by the notational parts of the score). Goodman is unmoved by these sorts of problems, partly, it seems, for reasons related to the overall systematicity of his account of artworks as symbols, and partly due to his more general philosophical preferences for certain sorts of variables in his analyses. But the resulting view is disastrous if we seek to clarify the manner in which the appreciation of performed works is mediated by our experiences of performances of those works. For given both the all-too-human nature of human performers and the artistic license we gladly accord to interpreters of works, it seems likely that few of us have ever heard a "Goodmanian" performance of many of the performed works we take ourselves to appreciate.

If we think it desirable to allow for performances of a work W that fail to be *correct* performances, then we need some criterion for being a performance of W that falls short of requiring strict compliance with the constraints specified in the work-focus of W. Philosophers seeking such a criterion have generally settled for one that combines two components: an "intentional" component – the performers must *intend* to perform W – and a "discernibility" component – it must be possible for a suitably qualified receiver to discern a performance of W in the performance-event.[8] Obviously, there is much more that needs to be said about each of these components, apart from more general concerns about the conditions under which individuals can form genuine intentions. In the first place, we need to clarify under what conditions someone can rightly be said to have an intention to perform a *particular* work. For example, must the performer be able to *name* the piece to be performed, and identify its *composer*? Is some minimum of further information about the piece required? I think that all of these questions should be answered negatively. That it is W, rather than some other work W', that a performer intends to perform on a particular occasion should be determined by applying the same principles that determine, more generally, when a particular entity is the intentional object of an agent's discourse or intentional states. Kripke and Putnam, among others, have argued against "descriptions" theories of reference for singular terms in a speaker's idiolect, and for singular objects of a speaker's thoughts. The descriptions theorist holds that the referent of such thought or talk is the entity, if any, that uniquely satisfies all, or a weighted subset, of a set of descriptions that the speaker or thinker associates with the singular term or mental object in question. Rejecting this view, Kripke and Putnam argue that its being Aristotle that I am speaking of in a given utterance depends upon the relevant singular term (not necessarily the term "Aristotle") in my idiolect standing in the right sort of historical relation to Aristotle. A similar analysis holds for its being Aristotle that I am thinking of at a particular time. Applying this to the case in hand, we may allow that a performer of W can be under some misapprehensions as to the properties of the work she is performing, as long as her intentions stand in the right sort of historical relationship to W.

As for the "discernibility" requirement, Levinson talks here of the performer not only intending to produce a correct performance of a given work, but also succeeding to a reasonable degree in fulfilling that intention. This is not, of course, an algorithm for deciding whether or not we

8   See, for example, Wolterstorff 1975; Levinson 1980.

have a performance of *W* on a given occasion, but anything resembling an algorithmic decision procedure in this instance would be *ipso facto* unsatisfactory. It is a matter of judgment upon which competent judges may disagree whether, in certain cases, we have a very *bad* performance of a work, or something that fails to be a performance of the work at all.[9] Given some plausible account that incorporates, as conditions, both an appropriate guiding intention and a measure of successful fulfillment of such an intention, we can then follow Levinson in distinguishing between *performances* – which satisfy the foregoing conditions – and *instances* (correct performances) which not only satisfy these conditions but also fully comply with the constraints established through the work-focus of *W*.

As noted above, it seems likely that the vast majority of the performance-events that we attend in theaters and concert-halls fail to be *correct* performances of the advertised musical and dramatic works. There are almost always slight flaws in the execution of the explicit constraints on performance, and deliberate departures from those constraints in the interests of realizing certain values in the interpretation of the work. Furthermore, very few modern performances of significantly earlier works will be correct, even if they comply with all of the constraints that are explicit in a script or score. For example, the manner in which performers contemporary to Shakespeare would have interpreted his playscripts is quite alien to the present-day performative community, and can be reconstructed only by dint of scholarship that modern directors usually lack or disregard. Similarly, while considerable attention has been paid to historical "authenticity" in the performance of musical works on the part of some performers, such concern has been criticized by many modern theorists and performers as unnecessary and ultimately stultifying.[10]

This might be thought to present a problem. For it seems that it is only by reference to correct performances – those that fully comply with the performative constraints specified in the focus of a work – that we can determine the artistic statement articulated in a performed work. But it appears that we rarely if ever experience correct performances of such works. However, even if most of the performances of works that we attend are incorrect performances of those works, we can use the notion of "correct performance" to explain how the experience of work-

---

9   See Levinson's remarks on this issue in his 1980.
10   For the debate over the significance of authenticity for the performance and appreciation of performed works, see, for example, S. Davies 1987; Young 1988; Levinson 1990a.

performances bears upon the appreciation of performed works. For, I have suggested, to appreciate a work in the performance arts as a generative performance completed by a work-focus, it is necessary to grasp both (1) a set of constraints that must be satisfied by correct performances of the work, and (2) the particular artistic and aesthetic values that are realizable in performances that comply with those constraints – the artistic statement articulated through them. A grasp of both (1) and (2) is necessary if we are to appreciate a work as a generative process completed by *this* work-focus. Given the modal nature of (2), however – its talk of what is *realizable* – appreciation of a performed work can be furthered not only through correct performances of that work, but also through *incorrect* performances, as long as the appreciable qualities we find in the latter do not depend upon those respects in which the performance fails to be correct.

To put this point another way, the aesthetic and artistic values realized in an incorrect performance of a work *W* can nonetheless bear upon the appreciation of *W*, if the values themselves *would* be realizable in a *correct* performance of *W* – one that met whatever conditions of correctness the performance in question fails to meet. Thus, even though most modern performances of Greek or Shakespearean drama may be incorrect, in that they fail to respect relevant staging conventions, we may still rightly take these performances as providing insights into the respective *works* in most cases. And, more obviously, even though a performance of Elgar's Cello Concerto may depart from the score in certain minor respects, we can still refer qualities found in the performance to the performed work as long as we take these departures to be inessential to the qualities in question. What matters, then, is *not* whether a performance of *W* in which a given quality is realized is *itself* a correct performance of *W*, but whether that quality *could have been realized in a correct performance of W*. Where we judge that it *could* have been, we refer the quality to the performed work, if one of two further conditions is satisfied: (1) it is a positive quality that increases the value of the work, or (2) if it is a negative quality, we take it that *any* correct performance of the work would have that quality, or (weaker) would be likely to have that quality – that is, that the weakness lies *in the set of constraints*, not in a particular way of interpreting that set of constraints.

This has one surprising implication. We can refer back to *W* qualities found in performances of *W* that are not instances – correct performances – as long as we take those values to be *realizable* in instances. But consider where the performance-event is not even a performance of *W*. For example, it may be a performance of another work with an identical or closely related set of constraints, as in Currie's "Twin Beethoven" example, or, better, Levinson's example of the identically scored piano sonatas by Brahms and Beethoven. If the role of performance-events in the appreciation of performed works is to enable the receiver to grasp the aesthetic and artistic qualities realizable in instances of the performed work, then my appreciation of a performed work *W* may be heightened by a performance-event that is neither an instance nor a performance of *W*, and that is not even intended to realize the qualities I find in it.

9.3 Work-Performances and Performance-Works

We have yet to say anything about the nature and appreciation of those performance-events that we have thus far identified with work-performances – performance-events that are performances of performed works. Nor have we said anything about another class of performance-events that enter into our appreciation of the arts – performance-events that are *not* intended to instantiate any set of constraints imposed by a performed work, but that, as improvisations of some kind or another, stand alone as performances subject to artistic appreciation. I shall say more about improvisation in the next section. I shall assume for the present, however, that Keith Jarrett's *Köln Concerts* and similar performance-events are themselves artworks, or elements in artworks, and that this must be accounted for by an adequate theory of performance as art.

I suggest that performance-events of the two kinds just distinguished share a particular status, in spite of the different relations in which they stand to performed works. In each case, the performance-event is itself part of the work-focus of a work, a work which is to be identified with a generative performance completed by that performance-event. If, as I am assuming, performance-events are in principle publicly observable occurrences taking place upon a stage or in a room or in an external location, then performance-events of both kinds are vehicles that serve to articulate artistic statements. Such events are thereby part of the work-focus of what I shall term a *performance-work*. There are, then, two kinds of performance-work, differing as to whether or not the performance-event serving as vehicle is constrained by the requirements of a performed work. When the performance-event is not so constrained, we have what

I shall term a *pure performance work*. When the performance-event is so constrained, the work in question is what I have termed a work-performance. The task in the rest of this section is to defend the proposal that work-performances are themselves performance-*works* of a particular kind, so that, when we attend a performance-event that is constrained by the requirements of a performed work, there are *two* works available to us for appreciation.[11]

The primary intuition underlying the claim that work-performances are performance-works is that our critical and appreciative discourse about work-performances has those features which were determined, in chapters 2 and 3, to be distinctive of our discourse about artworks. The appreciation of an entity as an artwork, it was argued, requires that we refer that entity to the creative act through which it was generated or specified. This permits us to ascribe to the entity "artistic" properties that it possesses in virtue of a history of making that is itself located in a broader context of artistic activity. This conception of artistic appreciation was contrasted with the aesthetic empiricist view of writers such as Clive Bell and Alfred Lessing. As I went on to argue, artistic properties of works – properties that bear upon the ascription to them of artistic values – depend, inter alia, upon relations between works, the manner in which the artist's specificatory activity makes reference to what other artists have done, the values an artist was trying to realize in her work, the sorts of materials with which the artist worked and their resistances to manipulation, and other contextual and conventional features of the context in which the work-focus was specified. These things bear on the *appreciation* of the "manifest work" because they enable us to understand *why* the artistic vehicle has the manifest properties it does by placing those properties in a context of artistic making, and to determine the artistic statement articulated through that vehicle.

If we examine our critical and appreciative discourse about performance-events in the performing arts, however, we see that the appreciation of *work-performances* proceeds by reference to analogous qualities. We, as critical receivers of such performance-events, take account of how a given performance of a work stands in relation to *other* performances, how the *performer* related what she did to what had already

---

11   I should note that, while I find the considerations adduced in the following paragraphs compelling, nothing crucial hangs on the reader's agreeing with me in my assessment. A reader who is unconvinced need only grant that work-performances are *like* performance-works in significant ways, even if they are not themselves performance-works.

been done (including other performances of her own), what values the performer was trying to realize in the performance, the qualities and potentialities of the instruments on which the performer plays or the theatrical resources that the performers use, and other conventional and contextual features of the context of the performance-event. Performances, construed as *interpretations of works*, are subject to all of these kinds of assessments and appreciations. *Appreciating* such a performance-event, like appreciating the work of which it is a performance, is a matter of locating a *focus of appreciation* – the performance-event and the artistic statement it articulates – in the context of a broader performance through which that focus is specified.

If work-performances are performance-works, then their constitutive properties will include those prior manipulations of the vehicular medium that guided the performer in her decisions as to how the performed work should be presented to receivers, motivating the "performative interpretation" of that work presented in the performance-event that is the vehicle of the performance-work. We must also take account of more general theoretical motivations that ground the interpretations of performed works by particular performers. This would apply, for example, to the work-performances of Glenn Gould. A knowledge of both kinds of motivations is necessary if the receiver is to appreciate why the performance-event has certain of the manifest properties that it does. Similarly, artistically appreciating a performance of a play requires an understanding of the motivations guiding the "performative interpretation" of the play by the director and actors. Appreciation of the performance-work, as a creative performance that articulates an artistic statement through a performance-event, will also require that one take account of manipulations of the medium prior to that event – rehearsals of a musical piece or play, and changes made in the performance-event as a result of developments and insights arising in those rehearsals. Finally, as in the case of non-performance works, the intentions of the performers that guide them in crafting the performance-event, as vehicle, may *not* be realized in the artistic statement articulated through that vehicle, but may nonetheless be relevant to an appreciation of the performance-work. That Gould intended his performance of a work W to express a quality he found in different works by the same composer, and that, while succeeding in expressing that quality in performances of those other works, he failed in respect of the performance of W, may be relevant to our artistic appreciation of the performance of W. It may, for example, explain otherwise puzzling features of the performance-event.

Let me briefly address a couple of sources of concern regarding the proposal that we see performances of performed works as themselves performance-works. First, it might be said that, my claims to the contrary, this goes against our customary way of thinking about and treating performance-events in the arts. The short answer to this is that, as noted above, we clearly *do* treat some performance-events as works, where such events are *not* performances of separately identifiable works. For example, this is how we treat free improvisations in both jazz and avant-garde theater. The *Koln Concerts,* considered as free improvisations, involve performance-events through which an artistic statement is articulated. Each improvisation is a realization of what Levinson terms a "sound/ performance means-structure" on an occasion which is neither subject to pre-existing constraints stemming from the focus of a performed work nor perhaps plausibly viewed as defining such a work.

But, it might be objected, what is crucial here is that, in performances of pre-existing works, the performer *is* constrained by the demands or at least the solicitations of another work, and this is why we shouldn't think of work-performances as performance-works. However, it is difficult to find a plausible generalizable principle to justify excluding from workhood the products of performances taken to be subject to pre-existing constraints. For many canonical works of Renaissance visual art are the products of analogous performances of interpreting within the constraints of a *tradition.*[12]

Third, it might be objected that performances of works in the performance arts fail to satisfy one necessary condition of arthood – namely, that there be an identifiable *artist* to whom such putative works can reasonably be ascribed. This objection counts, at best, against those performances that involve the collaborative creative efforts of multiple individuals, but even in such cases the denial of arthood on such grounds seems ill-motivated. Even in the visual arts, the idea of single authorship of a work is often no more than a convenient labeling fiction, and, as Berys Gaut has forcefully argued,[13] this idea has little purchase on the realities of cinematic art. Once we acknowledge the phenomenon of multiple authorship of works outside the performance arts, we should not be troubled by the prospect of multiply authored works within that domain. And, of course, most of the pure performance-works in jazz are multiply

---

12　See, for example, Baxandall's discussion of Piero's *Baptism of Christ* in his 1985, and his more general discussion of the conditions under which early Renaissance paintings were produced in his 1972.
13　See Gaut 1997.

"authored" – indeed, this has been taken to be one of the defining features of jazz improvisation by exponents such as Miles Davis.

Finally, it might be said that, in many cases, the proposed division between a performed work and performance-works that provide it with performative realizations cannot be sustained, because the process of composition itself involves mediating performances – either on the part of the individual (or individuals) who specifies the performative constraints of the performed work, or on the part of others. We might balk at the idea that we have genuine *performances* in at least some of these cases – for example, where a composer writes "at her instrument." In other cases, however, the phenomenon is more clear cut. For example, the "finished" version of a stage play often results from a series of trials (usually in "the provinces"), and the input of both performers and audiences is instrumental in bringing about considerable modifications in the vehicle of the performed work. However, this hardly counts against the idea that, where we have an established set of constraints on performance furnished by a performed work, interpretations of those constraints by performers should themselves be conceived and appreciated as works. What it *does* raise is interesting questions about the manner in which we individuate performed works by reference to an intentional unity in a series of activities by one or more individuals taken to be instrumental in the specification of a single set of performative constraints. That work-individuation depends in this manner on the reconstruction of a process of specification may be seen to support the idea that it is a performance of specifying a particular work-focus, rather than the focus as specified through that performance, that is the proper locus of our critical and appreciative interest in something as an artwork in the performance arts.

Let me conclude this section by offering a few remarks on the appreciation of work-performances as performance-works. As noted earlier, when I attend a performance-event that presents a performed work, my experience of that event bears upon the appreciation of two distinct works – the performed work whose vehicle is the set of constraints guiding the performance-event, and the performance-work whose vehicle is the performance-event itself, viewed as a sound-sequence produced by a given performance means. As a consequence of the relation in which it stands to the performed work, we often value a work-performance for the manner in which it elucidates the artistic statement articulated in that work, its making manifest how the performative constraints that are the latter's vehicle engender performances that are interesting, illuminating, or otherwise aesthetically valuable.

But it would be wrong to conclude that what we value in a work-performance is always parasitical upon its contribution to our appreciation of the work performed. In many respects, our appreciation of a work-performance mirrors our appreciation of a pure performance-work. An *incorrect* performance *P* of *W* may realize certain aesthetic or artistic values that *cannot* be referred to *W* because they could *not* be preserved in a performance that rectified the departures in *P* from the constraints on correct performance of *W*. But the presence of these values in *P* is relevant to our appreciation of *P* as a performance-work nonetheless. Also, we may value a work-performance for the *originality or boldness* of its performative interpretation of a performed work, even if the qualities of the work that are manifest in the performance are not themselves novel. The director or conductor may have come up with a new way in which to bring out established qualities of the work in a performance. For example, an established thematic construal of a play may receive a novel presentation through a performance that locates the play, with its established theme, in a contemporary setting that is itself provocatively viewed in such thematic terms.

In fact, different aspects of a work-performance bear upon the two kinds of artistic appreciation that attend our engagement with the performance-event. First, insofar as we appreciate a performed work *through* the performance, we are concerned only with artistic and aesthetic qualities realized in the performance-event. As we have seen, what is at issue, here, is the qualities that are *realizable* in instances of the performed work, and, provided we are sufficiently familiar with the constraints definitive of a given performed work, we can be enlightened on this question by performance events that are neither instances nor performances of that performed work. In this respect, we are not concerned with any features of the broader performance that results in the performance-event in question. None of the intentions that guide the performer's activity prior to the performance-event, not even her overriding intention to be interpreted according to the norms of a particular interpretive community, bear on our appreciation of the performed work through that performance-event. On the other hand, insofar as we are interested in the work-performance as an artwork in its own right – as a performance-work – our appreciation must take account of all such aspects of the motivated manipulations that precede the performance-event, as well as the properties of that event itself.

A parallel analysis holds with respect to the aspects of the performed work that are relevant to *appreciation of the work*, and to the *performative interpretation* of that work on the part of performers. The performer who wishes to generate a performance of a work *W*, correct or otherwise, need concern herself only with the set of performative constraints comprised by the work-focus in virtue of its vehicle and its artistic medium – the explicit constraints on correct performance and the performative norms of the indexically indicated performative community. Only those intentions that are partly determinative of the work-focus so construed bear upon the activity of the performer. But the appreciation of the performed work requires that all relevant aspects of the performance generative of that work-focus be taken into account.

9.4 Performance-Works and Improvisation

In order to bring our discussion to bear on the various examples of performed works and artistic performances with which we began, we need to inquire about the status of artistic performances that are *not* work-performances in the prescribed sense – that is, artistic performances that are not performances of pre-existing works, and thus are not guided by an intention to comply with pre-existing constraints on right performance. These are what I have termed pure performance-works. The clearest examples are certain kinds of *improvisational* performances, and the latter are best approached by way of a more general reflection on the ways in which improvisational performance can occur in the arts.[14]

There has been some debate as to the distinguishing feature of *improvisation* in the performing arts. Philip Alperson (1984) has proposed that a musical performance is improvisational if it involves the *spontaneous* creation of a musical work, where the "work" in question is a performance-event that comprises a sequential structure of sounds. As a rule, this performance-event is neither guided by, nor constitutive of, the performative constraints of a performed work. Thus it differs from work-performances in that it does not involve *interpretation*. It has recently been argued, against Alperson, that there is no difference in kind, but only a difference in degree, between interpretation and improvisation (Gould and Eaton 2000; Cochrane 2000). All performances, on this view, involve improvisation to some degree, because all performances involve interpretation. There is improvisation whenever a performer exhibits "fluency" in departing from a score (or, in the literary arts, a script). It is

14   There has been considerable recent interest in improvisation, much of it stemming from Philip Alperson's 1984. See the papers contained in the spring 2000 issue of *Journal of Aesthetics and Art Criticism*.

difficult, however, to see how the "fluency in departing from a score" reading of improvisation can accommodate what I have termed "pure performance-works," where there seems to be *no score to depart from*. In what follows, therefore, I shall assume that Alperson is correct in tying improvisation to spontaneity, although more needs to be said about cases where improvisation *is* guided by a set of constraints.[15]

We can distinguish three ways in which improvisation can be a significant aspect of a performance-event in the arts. A performance-event may involve what I shall term *improvisational interpretation*, *improvisational composition*, or *pure improvisation*. A given performance-event may, in fact, incorporate elements of more than one kind of improvisation, but usually only a single kind of improvisation will be involved. Furthermore, as we shall see, each kind of improvisational performance presents a distinct type of appreciative task for the receiver.

Improvisational interpretation, as I am using the term, begins with an existing performed work, and involves an improvised performance of that work, whereby certain aesthetic and artistic qualities valued in performances of this kind are realized. We may distinguish two kinds of cases. First, the work-focus of the performed work may impose certain constraints that are *intended* to function as a framework for improvisation. This is clearly the case with *All Blues*, and other pieces by Davis, Mingus, Monk, Coltrane, etc. In this case, the aesthetic and artistic qualities realized in different improvisational interpretations that conform to the specified constraints are rightly taken to bear upon the appreciation of the performed works themselves. Such performed works, therefore, formally resemble classical performed works, such as Elgar's Cello Concerto. All that differs is the nature of the constraints and often the vehicle used to convey them.[16] It is important, however, to place some limits on what can count as a set of constraints capable of determining the class of performances of a performed work. It is implausible, for example, to allow that such a set of constraints is given by the sum of the shared understandings in a community of improvising musicians over a given period of time. If

15   See Matheson and Young 2000.
16   Usually, the vehicle for performed works of this kind is a "chart" rather than a score strictly speaking, which gives a chord progression and a correlated melody. The interpretive norms may include accepted substitutions for the specified chords. But the vehicular medium differs quite radically from conventional scoring in certain cases. For example, Mingus distributed the performative "constraints" for one of his pieces to the members of his ensemble in the form of individual drawings – one for each musician – of such items as a coffin. See Priestley 1982. Another example of this kind is John Zorn's *Archery*, one of his "game" pieces.

we allowed this, then all of the "free improvisations" played by members of that community in that temporal interval would count as performances of the same work.[17]

On the other hand, where a performed work not *designed* for improvisational interpretation is *used* for such purposes, we may not be able to refer qualities of the performance-event to the appreciation of the *performed work*. An improvisational interpretation of this sort may violate both explicit constraints and implicit conventions obtaining in the performing community to whom those constraints were addressed to such an extent that none of the distinctive values realized in the performance-event would be realizable in a correct performance of the performed work. Arguably, this applies to Coltrane's performances (or perhaps his *later* performances) of "My Favourite Things," even though these performances show how wonderfully the piece lends itself to improvisational interpretation.

Improvisational composition, as I use the term, does not involve the performance – correct or otherwise – of a pre-existing work, but is nonetheless a work-performance, being the initial performance of a work whose work-focus is specified through this very act of improvisational composition. Improvisational composition is possible as long as there are conventions whereby an improvised performance *specifies a set of performative constraints for a performed work* – that is, a set of constraints in virtue of sufficiently satisfying which a future performance, guided by the appropriate intentions, might qualify as another performance of the same work. Whether improvisational composition, so construed, is possible in a performance art at a given time will depend upon whether there are indeed such conventions obtaining in the performing community, or whether a performer can establish such conventions. But the *presence* of such conventions is not by itself sufficient for improvisational composition, if we assume (correctly, I think) that composition is an act with a determinate intentional structure. A performed work, I have argued, exists through, and is appreciated as, a generative performance whereby a set of constraints is established as a basis for a class of performances which articulate a particular artistic statement. A work-focus of a performed work is specified only given an intentional context in which such specification can occur – for example, a context in which the putative specifier has intentions concerning how explicit constraints are to be interpreted (including

---

17   Richard Cochrane 2000 comes close to endorsing such a view of the Chicago "free jazz" tradition, although he refrains from talking of performances of the same *work*, and talks instead of performances of a *type*.

the "null" intention, "any way you please"!), and the governing intention that what she is doing serves to establish such a set of constraints. That an individual engages in an improvisation not intended as a performance of any existing performed work, and in a context where certain conventions exist that permit improvisational composition to take place, does not by itself entail that the individual's performance is the improvisational composition of a performed work open to interpretation in future work-performances.

Whether there are any actual instances of improvisational composition in a given performance art is an empirical matter. It is not difficult to imagine how such instances might come about, however. For example, it is not difficult to imagine a work like *All Blues* resulting from improvisational explorations on the part of a group of musicians, where (1) the initial performance has the sort of integrity required if it is to count as a performance-event (rather than a process of composition where the composer has recourse to instruments as a compositional device), (2) conventions exist that permit improvisational composition to take place, and (3) the intentions required for the performance to count as the specification of a piece crystallize during the performance-event. There may also be instances of improvisational composition in the area of dance, where a choreographer may leave a section open to free improvisation on the part of the dancer, yet a dancer dancing that part of the work may establish *how* that section is to be danced in future in legitimate performances of the piece.[18]

Evidence suggests that works like the *Koln Concerts* are not improvisational compositions. Both the necessary conventions and the appropriate intentions seem to be lacking. More plausibly, the *Koln Concerts* are viewed as an example of what I term *pure improvisation*. This comprises all improvisational performance-events that are not improvisational interpretations, and that occur in the absence of the conventions and intentions necessary for a performance to determine a set of performative constraints for a performed work. Pure improvisation neither specifies the performative constraints for a new work nor interprets an existing work. Rather, the improvisational performance-event is the vehicle in a pure performance work. The work itself is to be identified

---

18   However, this is open to another interpretation, where the performance in question is taken to be part of a temporally extended process of specifying a set of constraints for a performed work – in this case, we might take the work to be collaboratively composed, as is the case with certain theatrical works.

with a more comprehensive performance on the part of the performer, and artistic appreciation of the work requires that the vehicle
be located in an artistic medium and referred to the generative
performance that it completes. If a performance-event is a genuine
instance of pure improvisation, then no degree of similarity in a subsequent performance-event renders the latter another performance of the
same work. One who acted with the intention of reperforming the earlier
work would have *misunderstood* the status of the original performance-
event. Pure improvisations are performance-events that complete generative processes, and, as the vehicles specified through such processes, are
to be appreciated for the artistic statements that are articulated through
them.

We may now return to the other, non-musical examples of artistic performance-events listed at the beginning of this section. As we noted, the
pieces by LeWitt, Acconci, and Naumann look, on the surface, to be
performed works analogous to Miles Davis' *All Blues*. If they are
indeed performed works, then their appreciation will be mediated by
performance-events which enable the receiver to determine the artistic
statement articulated through the specified constraints on performance.
Such an analysis looks implausible in the case of Naumann's piece, if there
are indeed no performance-events satisfying the specified constraints and
if, as seems plausible, this does not somehow compromise our ability
to appreciate the work. But in the case of the pieces by LeWitt and
Acconci, there are performance-events that might be viewed as work-
performances of a performed work. Furthermore, it is not uncommon
for there to be multiple enactments of the prescriptions for performance
specified by LeWitt in pieces like the one cited. Are there, then, at least
some late modern pieces that are properly analyzed as performed works,
with realizing performance-events playing an essential role in their
appreciation?

I shall argue that none of the late modern works in question is properly so analyzable, although their proper analyses differ in significant ways.
Consider, first, LeWitt's piece. If we try to read the piece as a performed
work, the claim must be that physical *executions* (product, not process) of
the specified constraints realize certain qualities that bear upon the artistic statement articulated and, thereby, upon the appreciation of LeWitt's
work. So read, LeWitt's piece is structurally analogous to the performed
works of Elgar and Miles Davis, save in two respects. First, the thing that
makes manifest the artistic statement articulated through the specified
constraints – the thing that functions in the way a performance of *All*

Blues functions in the appreciation of that performed work – is the physical realization of the specifications on the wall of a gallery, not the act of bringing about that physical realization. Qualities of the act of execution itself will not bear upon the appreciation of the performed work. Second, whereas, in the case of musical performed works, performance-events that realize the work are themselves performance-works, it is not clear that there is more than one *work* involved in the appreciation of the LeWitt piece. For it is not obvious that the "execution" of LeWitt's specifications is itself a performance that specifies a focus of appreciation in an appropriate sense. If we do think of it in this way, then we must construe Lewis' executory performance as a standard visual artwork whose vehicle is a physical realization of LeWitt's specifications. Lewis's work will then be analogous to Renaissance paintings executed to fulfill specifications dictated by a patron! On the other hand, we might take what Lewis did to be simply a second stage in the specificatory performance identifiable with a single work. In that case, we will have something like print-making, save that the first stage issues in a set of specifications rather than a plate or mold. In either case, it seems that there is no *performance-work*, even though there is a performed work whose appreciation depends upon a performance-event that satisfies a set of performative constraints.

We should note, however, that LeWitt's own pronouncements suggest that he would strongly resist an analysis of his piece as a performed work. In his "Paragraphs on Conceptual Art," he writes as follows:

> I will refer to the kind of art in which I am involved as conceptual art. In conceptual art, the idea or concept is the most important aspect of the work. (In other forms of art, the concept may be changed in the process of execution.) When an artist uses a conceptual form of art, it means that all of the planning and decisions are made beforehand and the execution is a perfunctory affair. (1967)

Significantly, we may note, LeWitt's specifications for the piece leave indeterminate the very features of a physical realization of those specifications that would make the latter a particular object of "intentional visual interest," to cite again Michael Baxandall's phrase. When one actually encounters a realization of a LeWitt piece, one may not feel, as is the case with standard performed works, that appreciable features of the "performance" – here, the physical realization of the specifications – can be referred back to the performed work to illuminate the artistic statement articulated in the latter. Rather, such an encounter simply reinforces LeWitt's own insistence on the purely conceptual nature of the work.

Take, for example, LeWitt's *Wall Drawing No. 623 Double asymmetrical pyramids with colour ink washes superimposed* in the National Gallery of Canada. What confronts one is a very large mural, taking up most of two walls that meet at right-angles. Upon those walls has been painted a pair of pyramid-like figures in a very pleasing arrangement of visually rich colors. One's initial impression upon confronting the mural is of an object of considerable visual interest, pleasing in both its structure and use of color. What one learns, in reading the title and description of the work, is that the constraints laid down by LeWitt in no way mandate any of the formal and design features that give the mural its initial attractiveness. The constraints read as follows: "colour ink wash: the background is grey, blue, grey, blue; left pyramid: the apex is left – four sides: 1 – red, blue, blue, red, blue; 2 – yellow, blue, grey, blue; 3 – grey, grey, blue, red, red; 4 – red, grey, red; right pyramid: the apex is centre – four sides: 1 – grey, grey; 2 – grey, red, yellow; 3 – yellow, grey, blue, blue; 4 – grey, blue, red, red." What is clear from the verbal characterization of the piece is that most of the visually attractive features of the exhibited mural are *contingent* features of the piece. Visual structures lacking those features could equally well comply with LeWitt's specifications, and the visual structure in the National Gallery could accord with quite different sets of specifications of the same general sort. Given that visual structures differing widely in their perceptible properties, and in the experiences they engender in receivers, can serve as realizations of LeWitt's constraints, it seems that the experiences elicited by particular instantiations do not bear upon the appreciation of the piece, save that we require an encounter with an instantiation, together with LeWitt's specification of the piece, for this point to be brought home to us.

Other candidates for late modern "performed works" are Damien Hirst's "spot" paintings. These paintings – colored spots on white canvas, arranged with geometric precision, which appear to be moving around – are conceived by Hirst in Cornwall and "executed" by assistants in London. Many hundred such paintings have been executed. Hirst specifies that the executors must employ household gloss paint, and must preserve an identity between the size of the spots and the size of the distances between the spots. He also specifies the size of the painted canvas.[19] But whether these should be viewed as "performed works" with the executed canvases as intermediaries depends upon how one demarcates the artistic process generative of the vehicle. It seems more plausible to see this process as analogous to the one whereby early Renaissance paintings were produced by artists working under the supervision of a principal artist and to the specifications of one who commissioned the painting.[20] The executory "performance" will then be internal to the process of generating the artistic vehicle, as is the case with the "executory performances" that enter into the generation of the artistic vehicle in architecture and in film.[21]

But if LeWitt's pieces are not to be analyzed as "performed works" whose appreciation is mediated by physical realizations of the specified constraints, how do these constraints enter into the identity of the work? Surprisingly, I think, they enter into its identity in pretty much the same way as Naumann's specifications enter into the identity of his work. In both cases, the vehicle through which an artistic statement is articulated for receivers is neither a class of performances that comply with a set of constraints, nor a single performance that so complies. Rather, the vehicle is the *idea* of carrying out a performance as characterized in the specifications. It is this that makes the works conceptual, as LeWitt himself maintains. The fact that there are actual enactments of LeWitt's constraints, whereas there are no such enactments of Naumann's constraints, bears upon the appreciation of the work only by, as we might put it, "enlivening" the idea, supplementing the intensionality of the vehicle as verbally specified. What we gain from our encounters with physical realizations of LeWitt's specifications is a clearer sense of what it would mean to carry out the kind of performance conceptualized in the vehicle of the work. This enables us to comprehend more clearly the artistic statement articulated through the idea of such a performance. In the case of Naumann's piece, the absence of any enactment of the constraints, and, a fortiori, of any photographic documentation of such an enactment, means that the idea of a particular kind of performance, which serves as the vehicle, is fashioned through the manipulation of a purely verbal medium. This indicates to the receiver the irrelevance, for appreciation of the work, of her inability to witness a "performance" of the piece.

20   See Baxandall 1972, especially ch. 1.
21   But then we might take these analogies to be part of the point of Hirst's works – in which case the vehicles of the works will be more complicated performances, as with Acconci's *Conversions* as analyzed in section 8.2 above.

What should we say about Acconci's *Following Piece*, and, by extension, about the other pieces by Acconci that were discussed in chapter 8? One possibility would be to regard these pieces as performed works, with analyses that parallel the one given of Davis' work. The vehicle, then, will be a set of constraints on a class of performance-events, and the articulation of an artistic statement will be mediated by Acconci's executing a performance-event falling within that class.[22] On this reading, Acconci's work falls within the performance arts as we have understood them, and the appreciation of his work will require that we take account of an artistic statement articulated through manifest properties of the performance-event.

I think, however, that this is not a tenable construal of Acconci's work. First, it is characteristic of performed works that different work-performances may bring out different features of the artistic statement articulated in the work. Indeed, one of the things that we value in performed works is the richness of their content, which is not exhausted in any particular performance. Different performances of a performed work deepen our appreciation of that work by making that richness apparent. But, while nothing in the performative constraints for *Following Piece* rules out further performances, it is difficult to imagine that such performances would add to our understanding of the piece, or that anything bearing upon the artistic statement articulated in the work would be learned from them. This is related to a second point, that our inability to observe Acconci's enactment of the performative constraints of *Following Piece*, and the fact that we possess only very limited photographic "documentation" of the performance-event, is not experienced by us, as receivers, as an obstacle to our properly appreciating the piece. But, if so, then it seems that the performance-event cannot play the intermediary role we have ascribed to work-performances in the performance arts – the role of making accessible to receivers the artistic statement articulated in the work.

Should we, then, analyse Acconci's piece in a manner parallel to our analysis of LeWitt's and Naumann's pieces? On this reading, there will be no performed work, and therefore nothing that counts as a work in the performance arts. Acconci's work, like LeWitt's, will have as its vehicle an action-*type* – the action-type defined by the set of performative constraints

---

22   In fact, Acconci's actions, so viewed, would be a performance but not an instance of the performed work, because he omitted to carry out the prescribed exercise on some of the days!

given in the description of the piece. The "documentation" of Acconci's performance-event will then serve merely to "enliven" the idea of performing an action of the prescribed type. The artistic statement articulated through the artistic vehicle will depend only in this indirect way upon manifest properties of that performance event.

While this is a possible reading of the piece, I think we should prefer a third alternative, which takes the artistic vehicle to be not the *idea* of a particular kind of performance, but the unique performance-event enacted by Acconci (more or less) in accordance with the prescribed constraints. On this reading, there is, again, no performed work, and therefore nothing that counts as a work in the performance arts. But Acconci's work has as its vehicle a particular performance-token. It is through that performance-token that Acconci articulates an artistic statement. But the use of photography in a minimal documentary role is understood by the receiver as indicating that visible features of the actual performance not preserved on film are not important for the appreciation of the work. The photographs serve to isolate those features of the performance-event, as vehicle, that bear upon the articulation of an artistic statement, rather than further enriching by pictorial means the conceptual content of an idea.

As argued in chapter 8, I think this analysis of *Following Piece* allows us to see other works by Acconci – *Adaptation Studies* and *Conversions*, for example – as similar in having performance-events as their vehicles, but as differing in how the performance-events contribute to the articulation of an artistic statement. In the case of *Adaptation Studies*, manifest properties of the performance-event, as preserved in the cinematic record, play a much more significant role in the articulation of content, whereas in *Conversions* the cinematic recording of activity is itself part of the performance serving as artistic vehicle.[23]

The analysis offered, here and in the preceding chapter, of different late modern works is intended to fulfill, at least in part, the undertaking, given in chapter 1, to provide a more systematic response to Wolfe's critique of such works. My claim is that there is a fundamental continuity in the structure of appreciation that unites such works with more traditional pieces in the visual arts, and with works in the other arts, traditional and modern. I have proposed a way of analyzing late modern works that clarifies what the appreciation of such works involves, and what, if anything, one is supposed to do with the objects displayed in galleries that in some way represent these works. In the final chapter, I shall discharge one other

23   See the much fuller discussion of these issues in section 8.2 above.

outstanding obligation – to say something about what makes a medium, and a statement articulated through that medium, "artistic." I shall also venture some remarks on the implications of the performance theory for the theory of artistic value.

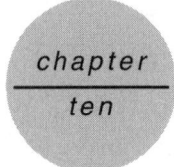

chapter

ten

Defining "Art" as Performance, and the Values of Art

10.1 Notes Toward a Definition of "Art"

At the beginning of chapter 4, I noted that, if our concern were merely to identify the more general ontological category to which artworks belong, we could express the performance theorist's claim as follows: art-works are token performances whereby a content is articulated through a vehicle on the basis of shared understandings. This way of formulating the performance theory is at the same level of generality as Currie's ATH, which asserts that artworks are action-types that involve discoverings of structure-types by heuristic paths. In both cases, what is offered is only a necessary condition for being an artwork, and in neither case would it be plausible to take it as a sufficient condition. For example, my coming up with the previous sentence in the way that I did is a token performance that articulates a content through a vehicle on the basis of shared under-standings. It is also a token of an action-type that satisfies the require-ments of the ATH. However, whatever I might rightly be taken to accomplish through my present activity, I am surely not bringing an artwork into existence. Indeed, given that the notion of "articulated content" is broadly construed, the class of performances fitting the above formulation of the performance theory will include such patent non-art-works as the baking of a birthday cake for a child, the writing of a student term-paper, the giving of a Christmas present, and the application of "devil" make-up by one about to attend a Halloween party.

If we are to move beyond the sorts of ontological claims just canvassed, in the hope of arriving at a characterization that would apply more selectively to artworks, we must trespass upon terrain traditionally occupied by those who seek a definition of "art" or "artwork." Throughout this book, I have operated with something that might be viewed as a place-holder for such a definition. In presenting and defending the performance theory, I have spoken not in the general terms employed above, but, rather, of artworks as performances whereby one or more individuals articulate an *artistic* statement by working in an *artistic* medium when manipulating a vehicular medium. This is at best a place-holder for a definition because no attempt has been made to clarify what makes a statement or medium *artistic*. Rather, I have relied upon examples drawn from the different arts to give some content to these remarks. While an appeal to the pragmatic constraint might justify the assumption that the examples in question are themselves genuinely artistic, this in no way explains what it is that *makes* them artistic, where the other examples cited in the previous paragraph fail to be so. In chapter 4, I promised that, in the final chapter, I would offer some suggestions as to how we might remedy this lacuna, and seek a more principled distinction between artworks and those performances of related kinds that are not artworks. It is now time to make good on that promise.

If we had an independent way of characterizing what is distinctive about the contents articulated by artistic vehicles, we could then define an artistic medium as the means whereby such contents are articulated. If, on the other hand, we had an independent way of characterizing what makes an articulative medium an *artistic* medium, we could define an artistic statement as a content articulated through such a medium. As it is, we have as yet neither kind of independent characterization. Nor, it should be noted, would our current situation be improved by taking works to be contextualized products rather than generative processes whereby such products are specified. We would face an analogous task in saying what makes an indexing convention (Binkley), a historically evolving system of productive practices (Danto), or the taking of a structure as normative for a class of performances (Levinson), distinctively "artistic" or part of an "artworld."

Another prima facie promising strategy appeals to a difference in our appreciative practice. One thing that was stressed in chapter 3 is that our appreciative interest in artworks is an interest not merely in an articulated content, but in the manner in which a content has been articulated in a medium. As was suggested, this is one way of fleshing out the idea that the vehicles through which artistic statements are articulated are valued "for their own sakes," or that they possess "intrinsic" rather than merely instrumental value. But, if there is indeed such a difference between the kind of appreciation we accord to artworks and the kinds of appreciation we take to be appropriate in the case of other performances that articulate a content through shared understandings, this is surely something that is *consequent upon* a perceived difference between artworks and other performances or contextualized entities, rather than something that can serve as the basis for such a difference.

We may therefore turn, in hope of enlightenment, to the proposals offered by those who have attempted to define "art" or "artwork." What resources do they offer that might help us to further refine the performance theory by offering a principled distinction between artworks and other performances of the same generic kind? While attempts to define "art" have been legion, it is possible, without doing too much violence to the diversity of proposals, to distinguish two or three broad definitional strategies. In a comprehensive critical survey of the definitional enterprise, Stephen Davies has argued that all attempts to define "artwork" are either transparent or concealed variations on two kinds of approach. These approaches, which he labels "functionalism" and "proceduralism," are described in the following manner: "The functionalist believes that, necessarily, an artwork performs a function or functions (usually, that of providing rewarding aesthetic experience) distinctive to art. By contrast, the proceduralist believes that an artwork necessarily is created in accordance with certain rules and procedures" (1991: 1). As Davies points out, we might expect functionalism and proceduralism to be complementary, in that the relevant procedures will be ones that ensure that their issue is something that can perform the relevant function. But, he believes, much of the confusion about late modern art is the result of the falling apart of the functional and procedural aspects of artworks, something that occurs when "the procedures under which a thing is created part company from the point of our having such things, from the functionality of the thing in question" (1991: 1). Davies also argues that attempts to define art in terms of the intentions of makers are in fact reducible to forms of functionalism or proceduralism, and defends a sophisticated form of proceduralism against standard objections raised against other proceduralist accounts.

Davies' general framework for thinking about the definitional enterprise is useful, and I shall draw upon it in the following discussion. However, it cannot suffice for our current inquiry, for at least three reasons. First, as is clear from the above quotations, Davies assumes that artworks are the *products* of some kind of creative activity, where the performance theory identifies works with the processes whereby those products are generated. Since the performance theorist takes the intentions that guide the manipulations of a vehicular medium to be partly constitutive of the work, she will presumably resist the idea that the intentional component of arthood can be reduced either to the functionality of the product or to the procedures whereby it is manufactured. Second, for reasons that I shall come to shortly, I think that even a sophisticated proceduralist account of the sort proposed by Davies cannot, by its very nature, give us the kind of principled distinction between artworks and other ontologically similar things that we are seeking. This leads to the third and most important point. Davies' way of approaching the definitional enterprise assumes that "functionalism" and "proceduralism" are two approaches to a single question about the defining properties of artworks, and that intentionalist accounts are a further attempt to answer this question. However, as I shall argue, we need to distinguish two overlapping concerns that enter into disputes about the definition of art, one of which admits of a broadly proceduralist answer (though not of the kind favored by Davies), and the other of which can only be answered in functionalist terms.

If we turn to the traditional enterprise of defining art, we quickly see that the proposed definitions are either explicitly or implicitly functional in nature. We find two kinds of broadly functional definition: those that classify things as "artworks" by explicit reference to some function they perform for us ("pure functionalism," we might say), and those that classify things as "artworks" on the basis of their possession of certain manifest properties in virtue of which they can perform some function ("aesthetic functionalism"). An example of the former is Tolstoy's characterization of art as "a human activity consisting in this, that one man consciously by means of certain external signs, hands on to others feelings he has lived through, and that others are infected by these feelings and also experience them" (1960: 51). An example of the latter is Bell's claim that artworks are to be distinguished from other things by certain of their manifest properties, those which constitute "significant form" in the appropriate medium (1914: 8). The *significance* of "significant form" is functional in nature – it is that property of visual artworks that is responsible for the eliciting of the "aesthetic emotion" in receivers. It is only on the basis of a prior functionalist conception of art that Bell arrives at his definition in terms of significant form (1914: 6). In fact, most pure functionalist definitions, when read in context, offer some indication as to the kinds of manifest properties that are required to perform the specified function, and most aesthetic functionalist definitions, read in context, identify the function served by the specified manifest properties.

There are a number of problems with functionalist definitions of art of either stripe, problems that have been much rehearsed in the literature starting with a number of papers influenced by the work of the later Wittgenstein. One problem is that, in making the performance of a particular function, or the possession of properties that are required for the performance of that function, the defining condition of arthood, such definitions leave little if any room for *failed* artworks. In this respect, they may be thought to run together what Morris Weitz (1956) termed the "descriptive" and the "evaluative" uses of the term "work of art." Used evaluatively, the term serves to commend that to which it is applied, whereas used descriptively it merely classifies. Weitz argued that traditional functionalist theories of art of the sort just surveyed are properly viewed as attempts to highlight certain sorts of values to be found in art, rather than as descriptions of the conditions under which the term "artwork" is correctly employed in a classificatory sense.

Second, the very diversity of proposed functionalist definitions of art suggests that there is no single "point" to art, but that artworks can quite legitimately serve a range of functions. The converse of this is that, for each of the proposed defining functions of art, we should expect that there are legitimate artworks that fail to serve that particular function. Not all of Bell's paradigm cases of visual artworks possessed of significant form are plausibly viewed as transmitters of Tolstoian feelings, for example. And some of the works praised by Tolstoy seem unlikely to meet Bell's requirements for being artworks. Weitz, citing exhibited pieces of driftwood, argued that even what might seem the least controversial "necessary condition" of arthood – that a work be an artifact of some kind – is not without exceptions. Relatedly, to the extent that arthood is supposed to be a matter of possessing certain kinds of manifest properties, the functionalist cannot explain how entities that share all such properties may differ in terms of arthood, a phenomenon familiar to us from the Readymade tradition and from our discussions of forgeries.

A third problem with functionalist theories is that even a liberalized functionalism must place constraints on the functions legitimately served by artworks. Weitz maintains that it is not merely that artworks failing to serve a widely accepted function of art *happen* to arise. Such artworks often arise precisely because artists wish to challenge, in their works, accepted conceptions of how artworks are supposed to function. Thus, so it is argued, any functionalist definition, whether pure or aesthetic in nature, would run counter to the very activity of art, by acting as a constraint on the essentially creative and innovative nature of artistic activity.

Weitz himself raises these sorts of problems for traditional functionalist definitions of "art" as part of a broader Wittgensteinian attack on the very project of defining "art." The conclusion we should draw, he maintains, is that there are no defining conditions of arthood. "Art" is an open concept, whose extension to novel cases requires a decision based on overlapping strands of similarity between such cases and those things already classified as artworks. As Binkley (1976) points out, "art" is in fact a *radically* open concept for Weitz, in that any attempt to "close" the concept would be forlorn, given the essentially creative nature of the artistic enterprise.

However, two other kinds of response are open to us if we grant the case just sketched against functionalism. One kind of response is exemplified by Jerrold Levinson's "historical" definition of "art," which also takes into account the intentions with which something is made (Levinson 1979, 1989). Abstracting from the details of his view, Levinson's strategy is to define "artwork" in terms of (1) a historical tradition of regarding artworks in particular ways, and (2) a maker's intention that the product of her making be regarded in one of those ways in which artworks have been rightly regarded. There is an air of circularity in such a definition, but this is claimed to be harmless. For what is proposed is an account of what it is for something to be art at a time t in terms of intentions accountable to historical facts about how certain things have correctly been regarded prior to t. Levinson also insists that the reference, in characterizing the maker's intentions, to the ways artworks have correctly been regarded prior to t should be given both an opaque and a transparent reading. Read opaquely, the maker consciously refers the product of her activity to a history of artistic making and artistic regard. Read transparently, the maker's intentions involve no such conscious reference: it is just that the way in which the maker intends the product of her making to be regarded is *as a matter of fact* one of the ways in which artworks have been correctly regarded prior to t. This allows for artworks created by individuals who act in complete isolation from a tradition of artistic making, if their intentions happen to coincide with a way in which works have been regarded in such a tradition.

It should be clear how Levinson's "historical" definition avoids the first two objections to functionalist accounts. By making arthood a function of the maker's intentions, we allow for genuine artworks which are nonetheless unsuccessful because the maker's intentions are not realized in the products of their making. And by talking of ways in which artworks have been correctly regarded in an evolving artistic tradition, we allow for a plurality of functions which artworks may serve, with no particular function being a necessary condition of arthood. Levinson also claims that his definition answers the third objection against functionalism in allowing for "revolutionary" art that is intended to be regarded in a novel way. Even the revolutionary artist, Levinson argues, must intend that her product be regarded in a way that is understood *by reference to* existing ways of regarding artworks if what she produces is to be art, rather than something else.

Levinson's historical definition challenges the idea that art-making is possible only for one who acts with conscious reference to a social or cultural framework with established understandings or procedures. If we use the term "institution" in a broad sense, so that a socially embodied set of understandings and practices bearing upon a particular matter counts as an "institution," then Levinson opposes the idea that art is essentially institutional. He wants to allow for artworks whose maker's intentions in no way implicate the existence of any artistic institutions in this sense. He also wants to allow for cases where the status of an object as an artwork becomes apparent only some time after its manufacture, when the ways of correctly regarding entities within the structures of such an artistic institution have evolved so as to encompass the sort of regard intended by such a culturally isolated maker.

In so doing, Levinson is rejecting broadly "institutional" theories of art, which maintain that some kind of certification within an institutional framework is the defining condition of arthood.[1] "Institutional" definitions of "art" are procedural in Davies' sense. They represent a third kind of response to Weitz's critique of functionalist definitions, one that takes its inspiration from Maurice Mandelbaum's observation (1965) that Weitz's anti-definitional arguments have force only as long as one restricts oneself to pure or aesthetic functionalist definitions of "artwork." Such definitions, as we have seen, require that works have those manifest or exhibited properties that are necessary to perform the specified functions of art, and that they be able to perform such functions in virtue of possessing such properties. Weitz's argument is persuasive against definitions in terms of properties like "has significant form," or "expresses feeling through the organization of elements," for it is easy to think of accepted works that fail to have the designated property, and any definition in terms of such properties would inhibit the development of art. But, Mandelbaum points out, the defining property of arthood may neither be exhibited nor entail any particular kind of exhibited property. Indeed, even the concept always cited by Wittgensteinians opposed to the

---

1   For another anti-institutional argument of this sort, see Beardsley 1976.

definitional enterprise – the concept "game" – may be definable in terms of some non-exhibited property.

Mandelbaum himself offered no particular candidate for a non-exhibited defining property of arthood. George Dickie, however, taking up the challenge, has proposed an "institutional" theory of art, according to which artworks are distinguished from non-works not through the possession of any exhibited property, but through having acquired a certain kind of status within a broadly institutional context.[2] Dickie calls this institutional context "the Artworld," a term he takes from Danto. As Danto himself notes (1981: vii), Dickie gives this term a different sense from the one originally accorded to it. For Danto (1964: 580), an art-world is constituted by "an atmosphere of artistic theory, a knowledge of the history of art," something which is necessary in order "to see something as art," and for the creation of artworks. For Dickie, on the other hand, the term refers to "the broad social institution in which works of art have their place" (1974: 31). This "institution" is a system of "established practices" corresponding to the different art forms. Each such system functions as "a framework for the *presenting* of works of art." In the theater, for example, "the roles of the actors and the audience are defined by the traditions of the theater. What the author, management, and players present . . . is art because it is presented within the theater-world framework. Plays are written to have a place within the theater system and they exist as plays, that is, as art, within that system" (1974: 30).

Arthood, then, is defined as a status conferrable by one who acts on behalf of the artworld so conceived. Dickie's original definition states that an artwork, in the classificatory sense, is "(1) an artifact (2) upon which some person or person acting on behalf of a certain social institution (the artworld) has conferred the status of candidate for appreciation" (1971: 34). This definition was later amended, however, so that it is *a set of the aspects* of an artifact that acquires this conferred status (1974: 101). Dickie maintains that one of the achievements of artists like Duchamp was to make us aware of the act of status conferral that is necessary and sufficient for something to be a work of art:

> Painters and sculptors . . . have been engaging all along in the action of conferring [the status of art] on the objects they create. As long, however, as the created objects were conventional, given the paradigms of the times,

2 I shall restrict my discussion to the earlier formulations of Dickie's view, in his 1971 and 1974. Later refinements in Dickie's position do not, I think, affect the points I wish to make in the following pages.

the objects themselves and their fascinating exhibited properties were the focus of attention of not only spectators and critics but of philosophers of art as well . . . When, however, the objects are bizarre, as those of the Dadaists are, our attention is forced away from the object's obvious properties to a consideration of the objects in their social context. (1974: 32)

I shall not survey here the full range of objections that have been brought against the institutional theory, or the range of responses forthcoming from its proponents. I shall simply note some salient points that may assist in the search for a definition of art that would complement the ontological claims of the performance theory. We may note, first, that Dickie's "artifactuality requirement" seems to do little work, given that Dickie allows that it is satisfied even by exhibited driftwood which somehow has artifactuality "conferred" upon it in the process of acquiring the status of artwork.[3] Second, we may wonder how the act of status conferral is supposed to take place, and why it presupposes the institutional framework of an artworld. Dickie does not want to say that something becomes a work only when it is actually performed in a theater or exhibited in a gallery. He grants that "many works of art are seen only by one person – the one who creates them – but they are still art" (1974: 37–8). The artworld gets into the picture because the conferred status is itself defined by reference to the presentational practices that make up systems of the artworld. The conferred status is candidacy for appreciation in accordance with the presentational practices of the relevant system. But, since Dickie is at pains to insist that there is nothing distinctively "aesthetic" about the appreciation at issue here,[4] it seems that what the conferral of the relevant status requires is the conferrer's intending that an entity be regarded in whatever is the appropriate way in the artworld system in question. If so, one can sympathize with Levinson's suggestion that we should also count as artworks those things whose makers intend them to be so regarded *transparently construed* – that is, regarded in a particular way, characterizable without reference to the presentational practices of the artworld, which happens to coincide with a way of regarding things licensed by the artworld. If the purported essential institutionality of art is to be understood in the manner proposed by Dickie, it seems unmotivated.

---

3   Binkley 1976: 100 suggests that Dickie's "artifactuality" condition serves "no apparent purpose outside securing a place for an artifactuality requirement in a definition" of art!

4   See Dickie 1974: 40–1: "All that is meant by 'appreciation' in the definition is something like 'in experiencing the qualities of a thing one finds them worthy or valuable,' and this meaning applies quite generally both inside and outside the domain of art."

Levinson's anti-institutionalism is plausible as long as an "artworld" enters only indirectly into the process whereby something becomes art, as is the case with Dickie's theory. If the conferral of the status of "artwork" is a matter of intending that an entity be "regarded" in a certain way by those who seek to appreciate it, where the presentational practices of an artworld serve to identify the relevant kinds of "regard," it seems unnecessary that one who intends such a regard be aware of such practices. However, our analysis of the fine structure of the focus of appreciation provides us with a much stronger argument for the essentially institutional (or perhaps, more accurately, socio-cultural) nature of art, given that we are taking the notion of "institution" in a broad sense that encompasses shared understandings embodied in the practices of a community of receivers. For, as argued in chapter 3, a crucial component in the focus of appreciation is the artistic medium in which an artist works when manipulating a vehicular medium. But the artistic medium is a set of presumed shared understandings upon which the artist draws in her attempt to articulate a particular artistic statement through these manipulations. An artistic medium is therefore "institutional" in the relevant sense. Indeed, this is explicit in one of the sources upon which I drew in developing the idea of an artistic medium. Binkley, we may recall, contends that a piece in the visual arts is specified by means of what he terms "artistic indexing conventions." While I have preferred to talk of "shared understandings" rather than conventions, an artistic medium, like Binkley's "conventions," is embodied in the understandings of an artistic community, understandings that provide a necessary link between artists and receivers of works. The existence of an artistic medium thus presupposes the existence of an "artworld" in something like Danto's, rather than Dickie's, sense of that term.

An artistic medium is a *necessary* link between artist and receiver, it will be recalled, because it mediates between the manifest properties of the vehicle and the artistic statement articulated through that vehicle. It is that in virtue of which certain of the manifest properties of the vehicle count as artistic properties and contribute to the articulation of an artistic statement. But, crucially in the present context, we saw in chapter 7 that the artistic statement articulated through a vehicle depends upon the artist's intending that her work be received according to the shared understandings of a particular community of receivers. Thus the artist must consciously operate by reference to certain presumed shared understandings in order for her manipulations of a vehicular medium to count as the articulation of an artistic statement. Put simply, an individual's manipulation of a vehicular medium can serve to specify the focus of appreciation of an artwork only if the artist is guided in her activity by her beliefs about shared understandings in virtue of which what she is doing articulates a particular artistic statement – that is, only if she is working in an artistic medium. Because a focus of appreciation of an artwork can be specified only by one who so orients herself to a community of receivers, art is indeed essentially institutional in the broad sense. This is why we should reject Levinson's suggestion that something can be an artwork even if it originates in the activity of one who is ignorant of the practices of an artworld *as* such practices, as long as her intentions fit with such practices. For without the appropriate intentional use of an artistic medium, there is no articulation of an artistic statement and therefore no artwork.

This argument also applies, mutatis mutandis, to Robert Stecker's "historical functionalism." Stecker's definition of "artwork," prior to refinements that do not concern us here, is as follows:

> An item is a work of art at time *t*, where *t* is a time no earlier than the time at which the item is made, if and only if (a) either it is in one of the central art forms at *t* and is made with the intention of fulfilling a function art has at *t* or (b) it is an artifact that achieves excellence in fulfilling such a function, whether or not it is in a central art form and whether or not it was intended to fulfill such a function. (1997: 50)

Stecker's (b) fails to be a sufficient condition of arthood because there is no reason to think that an entity that satisfies (b) will serve to articulate an artistic statement. In fact, for reasons that will be elaborated below, I think Stecker's (a) is also flawed in that, taken together with (b), it excludes works that make use of an artistic medium for purposes other than those that the medium is intended to serve.

The essentially institutional nature of art, therefore, is grounded directly in the preconditions for artistic creation, rather than being parasitic upon the presentational practices of a Dickian artworld. This relates to two other failings of Dickie's procedural theory identified by his critics. First, as Danto points out (1981: 31–2), Dickie's account of how artworks come into existence provides no insight into the particularity of works, the manner in which what is created is a *particular* work. The conferral of status in virtue of which something qualifies as an artwork seems to occur when whatever is responsible for the particularity of the work has already taken place. Whether it is an artifact, or a set of the aspects of an artifact, that has the status conferred upon it, this in no way explains how the process whereby an artifact is created bears upon the appreciation of the resulting artwork.

A second related criticism is developed by Binkley (1976). He argues that, given the vacuity of the "artifactuality" requirement and the openness of the notion of "appreciation," the substance of Dickie's definition is contained entirely in the idea that arthood is a conferred status. Binkley maintains that status conferral is an inadequate model for the process whereby artworks come into existence, and that we should prefer a model in terms of piece specification for at least two reasons. First, status conferral picks out its objects *extensionally*. An entity that has a status conferred upon it has that status however it is described. But artworks are individuated *intensionally*, so that the same object or structure can house more than one artwork. Dickie fails to meet this objection with his revised definition, where it is "sets of aspects" of artifacts, rather than artifacts, that have conferred upon them the status of candidate for appreciation, For he still identifies the work with *the artifact*, not with the set of aspects. Second, echoing Danto's criticism, Binkley argues that status conferral is a two-stage process, which requires some way of independently identifying an entity prior to conferring a status upon it. Art-making, on the other hand, is a one-stage process, where a piece is specified *as a particular piece* through the performance of some action on the part of the artist. An adequate theory of art should explain how something becomes an artwork by becoming a particular artwork, and the model of status conferral fails to meet this requirement.

I think these criticisms raise serious doubts as to whether any procedural definition of "artwork" in terms of status conferral can do justice to the process whereby artworks are created. The difficulties cannot be overcome by putting more substance into the institutional account by further elucidating the different roles that make up the artworld, as Stephen Davies (1991), for example, proposes. Davies thinks that the procedural account is defensible if we supplement it with an account of how one acquires the necessary "authority" to confer the required status on different kinds of objects in the artworld. This, for Davies, meets what he sees as the principal failing in Dickie's account, its inability to explain why only some individuals at some times are able to "transmute" urinals into artworks, for example. But, if the preceding reflections are correct, the problems with a procedural definition like Dickie's run much deeper. An adequate account must reconceive the nature of the "artistic act" through which an artwork comes into existence.

The requirement that such an artistic act draw in an intentional way upon the shared understandings constitutive of an artistic medium captures, I think, the kernel of truth in institutional, and more generally in procedural, definitions of art. But it should be apparent that we are still faced with our initial problem. We still lack a principled distinction between artworks and other performances of the same generic kind. For we have been offered no clarification of what it is that makes a medium, or an "indexing convention," *artistic*, nor have we clarified what makes an "artistic act" of the sort just mooted an *artistic* act. The challenge for any procedural or institutional definition of art is to provide a principled account of what makes a particular system of practices or procedures part of an "artworld," in one of the senses of this term. There appears to be a circularity at the very heart of the institutional theory, in that artworks are defined by reference to a status acquired in a system of the artworld, and an artworld system is defined as one in which the things that acquire status are artworks.

Proceduralists naturally try to downplay this difficulty. Dickie, for example, suggests that the "circle" is informative in virtue of everything that is said about different roles in the artworld and different presentational conventions. The "Artworld" is not simply defined as the context in which things have and acquire the status "work of art," but is described in some detail (1974: 44). He further suggests that this appearance of circularity will always be a feature of institutionally defined concepts, and that to expect more is in a sense to beg the question against the institutional theorist. Davies also charges (1991: 113) that those who think we need some account of the *point served* by conferring art-status are begging the question against the institutional theorist. But I think the difficulty is genuine, and undermines any claim on the part of institutional theorists to offer an adequate definition of art. To see why, let us test Dickie's claim about definitions of institutional concepts.

Consider the concept "legal currency," which seems to be an essentially institutional notion. Something is legal currency, we might say, if it has a particular status conferred upon it by individuals acting on behalf of a particular kind of social practice which we may term a "commerceworld." We can say a number of things about this sort of social practice. For example, there are some who have the authority to confer the status of "legal currency," and there are others who act in the role of "users" of that which has acquired the status. We can also point to particular examples of "legal currency" in different commerceworlds. If we are asked to say what makes a particular social practice a commerceworld, we might respond that it is a practice that is carried on by means of a legal currency. However, we can avoid any appearance of vacuity or circularity in our account by also saying something about the *function served by the institutions* that we have termed "commerceworlds." Such institutions exist because there is a division of labor in most human cultures, which leads to the need for a system of exchange so that individuals can acquire various goods that they do not themselves produce. In such a context, "legal currency" is whatever acquires or has conferred upon it the status of medium of exchange. It is because we are able to identify commerceworlds by reference to the function that such institutions serve that we are able to tell if a newly encountered set of social practices in a culture very different from our own is a commerceworld, and if something within that culture has the status of "legal currency."

The challenge, then, is to say what would permit us to identify a system of practices in another culture as an "artworld" system. If we can provide an answer like the one just proposed for identifying a social practice as a commerceworld, then a "procedural" account of how something becomes art in the context of an artworld needs to be supplemented by a *functionalist* account of what it is that makes an established way of doing things a system of the *artworld*. If, on the other hand, it is claimed that no such functionalist account is forthcoming, then the proceduralist account seems to be empty, for it merely tells us that, in our culture, we happen to use the same term to describe a number of different systems within which entities are produced and presented for appreciation. We would have no basis whatsoever for labeling practices in other cultures, or indeed in earlier stages in the development of our own culture, as "artworlds," and the things produced or certified within those practices as "artworks."

Can we, then, say anything of interest about the function or functions performed by those practices within which the things we term "artworks" are created and appreciated? I shall only gesture here at how I think we might try to provide a positive answer to this question. A promising route, I think, is to look at one of the most sophisticated forms of pure functionalism. In repudiating institutional and standard functionalist conceptions of the artwork, Nelson Goodman argues that arthood is not so much a matter of what a thing *is* – what properties it possesses – as of what a thing *does*, the function that it performs in a given context. While functionalist definitions tend to classify things in terms of how they usually function, or how they were designed to function, Goodman maintains that arthood, in the strict sense, is something that an object possesses only when it functions as a symbol of a certain kind:

> Just by virtue of functioning as a symbol in a certain way does an object become, while so functioning, a work of art. The stone is normally no work of art while in the driveway, but may be so when on display in an art museum. In the driveway it usually performs no symbolic function; in an art museum, it exemplifies certain of its properties – e.g., shape, colour, texture. The digging and filling of a hole functions as a work insofar as our attention is directed to it as an exemplifying symbol. On the other hand, a Rembrandt painting may cease to function as a work of art when used to replace a broken window or as a blanket. (1978: 67)

Given our discussion of the sense in which art is essentially institutional, we can see why this view is unacceptable as it stands. First, what matters for something's being an artwork of a particular kind is that it involves the articulation of an artistic statement through the use of an artistic medium. This is a matter of the symbolic functions that a vehicle can perform in virtue of its history of making, not of those functions that might be conferred upon it by users independently of that history of making. Second, we want to allow for artworks that fail to achieve any real artistic merit, and this failure may be a failure to perform the sorts of symbolic functions normally valued in art.

We can, however, consider Goodman's account not as providing conditions under which we have an artwork, but as providing conditions under which a practice of making counts as a practice of *artistic* making. So construed, what Goodman clarifies is the conditions under which a set of shared understandings counts as an *artistic medium*, so that vehicles generated by agents who rely upon those understandings in articulating a content are rightly taken to articulate artistic statements. The idea, here, is that artistic media serve to articulate their contents in distinctive ways, to be glossed in terms of the sorts of symbolic functions that are conferred upon artistic vehicles by those who employ such artistic media in their manipulations of a vehicular medium. In spelling out the sorts of symbolic functions that are characteristic of artworks, Goodman talks of "symptoms of the aesthetic." He identifies five such "symptoms":

> (1) syntactic density, where the finest differences in certain respects constitute a difference between symbols . . . ; (2) semantic density, where symbols are provided for things distinguished by the finest differences in certain respects . . . ; (3) relative repleteness, where comparatively many aspects of a symbol are significant – for example, a single-line drawing of a mountain by Hokusai, where every feature of shape, line, thickness etc., counts, in contrast with perhaps the same line as a chart of daily stock-market aver-

ages, where all that counts is the height of the line above the base; (4) exemplification, where a symbol, whether or not it denotes, symbolises by serving as a sample of properties it literally or metaphorically possesses; and finally (5) multiple and complex reference, where a symbol performs several integrated and interacting referential functions, some direct and some mediated through other symbols. (1978: 67–8)

The suggestion, then, is that an artistic medium is a set of shared understandings in virtue of which the manipulation of a vehicular medium may issue in a vehicle which articulates a content in virtue of functioning as an "aesthetic" symbolic in something like Goodman's sense. It is because certain systems of shared understandings promote the articulation of a content in this way that we classify the products of articulative acts that employ those understandings as artistic vehicles, and the articulative performances as artworks. It is, then, the functions served by the medium of articulation that makes an articulative system a system of the "artworld." But this doesn't amount to a functionalist definition of "artwork," because something is an artwork in virtue of its being an articulative performance that takes place within such a system, not in terms of its functioning as an "aesthetic symbol" to a greater extent than things which are not artworks. Many things that are not artworks can function as Goodmanian aesthetic symbols, and many artworks, while they articulate their content by means of articulative conventions that facilitate functioning as an aesthetic symbol, do not themselves function as such symbols to a greater extent than non-artworks. This will be the case with artworks that fail, and artworks that are deliberately "non-aesthetic."

While I cannot develop these ideas here in detail, it is worth noticing how many interesting late modern artworks *do* articulate their content through functioning as "aesthetic symbols" in Goodman's sense. In particular, late modern works which lack manifest "aesthetic properties" of the traditional kind tend to articulate an artistic statement through what is exemplified by their vehicles (which may not themselves be objects, as we saw in chapter 8), through multiple symbolic functioning, and through the repleteness of the vehicular medium. Take, as just one example, one of the more infamous works of "Young British Art," Damien Hirst's dead shark suspended in a tank of formaldehyde. This is the way the piece is usually characterized, but it has a title which may be read as crucial to the artistic statement articulated by Hirst through the exhibited object as vehicle. The title is *The Physical Impossibility of Death in the Mind of Someone Living*. Critics have remarked the obvious symbolism of the piece

– the shark presumably represents death, and the tank then represents the mind, or something like that – and have assumed that the piece is intended to work through shocking the viewer. If this were a proper reading of what Hirst is about in this piece, it might be tempting to opt for an analysis like the one proposed in chapter 8 for some other late modern works, where the vehicle is not the displayed object but the gesture of displaying such an object in a gallery. If one observes how the displayed object is generally received when exhibited in a gallery, this would further encourage such a reading.

But I think the work is open to a much richer and more interesting analysis, according to which it involves an articulation of content by means of "aesthetic" symbolism of a Goodmanian kind. First, one needs to attend much more closely to the properties of the vehicle displayed in the gallery, rather than simply registering that there is a rather fearsome-looking shark in a tank. In particular, one needs to walk around the tank while looking at the shark. If one does so, one quickly becomes aware that the shark always presents itself to the eye as being adjacent to the side of the tank closest to the viewer. Because of the optical properties of the material of which the enclosure containing the shark is constructed, the shark will "follow one around" as one circles the tank. More significantly, however, the shark, as presented to the eye of the receiver, is a physically impossible object. For it is clearly not *moving* in the tank – it is a dead shark, after all – yet there is no enduring physical location in the tank at which one can visually situate the shark as one circles the tank. If the shark in some sense symbolizes death, and the tank symbolizes the mind, therefore, the vehicle as a whole can be taken to symbolize precisely what the title says.

In specifying the piece, Hirst can assume that the receiver will be open to the idea that the vehicle performs the sorts of complex symbolic functions just mooted. As a receiver, one anticipates that the vehicle is syntactically "replete" in a way that an indistinguishable object in a natural history museum would not be. The optical properties of the physical medium bear upon what is represented both at a first-order level and at a higher level of meaning, whereas they have no such bearing on the "meanings" articulated by a shark displayed in a museum. Furthermore, a physical engagement with the vehicle is necessary in order to determine what is being articulated, as is the case with more traditional works of visual art. This is why it would be a mistake to treat the work as a conceptual piece. The vehicle, through its representational content – the shark, as a symbol of death, represented as physically impossible – gives a concrete embodiment to an abstract idea, in a manner reminiscent of

Kant's claim that artworks are the expressions of "aesthetical ideas," visual realizations of abstract ideas of reason that occasion much thought without being adequately represented by any concept.

Our quarry, in this section, has been a principled distinction between artworks, as performances articulative of content, and other performances of the same generic kind, a distinction that might serve as a definition of "artwork." Our brief examination of the definitional enterprise has yielded the following proposal: an artwork is a performance which articulates a content through a vehicle via an "artistic medium," a system of articulatory understandings in a system of the artworld, in something like Danto's sense. An artworld system is a system whose articulatory understandings facilitate the articulation of content through vehicles that perform symbolic functions that are "aesthetic" in Goodman's sense. "Artwork" is defined procedurally, by reference to a performance that intentionally draws upon an established system of articulatory understandings, and functionally in that it is by reference to the facilitating of a particular kind of symbolic functioning that a system of articulatory understandings counts as an artistic medium.

If this kind of story is correct, then we have a distinction which is principled, but not one which will issue in a clear boundary between art and non-art. For the classification of a system of articulatory understandings as part of the artworld will rest upon a judgment as to whether the manner in which contents are articulated within this system of understandings is sufficiently "aesthetic" to count as an artistic medium. Here is where Weitz's talk of "family resemblances" seems appropriate. Should we, for example, include such practices as carpet-weaving, figure-skating, cake design, and pottery among the arts? These activities have always occupied an uncertain position on the fringes of the artworld, and this suggests that we should not be looking for a sharp division between art and non-art at this level of analysis. Within an acknowledged system of the artworld, however, we have a sharp division, but this again seems right. While there is much more to be said on these issues, I think the sort of approach sketched in this section is the right way to make progress, whether or not one subscribes to the more specific ontological thesis of this book.

10.2 The Values of Art

In chapter 1, it was noted that the "common-sense" theory of art contains, in germ, an entire philosophy of art – an ontology, an epistemology, an axiology, and a definition of "art." We also noted that the common-sense theory embodies some broadly "empiricist" views about artistic appreciation and artistic value. Works are given for appreciation in an experiential encounter with a perceptible entity – a canvas on a gallery wall, or the sequence of sounds produced by an orchestra – and artistic value is essentially a matter of the kind of experience elicited in such an experiential encounter. We looked, in chapters 2 and 3, at arguments that can be offered against naive or sophisticated versions of "aesthetic empiricism" – the common-sense account of artistic appreciation. Opponents of aesthetic empiricism maintain that the properties rightly ascribable to artworks in our critical and appreciative practice are not confined to manifest properties, or properties that supervene on manifest properties, or properties that supervene on manifest properties and category of art. Rather, a work's artistic properties depend in part upon broader features of the art-historical context in which an artist was working. Thus only if our encounter with a manifest work is informed by a proper understanding of this context can we grasp the distinctive artistic properties of a work, and thereby come to properly appreciate that work. The rejection of aesthetic empiricism provided us with the epistemological premise needed in order to mount an "epistemological argument" against common-sense ontology. Finally, in the preceding section, we have looked at the prospects for a definition of art that departs significantly from what is implicit in our common-sense understandings of art. Thus our dismantling of the common-sense view is complete, save for the common-sense axiological view that the value of an artwork resides in the experiences elicited in receivers who appropriately engage with that work.

One might think that empiricist axiology stands or falls with empiricist epistemology of art. Certainly, the notions of artistic value and artistic appreciation seem to be intimately related. Artistic value is presumably the value that can be determined through a proper appreciation of an artwork, and a proper appreciation is one that enables the receiver to determine a work's artistic value. However, empiricist axiology has proved more resilient than the other elements in the common-sense view of art. Indeed, it is taken by many to be the kernel of truth in that view, the thing to be preserved from the dismantling of the broader empiricist conception of art. This residue of empiricism is to be found even in the writings of a philosopher like Levinson, who has been among the most trenchant critics of aesthetic empiricist theories of appreciation. Taking appropriate account of the epistemological relevance of provenance does not, it might be argued, call into question the basic principle of empiricist axiology, that the artistic value of a work resides in qualities of the experience it elicits in an appropriately primed receiver. What is called for is a *refinement*, but not a repudiation, of the empiricist view. Following a suggestion by Matthew Kieran, one of its proponents, I shall term this combination of an anti-empiricist epistemology and an empiricist axiology of art, "enlightened empiricism." Proponents of enlightened empiricism include Malcolm Budd (1995), Matthew Kieran (2001), Roman Bonzon (2003), and (arguably) Jerrold Levinson (1992b).

Before critically assessing enlightened empiricism, it is important to clarify what kinds of experiences are supposed to enter into determining artistic value, and how their bearing on artistic value is to be understood. In its simplest form, the idea behind an empiricist axiology of art is that the value of an artwork resides in the experiences it elicits in the receiver. A crude form of empiricist axiology might take account only of experiences elicited directly in a perceptual encounter with a work. The view becomes much more plausible, however, if we include not only those experiences directly elicited in an encounter with an instance of a work, but also those imaginative exercises prompted by that encounter. As it stands, however, this characterization is still inadequate. For it is surely not the case that *all* of the experiences elicited through imaginative engagement with an instance of a work bear upon its artistic value. Standing in front of a painting, an art thief may experience great pleasure as a result of imagining just how she might be able to remove the painting from the gallery and sell it to a collector, but this surely does not reflect upon the value of the work as art. To clarify which experiences are relevant to the artistic value of a work, we will need to appeal to something like the very slippery Kantian notion of "disinterested" response. We will also have to tie the work to the experience in an intimate manner to avoid a purely instrumental conception of artistic value. It would surely be unacceptable to maintain that artistic value consists in some *detachable* experience elicited by a work, which we could imagine being elicited in other ways. The experiences must be properly grounded in experienced qualities of the work, and they must be inseparable from the engagement with the work so that a proper characterization of the experience in question cannot be given without referring to details of the work.[5]

5   See Budd 1995 and Kieran 2001 for good discussions of these issues.

We may also ask how a work's eliciting certain kinds of experiences can confer value upon the work. If the experiences are those directly elicited in a perceptual encounter with an instance of a work, then one might argue, like Bell, that the value-conferring experiences are inherently valuable experiences of an "aesthetic emotion." If, however, one's empiricist axiology also embraces those exercises of the imagination prompted by an encounter with an instance of a work, one is more likely to hold that the experiences elicited by works are valuable in a number of different ways that bear upon the artistic value of the works themselves. Kieran and Levinson each take such a line. Levinson (1992b), examining the view that artistic value is a matter of the enduring pleasures to be found in active engagements with works, cautions that the experiences engendered by artworks have value for us not merely in virtue of their being pleasurable or yielding some other immediately affective reward. Rather, they may be intrinsically valuable

> because one's cognitive faculties are notably exercised or enlarged; because one's eyes or ears are opened to certain spatial and temporal possibilities; because one is enabled to explore unusual realms of emotion; because one's consciousness is integrated to a degree out of the ordinary; because one is afforded a distinctive feeling of freedom or transcendence; because certain moral truths are made manifest to one in concrete dress; or because one is provided insight, in one way or another, into human nature. (1992b: 18–19)

It is indisputable, I think, that the sorts of cognitive and affective values catalogued are among the things for which we value works of art, and that the imaginative experiences elicited in receivers in their encounters with instances of works – objects in galleries, performances of musical and theatrical works, films projected in auditoria, copies of literary works – are crucial to the realization and appreciation of those values. What is distinctive of empiricist axiology, however, is the claim that artistic value is to be *equated* with the value that resides in such imaginative experiences. It is this claim that may seem difficult to reconcile with the repudiation of empiricist epistemology of art. If the appreciation of artworks requires that we take account of the history of making of the artistic vehicle with which we engage in our encounter with an instance of a work, why should we think that the only sort of artistic value properly ascribed to works in our appreciation of them is empiricist in nature? Our first question, therefore, is how enlightened empiricists achieve such a reconciliation of non-empiricist epistemology and empiricist axiology.

The key to being an enlightened empiricist lies in a particular way of understanding the case against empiricist epistemology of art. As noted earlier, for those like Levinson who argue from the rejection of an empiricist epistemology of art to a contextualist ontology of art, empiricist epistemology is flawed because it fails to take account of the manner in which the history of making of a given artistic vehicle partly determines *properties of the focus of appreciation* specified by the artist – what is represented or expressed, for example. For the contextualist, who wishes to identify the work with the focus specified in a particular context, knowledge of features of provenance is necessary for the proper appreciation of works because provenance determines salient features of that focus – in particular, it determines properties of the artistic statement articulated through the vehicle of the work.

But if this is how we understand the argument against empiricist epistemology of art, then there is no reason to question the basic empiricist axiological thesis that the value of a work is a function of the experiences elicited in a receiver. We need only refine this thesis to make explicit the requirement that the receiver take account of those properties of the work-product that are not given in an uninformed encounter with the manifest work, but that require knowledge of provenance: what matter are the experiences elicited in an encounter with a work *understood in the contextualist sense*. Levinson, for example, addressing the idea that the value of an artwork is a function of the qualities of the imaginative experiences it engenders in receivers, stresses that

> the pleasure proper to an object as art is one that is fully cognisant of the background from which a work emerges, the process whereby it came to have the exact shape that it does, the challenges inherent in the medium and material employed, the problems with which the work is wrestling, and so on. The proper pleasure of art is an *informed* pleasure, and understands that its object – unlike the beauties of nature – is an artifact, has a history, and represents something done and achieved. (1992b: 16–17)[6]

There is no denying the intuitive appeal of enlightened empiricism. On the one hand, in offering a broad range of affective and cognitive values to be located in the experiences elicited by artworks, it promises to accommodate the diversity of artistic values that we ascribe to the works themselves. On the other hand, the "enlightened" nature of the empiricism ensures that the works to which such values are ascribed are properly con-

6   See also Kieran 2001: 217.

textualized. Even for such an enlightened empiricism, however, all artistic value must ultimately reside in characteristics of the experiences elicited in receivers in a suitably informed engagement with an instance of a work. This is the sense in which enlightened empiricism still comprises an *empiricist* theory of artistic value. Thus it is open to challenge if there are factors that enter into our assessments of artistic value that are not reducible to the experienced effects of works. Reflection on examples discussed in chapter 3 above provides us with the basis for just such a challenge.

Recall, first, Clark's account of Turner's *Snowstorm*. Clark maintains that, whereas in earlier attempts to represent the power of nature Turner relied on design and composition, in the *Snowstorm*,

> the dramatic effect of light is not achieved by contrast of tone . . . but by a most subtle alternation of colour. As a result, oil paint achieves a new consistency, an iridescence, which is more like that of some living thing . . . than a painted simulacrum. The surface of a late Turner is made up of gradations so fine and flecks of colour so inexplicable that we are reminded, whatever the subject, of flowers and sunset skies. (1960: 146)

It is not implausible to think that the artistic values of the painting to which Clark alludes could be captured by the enlightened empiricist analysis. But, as noted in chapter 4, Clark continues that "to substitute colour for tone as a means of observing enlightened space could not be achieved by mere observation: it was a major feat of pictorial intelligence and involved Turner in a long struggle," a struggle involving years of "experiments" (146). Turner's *Snowstorm* represents "a major feat of pictorial intelligence" because of what was involved in articulating a particular artistic statement by finding novel ways in which to employ the vehicular medium of oil paint as an artistic medium.

If we think that the artistic value of Turner's painting is at least in part a matter of its involving such a "major feat of pictorial intelligence," is it plausible to say that this value resides in features of the imaginative experience elicited in us when we contemplate the picture in light of what Clark has told us? It is certainly conceivable that my "informed" experience differs in certain respects from my relatively "uninformed" experience. But surely this is because I am now aware of *a value that the picture has*. The difference in experience is to be explained in terms of a *recognition* of a value ascribable to the work. This value does not itself *consist in* the difference of experience when I view the picture in light of what Turner did, as the enlightened empiricist must say, but itself *accounts for* the difference in experience. And even if the informed experience were to be identical, qua imaginative experience, to the uninformed experience, this would not affect the value rightly ascribable to the work in virtue of what Turner achieved in specifying such a focus of appreciation.

Another example discussed earlier is the "staining" technique discovered by Morris Louis, as described by Clement Greenberg: "Louis spills his paint on unsized and unprimed cotton duck canvas, leaving the pigment almost everywhere thin enough, no matter how many different veils of it are superimposed, for the eye to sense the threadedness and wovenness of the fabric underneath" (1960: 28). In exploiting new materials in this way, Louis was able to produce canvases described by Edward Lucie-Smith as "veils of shifting hue and tone: there is no feeling that the various colour configurations have been drawn with a brush" (1976: 106). Clearly, again, the enlightened empiricist has no trouble accounting for artistic values that are a function of the observable qualities of the paintings to which Lucie-Smith alludes. But, as with the preceding example, it is surely not the case that any artistic value ascribable to the work in virtue of Louis' ingenious exploitation of novel resources is a function of the imaginative experience elicited in us when we contemplate the canvas in light of what we know about its history of making. Again, it seems that any difference in our imaginative experience is grounded in, rather than grounds, a recognized difference in artistic value.

Finally, consider again van Meegeren's *Disciples at Emmaeus*. One virtue of rejecting an empiricist epistemology of art and admitting the relevance of provenance to the appreciation of works is that we can explain why our assessment of this canvas changes when we take it to be the work of a twentieth-century journeyman painter rather than the work of Vermeer. But the difference between the value ascribed to the work when the canvas was attributed to Vermeer, and the value ascribed to the work when the canvas is attributed to van Meegeren, is surely *not* grounded in the different experiences elicited in us, as receivers, when our perceptual engagements with the canvas are "informed" first by one piece of information about provenance and then by the other. That our experiences differ *reflects* the value we find in the work on each occasion. It isn't the *ground* of that difference in value.

I said earlier that enlightened empiricism follows from a particular way of understanding the argument against empiricist epistemology. For

Levinson and other contextualists, the problem with empiricist epistemology is that it fails to take adequate account of the role that a history
of making plays in determining properties of the focus of appreciation
specified by the artist. But, as noted in chapter 2, there is another way of
understanding the anti-empiricist argument, upon which I have tacitly
drawn in setting out the foregoing examples. Dutton and Currie, for
example, argue that what reflection on our critical and appreciative practice demonstrates is that the object of critical appreciation is not the
product of the artist's endeavors per se, but the artist's achievement
in producing such a product. It is because we cannot determine the
nature of an artist's achievement without referring the manifest work to
a history of making that the empiricist account of artistic appreciation is
mistaken.

If one's critique of empiricist epistemology takes this line, however,
enlightened empiricism is no longer an attractive option. For, on this way
of viewing things, provenance bears upon the appreciation of works not
only because it partly determines salient properties of the focus of appreciation, but also because it is essential if we are to grasp *what the artist
has done* in bringing such a focus into existence. In appreciating a work,
we appreciate a particular performance or doing on the part of an agent.
In the examples discussed above, it is such doings on the part of Turner,
Louis, Vermeer, and van Meegeren that enter significantly into the artistic value of their works. Differences in elicited experiences are the result
of differences in ascribed achievements.

How might the enlightened empiricist try to meet this sort of
objection? The strategy of choice is to argue that such assessments of
the artist's achievement do not bear upon the artistic value of works.
The enlightened empiricist is unlikely to find this response attractive in
its traditional empiricist garb, where it involves an appeal to a distinction between "artistic value" and "art-historical value." But another
empiricist line of argument has found favor with at least some
enlightened empiricists. It may be argued that we value artistic
achievements of the sort canvassed in the above examples only insofar as
they enhance the possibilities for the kinds of valuable experiences
comprised by the enlightened empiricist axiology of art (see, for
example, Lessing 1995: 20). Levinson's status as an enlightened empiricist depends upon whether one reads the following passage as an expression of such a defence, or as an attempt to distance himself from
empiricism. Considering the claim that "an art work is valuable, ultimately, only insofar as *experience* of it is in some way worthwhile," he
comments in a footnote that

Even this may be unduly restrictive. Artworks may be valuable to us artistically in ways that go beyond their value in experience to us, strictly speaking. Part of an artwork's value might reside in its art-historical relations to other artworks, e.g. ones of anticipation, or originality, or influence, independent of the value of experiencing the work in the appropriate manner. In other words, part of a work's value as art may consist in how the work is connected to an important artistic tradition. However, it will remain true that the value of such traditions themselves – what we might call *cultural value* – is not ultimately explicable except in terms of the enrichment of human experience. (1992b: 12)[7]

This line of reasoning is open to a number of different responses. First, we might question whether all of the "achievement-properties" cited in the above examples are matters of "cultural value" in Levinson's sense. It is far from apparent, for example, that the value we ascribe to Turner's *Snowstorm* in virtue of his "feat of pictorial intelligence," or the value we ascribe to Louis' works in virtue of his innovative painting techniques, are values that stem from the contributions that each painter made to a developing tradition that has served to enrich human experience. In neither case is the innovation one that has spawned a "school" or "tradition" of other painters whose works have realized the sorts of experiential values proposed by the enlightened empiricists.

Second, if it is said that in the Turner and Louis cases the "experiential" payoff of the artistic achievement is to be found in the very works themselves – the paintings by Turner and Louis where the innovations yield valuable experiences to receivers of the works – it is not obvious that even this must be the case in order for a work to have artistic value in virtue of what was done by the artist. Certain early twentieth-century "experiments" in performance, such as the "bruitism" of Marinetti and Russolo (see Goldberg 2001: ch. 1), possess neither cultural value, in Levinson's sense, nor obvious merit through directly enriching human experience. Yet what was done by the artists at this time has genuine artistic interest, of the same sort as the interest we take in those artistic doings that do have experiential value.

Third, even if it be granted that the artistic value that resides in what an artist does or achieves is always ultimately accountable to the ways in which artworks can "enrich human experience" through the various channels canvassed earlier, this will not save enlightened empiricism. For the

---

7 Matthew Kieran has suggested a similar defence of enlightened empiricism in private correspondence.

artistic value ascribable to works in virtue of what an artist has done is in no way a function of the experiences elicited in encounters with instances of that *particular* work. As argued earlier, the dependence, if any, runs in the opposite direction: it is through our recognition of the value of what was done that we come to experience the work differently.

10.3 Conclusions: The Case Against Contextualism

The preceding investigations in the ontology of art have been lengthy and, in places, somewhat circuitous. Let me, therefore, try to draw together the different strands of my argument. I began with problems that late modern art and other aspects of our artistic practice present to those who subscribe, explicitly or tacitly, to the "common-sense" view of art. The latter, we saw, offers a broadly empiricist conception of artistic appreciation and artistic value, and a decontextualized conception of the artwork. I then rehearsed widely voiced criticisms of empiricist episte-mology of art, and sharpened these criticisms by providing an analysis of the fine structure of the focus of appreciation. This provided the basis for an "epistemological argument" against common-sense ontology of art.

However, as will have been apparent to the reader, it is not common-sense ontology, but rather contextualism, that has been the stalking horse in my extended argument in support of the performance theory. Con-textualism, as we saw, is the natural ontological response to the rejection of aesthetic empiricist epistemology – a response mediated by a positive epistemological argument whose epistemological premiss highlights the role that provenance plays in determining the artistic statement articu-lated through an artist's manipulation of a vehicular medium. The "cumu-lative" argument for the performance theory to which I alluded at the end of chapter 3 is, at the same time, a cumulative argument against contextualism. To properly gauge the force of the arguments for the performance theory, we must remind ourselves why the considerations adduced in support of the latter are also reasons to reject contextualism.

The analysis of the fine structure of the focus of appreciation in chapter 3 is a crucial first step in developing the case against contextualism. Drawing largely on ideas that are in play in the contextualist literature itself – in particular, in the writings of Binkley and Danto – we brought out the complex manner in which the different elements in the focus of appreciation are related both to one another and to the context of agency in which the focus is specified. This undermines the empiricist's appeal to a distinction between artistic properties and art-historical properties. But it also leads us to ask whether there is a principled way of excluding aspects of provenance not determinative of properties of the focus of appreciation from the appreciation of works. In chapter 4, I argued that the very logic of the anti-empiricist argument, as elaborated in the analysis of the focus of appreciation, calls into question the contextualist's attempts to exclude such aspects of provenance from the epistemology of art. I countered the response that the aspects of provenance cited in support of the performance theory are to be accommodated as *relational* properties of the work-focus, by suggesting that this misrepresents our interests in the appreciation of works. Once we recognize the different ways in which our appreciative interests in an artwork require that we take account of a generative performance, the burden of proof is on the contextualist to show why we should nonetheless think of the work as a contextualized product.

The "modal" argument of chapter 5 complements the arguments of chapter 4, but also provides an independent reason to question the adequacy of contextualism. The initial charge against a contextualist ontology such as Levinson's is that, in making certain types of features of provenance constitutive for all works, it lacks the resources to account for the work-relativity of modality. The performance theory, on the other hand, in identifying works with particular performances that share the general property of being specifications of focuses of appreciation, can easily accommodate the fact that our modal intuitions about works track our modal intuitions about the particular performances whereby focuses are specified, rather than being determined by a characterization of some general property that such performances share. Contextualism fails to reflect the fact that aspects of provenance bear upon our modal judgments with a *variable* force that reflects *our overall sense of what is to be appreciated* in a given work Even a revised contextualism that identified works with work-focuses as specified through a particular manipulative performance would be open to this criticism, for we can say nothing about what it is that makes these performances distinctive.

These arguments in support of the performance theory are buttressed by the detailed elaboration of the theory in chapter 7, an elaboration informed by the critical assessment, in chapter 6, of the difficulties that attend Currie's ATH. In particular, it was spelled out in a principled way how the elements of provenance entering into the identity of the work are determined by our sense of what was done in specifying a focus of appreciation, and such specificatory performances were identified not with "basic actions" which may have their times of occurrence essentially, but with "doings" that admit of the sorts of variation in modal properties required by the work-relativity of modality.

Two further anti-contextualist arguments were presented in chapter 8. First, a standard contextualist charge against process ontologies of art – the so-called "revisionism" objection – was turned back upon the contextualist. When we ask whether contextualism is itself open to a parallel objection, we uncover a basic instability in the contextualist account. This is revealed in its starkest form in Julian Dodd's (2000) recent challenge to Levinson's brand of contextualism. If a time or another temporally indexed parameter is represented as a constituent feature of a work, as is the case with the "indicated-structure" theory, then, so Dodd charges, works would have to be event-like entities, since only such entities can have times or temporally inflected properties as their constituents. If, on the other hand, the times or temporally inflected properties are not taken to be constituents of the contextualist's works, then the works must be thought of as *structures* which are *individuated* in terms of their times of occurrences. Thus contextualism is unstable, collapsing, once subject to scrutiny, either into some kind of decontextualized ontology or into an event ontology like the performance theory. Dodd, summarily rejecting the idea that works are event-like entities, takes this as an argument for the reinstatement of a structuralist view of musical and literary works. If, however, we reject structuralism, our only option is to accept an event ontology like the performance theory. We may then accommodate the "revisionist" implications of such an ontology by availing ourselves of a principled distinction between talk of works and talk of the elements that enter into works – in particular, the elements that enter into the work-focus. The basis for making such a principled distinction was sketched in chapter 8.

A second anti-contextualist argument is implicit in the later sections of chapter 8, where I argue that contextualism cannot adequately account for crucial distinctions that must be drawn between different late modern works, and is also unable to make sense of our treatment of forgeries. The performance theory, I maintain, is much better equipped to account for these features of our artistic practice. This line of argument for the performance theory is further developed in chapter 9, where a detailed analysis is offered of the ways in which performance-events – such as performances of musical and theatrical works – enter into the being and being appreciated of artworks. The performance theory provides us with the larger framework in which we can embed this analysis of performance-events so as to draw important distinctions between late modern artworks, and between different kinds of performance-events in the arts.

The analyses presented in the first two sections of this chapter complete the critique of the common-sense theory of art begun in chapter 1. I have sketched a way in which we might define an "artwork" as a kind of performance, and have proposed a theory of artistic value that, while embracing the sorts of experiential values celebrated by the enlightened empiricist, also allows for works to have artistic value in virtue of being particular performances or "doings." This also completes the elaboration of a broader philosophical framework for thinking about artworks – their being, their being appreciated, and their being valued – grounded in the performance theory. I suggested in chapter 1 that recent writers in the ontology of art are in agreement on the "pragmatic principle," according to which we must evaluate ontological proposals on the basis of their fit with a more comprehensive philosophical framework that makes sense of our artistic practice as that practice is "codified" upon rational reflection. It is its place within the broader philosophical account of our artistic practice elaborated in this book – a framework that exhibits both continuities and salient discontinuities between traditional and modern art, and between different artistic disciplines – that provides the ultimate measure of the performance theory as an ontology of art. The burden now falls upon the contextualist to propose a contextualist ontology that can outperform the performance theory when measured in this way. Contextualism is not, as its defenders may like to think, the "only game in town" if we accept the epistemological argument against decontextualized ontologies such as structuralism. Even if this book has not converted all of its readers to the performance theory, I would like to think that it has at least succeeded in redressing the balance of proof in the ontology of art. Such success would, I think, be reward enough.

References

Aagard-Mogensen, L. (ed.) 1976: *Culture and Art*. Atlantic Highlands, NJ: Humanities Press.

Allen, R. 1995: *Projecting Illusion: Film Spectatorship and the Impression of Reality*. New York: Cambridge University Press.

Alperson, P. 1984: On Musical Improvisation. *Journal of Aesthetics and Art Criticism*, 43, 17–29.

Arnheim, R. 1938: A New Laocoön: Artistic Composites and the Talking Film. In Arnheim 1964: 199–230.

Arnheim, R. 1964: *Film as Art*. Berkeley: University of California Press.

Baxandall, M. 1972: *Painting and Experience in Fifteenth-Century Italy*. Oxford: Oxford University Press.

Baxandall, M. 1985: *Patterns of Intention: On the Historical Explanation of Pictures*. New Haven, CT: Yale University Press.

Bazin, A. 1967: *What Is Cinema?* Vol. I. Trans. H. Gray. Berkeley: University of California Press.

Beardsley, M. C. 1958: *Aesthetics: Problems in the Philosophy of Criticism*. New York: Harcourt, Brace, and World.

Beardsley, M. C. 1976: Is Art Essentially Institutional? In Aagaard-Mogensen 1976: 194–209.

Beardsley, M. C. 1982a: What Is Going On in a Dance? *Dance Research Journal*, 15, 31–7.

Beardsley, M. 1982b: Redefining Art. In M. J. Wreen and D. M. Callen (eds), *The Aesthetic Point of View,*. Ithaca, NY: Cornell University Press, 298–315.

Beardsley, M. C. 1983: An Aesthetic Definition of Art. In H. Curtler (ed.), *What Is Art?* New York: Haven, 15–29.

Bell, C. 1914: *Art*. London: Chatto and Windus.

Bell, C. 1992: The Aesthetic Hypothesis. In P. Alperson (ed.), *The Philosophy of the Visual Arts*. Oxford: Oxford University Press, 119–26. This is an excerpt from Bell 1914.

Beuys, J. 1985: Interview with Bernard Lamarche-Vadel. *Canal*, 58–9.

Binkley, T. 1976: Deciding About Art. In Aagard-Mogensen 1976: 90–109.

Binkley, T. 1977: Piece: Contra Aesthetics. *Journal of Aesthetics and Art Criticism*, 35, 265–77.

Bloor, D. 1981: The Strengths of the Strong Programme. *Philosophy of the Social Sciences*, 11, 199–213.

Bloor, D. and B. Barnes 1982: Relativism, Rationalism, and the Sociology of Knowledge. In M. Hollis and S. Lukes (eds), *Rationality and Relativism*. Cambridge, MA: MIT Press, 21–47.

Bonzon, R. 2003: Fiction and Value. In D. Lopes and M. Kieran (eds), *Imagination, Philosophy, and the Arts*. London: Routledge, 160–76.

Borges, J. L. 1970: *Labyrinths*. Harmondsworth: Penguin.

Budd, M. 1990: Review of Currie 1989. *British Journal of Aesthetics*, 30 (4), 69–72.

Budd, M. 1995: *Values of Art*. Harmondsworth: Penguin.

Burge, T. 1979: Individualism and the Mental. In P. French et al. (eds), *Midwest Studies in Philosophy* IV. Minneapolis: University of Minnesota Press, 73–121.

Carroll, N. 1986: Performance. *Formation*, 3 (1), 64–78.

Carroll, N. 1988: *Philosophical Problems of Classical Film Theory*. Princeton, NJ: Princeton University Press.

Carroll, N. 1992: Art, Intention, and Conversation. In Iseminger 1992a: 97–131.

Carroll, N. 2000: Interpretation and Intention. *Metaphilosophy*, 31, 75–95.

Carroll, N. and S. Banes 1982: Working and Dancing. *Dance Research Journal*, reprinted in D. Goldblatt and L. B. Brown (eds) 1997: *Aesthetics: A Reader in the Philosophy of the Arts*. Upper Saddle River, NJ: Prentice Hall, 290–6.

Clark, K. 1960: *Looking at Pictures*. London: John Murray.

Cleland, C. 1991: On the Individuation of Events. *Synthese*, 86, 229–54.

Cochrane, R. 2000: Playing by the Rules: A Pragmatic Characterisation of Musical Performances. *Journal of Aesthetics and Art Criticism*, 58 (2), 135–42.

Collingwood, R. G. 1938: *The Principles of Art*. Oxford: Clarendon Press.

Cook, N. 1998: *Analyzing Musical Multimedia*. Oxford: Oxford University Press.

Croce, B. 1922: *Aesthetic*. 2nd edn. Trans. D. Ainslie. London: Macmillan.

Currie, G. 1989: *An Ontology of Art*. New York: St Martin's Press.

Currie, G. 1990: *The Nature of Fiction*. Cambridge: Cambridge University Press.

Currie, G. 1991: Work and Text. *Mind*, 100, 325–40.

Currie, G. 1995: *Image and Mind: Film, Philosophy, and Cognitive Science*. Cambridge: Cambridge University Press.

Danto, A. 1964: The Artworld. *Journal of Philosophy*, 61, 571–84.

Danto, A. 1981: *The Transfiguration of the Commonplace*. Cambridge, MA: Harvard University Press.

Davidson, D. 1980: *Essays on Actions and Events*. Oxford: Oxford University Press.

Davidson, D. 1987: Knowing One's Own Mind. *Proceedings and Addresses of the APA*, 60, 441–57.

Davies, D. 1991: Works, Texts, and Contexts. *Canadian Journal of Philosophy*, 21, 331–46.

Davies, D. 1996: Fictional Truth and Fictional Authors. *British Journal of Aesthetics*, 36 (1), 43–55.

Davies, D. 1998: Artwork, Object, and Process. *Acta Analytica*, 20, 131–53.

Davies, D. 1999: Artistic Intentions and the Ontology of Art. *British Journal of Aesthetics*, 39 (2), 148–62.

Davies, D. forthcoming (a): Semantic Intentions, Utterance Meaning, and Work Meaning. *Philosophiques*.

Davies, D. forthcoming (b): Review of Stecker's *Interpretation and Construction*. *Journal of Aesthetics and Art Criticism*.

Davies, S. 1987: Authenticity in Musical Performance. *British Journal of Aesthetics*, 27 (1), 39–50.

Davies, S. 1991: *Definitions of Art*. Ithaca, NY: Cornell University Press.

de Duve, T. 1996: *Kant After Duchamp*. Cambridge, MA: MIT Press.

Dickie, G. 1971: *Aesthetics: An Introduction*. Indianapolis: Pegasus.

Dickie, G. 1974: *Art and the Aesthetic: An Institutional Analysis*. Ithaca, NY: Cornell University Press.

Dickie, G. and K. Wilson 1995: The Intentional Fallacy: Defending Beardsley. *Journal of Aesthetics and Art Criticism*, 53, 233–50.

Dodd, J. 2000: Musical Works as Eternal Types. *British Journal of Aesthetics*, 40 (6), 424–40.

Dutton, D. 1979: Artistic Crimes: The Problem of Forgery in the Arts. *British Journal of Aesthetics*, 19 (4), 304–14. Reprinted in Neill and Ridley 1995: 21–33.

Eldridge, R. 1985. Form and Content: An Aesthetic Theory of Art. *British Journal of Aesthetics*, 25, 303–16.

Gaut, B. 1997: Film Authorship and Collaboration. In R. Allen and M. Smith (eds), *Film Theory and Philosophy*. Oxford: Clarendon Press, 149–72.

Gerrard, N. 1999: Is This the Future of British Art? *Observer* Life, 10 January, 12–15.

Goldberg, R. 2001: *Performance Art*. Revised and expanded edn. London: Thames and Hudson.

Goodman, N. 1955: *Fact, Fiction, and Forecast*. Cambridge, MA: Harvard University Press.

Goodman, N. 1976: *Languages of Art*. 2nd edn. Indianapolis: Hackett.

Goodman, N. 1978: *Ways of Worldmaking*. Indianapolis: Hackett.

Goodman, N. and C. Z. Elgin 1988: *Reconceptions in Philosophy and Other Arts and Sciences*. London: Routledge.

Gould, C. S. and K. Eaton 2000: The Essential Role of Improvisation in Musical Performance. *Journal of Aesthetics and Art Criticism*, 58 (2), 143–8.

Greenberg, C. 1960: Louis and Noland. *Arts International*, 4 (5), 26–9.

Greenberg, C. 1961: Modernist Painting. *Arts Yearbook*, 4, 101–8.

Greenberg, C. 1962: After Abstract Expressionism. *Art International*, 6 (8), 24–32.

Greenberg, C. 1971: Counter-Avant-Garde. *Art International*, 15, 16–19.

Greenberg, C. 1976: Seminar Six. *Arts Magazine*, 50, 90–3.

Harrison, A. 1998: Medium. In M. Kelly (ed.), *Encyclopaedia of Aesthetics*. New York: Oxford University Press, 200–3.

Heidegger, M. 1971: The Origin of the Work of Art. In *Poetry, Language, and Thought*. Trans. Alfred Hofstadter. New York: HarperCollins, 17–87.

Hermeren, G. 1992: Allusions and Intentions. In Iseminger 1992a: 203–20.

Hirsch, E. D. Jr 1967: *Validity in Interpretation*. New Haven, CT: Yale University Press.

Hospers, J. 1956: The Croce–Collingwood Theory of Art. *Philosophy*, 31, 291–308.

Iseminger, G. (ed.) 1992a: *Intention and Interpretation*. Philadelphia: Temple University Press.

Iseminger, G. 1992b: An Intentional Demonstration. In Iseminger 1992a: 76–96.

Iseminger, G. 1996: Actual Intentionalism vs. Hypothetical Intentionalism. *Journal of Aesthetics and Art Criticism*, 54, 319–26.

Juhl, P. D. 1980: *Interpretation: An Essay in the Philosophy of Literary Criticism*. Princeton, NJ: Princeton University Press.

Kieran, M. 2001: Value of Art. In B. Gaut and D. M. Lopes (eds), *The Routledge Companion to Aesthetics*, London: Routledge.

Kim, J. 1976: Events as Property Exemplifications. In M. Brand and D. Walton (eds), *Action Theory*. Dordrecht: D. Reidel, 159–77.

Kivy, P. 1983: Platonism in Music: A Kind of Defence. *Grazer Philosophische Studien*, 19, 109–29.

Kivy, P. 1987: Platonism in Music: Another Kind of Defence. *American Philosophical Quarterly*, 24, 245–52.

Knapp, S. and W. B. Michael 1992: The Impossibility of Intentionless Meaning. In Iseminger 1992a: 51–64.

Kripke, S. 1980: *Naming and Necessity*. Cambridge, MA: Harvard University Press.

Kuhn, T. 1970: *The Structure of Scientific Revolutions*. 2nd edn. Chicago: University of Chicago Press.

Lakatos, I. 1970: Falsification and the Methodology of Scientific Research Programmes. In I. Latatos and A. Musgrave (eds), *Criticism and the Growth of Knowledge*. Cambridge: Cambridge University Press, 91–196.

Laudan, L. 1977: *Progress and its Problems*. Berkeley: University of California Press.

Lessing, A. 1995: What is Wrong with a Forgery? In Neill and Ridley 1995: 8–21.

Lessing, G. E. 1957: *Laocoön: An Essay on the Limits of Painting and Poetry*. Trans. E. Frothingham. New York: Noonday Press.

Levinson, J. 1979: Defining Art Historically. *British Journal of Aesthetics*, 19, 232–250. Reprinted in Levinson 1990a: 3–25.

Levinson, J. 1980: What a Musical Work Is. *Journal of Philosophy*, 77, 5–28. Reprinted in Levinson 1990a: 63–88. Page references are to the reprinted edition.

Levinson, J. 1984: Hybrid Artforms. *Journal of Aesthetic Education*, 18, 5–13. Reprinted in Levinson 1990a: 26–36. Page references are to the reprinted edition.

Levinson, J. 1989: Refining Art Historically. *Journal of Aesthetics and Art Criticism*, 47, 21–33. Reprinted in Levinson 1990a: 37–59. Page references are to the reprinted edition.

Levinson, J. 1990a: *Music, Art, and Metaphysics.* Ithaca, NY: Cornell University Press.

Levinson, J. 1990b: Authentic Performance and Performance Means. In Levinson 1990a: 393–408.

Levinson, J. 1992a: Critical notice of Currie 1989. *Philosophy and Phenomenological Research*, 52, 215–22.

Levinson, J. 1992b: Pleasure and the Value of Works of Art. *British Journal of Aesthetics*, 32, 295–306. Reprinted in Levinson 1996: 11–24.

Levinson, J. 1992c: Intention and Interpretation: A Last Look. In Iseminger 1992a: 221–56.

Levinson, J. 1996: *The Pleasures of Aesthetics.* Ithaca, NY: Cornell University Press.

LeWitt, S. 1967: Paragraphs on Conceptual Art. *Artforum.* Quoted in Lippard 1973: 28–9.

Linker, K. 1994: *Vito Acconci.* New York: Rizzoli.

Lippard, L. 1973: *Six Years: The Dematerialisation of the Art Object 1966–1972.* New York: Praeger.

Livingston, P. 1998: Intentionalism in Aesthetics. *New Literary History*, 29, 831–46.

Livingston, P. 1999: Counting Fragments, and Frenhofer's Paradox. *British Journal of Aesthetics*, 39 (1), 14–23.

Lucie-Smith, E. 1976: *Late Modern.* New York: Praeger.

Mackay, A. 1968: Mr Donnellan and Humpty Dumpty on Referring. *Philosophical Review*, 77, 197–202.

Mandelbaum, M. 1965: Family Resemblances and Generalisation Concerning the Arts. *American Philosophical Quarterly*, 219–28.

Margolis, J. 1976: Works of Art are Physically Embodied and Culturally Emergent Entities. In Aagard-Mogensen 1976: 32–45.

Margolis, J. 1980: *Art and Philosophy.* Atlantic Heights, NJ: Humanities Press.

Matheson, C. and J. O. Young 2000: The Metaphysics of Jazz. *Journal of Aesthetics and Art Criticism*, 58 (2), 125–33.

Nathan, D. O. 1992: Irony, Metaphor, and the Problem of Intention. In Iseminger 1992a: 183–202.

National Gallery of Art, Washington, 1995: *Johannes Vermeer.* New Haven, CT: Yale University Press.

Neill, A. and A. Ridley (eds) 1995: *Arguing About Art.* New York: McGraw-Hill.

Poggi, C. 1999: Following Acconci/ Targeting Vision. In A. Jones and A. Stephenson (eds), *Performing the Body/ Performing the Text.* London: Routledge, 255–72.

Priestley, B. 1982: *Mingus: A Critical Biography*. London: Quartet Books.

Putnam, H. 1975: The Meaning of "Meaning." In *Mind, Language, and Reality: Philosophical Papers vol. 2*. Cambridge, MA: Cambridge University Press, 215–71.

Rawls, J. 1971: *A Theory of Justice*. Cambridge, MA: Harvard University Press.

Ridley, A. 1997: Not Ideal: Collingwood's Expression Theory. *Journal of Aesthetics and Art Criticism*, 55, 263–72.

Ridley, A. unpublished: Collingwood on Imagination and Genre. Presented at conference on Imagination and the Arts, Leeds, July 2001.

Rudder Baker, L. 1997: Why Constitution is Not Identity. *Journal of Philosophy*, 94, 599–621.

Saville, A. 1987: *Aesthetic Reconstructions: The Seminal Writings of Lessing, Kant, and Schiller*. Oxford: Blackwell.

Scruton, R. 1983: Photography and Representation. In *The Aesthetic Understanding*. London: Methuen. Reprinted in Neill and Ridley 1995: 89–113.

Shields, C. 1995: Critical notice of Currie 1989. *Australasian Journal of Philosophy*, 73 (2), 293–300.

Sibley, F. 1959: Aesthetic Concepts. *Philosophical Review*, 68, 421–50.

Sibley, F. 1965: Aesthetic and Non-Aesthetic. *Philosophical Review*, 74, 135–59.

Steadman, P. 2001: *Vermeer's Camera*. New York: Oxford University Press.

Stecker, R. 1997: *Artworks*. University Park, PA: Penn State Press.

Stecker, R. 2003: *Interpretation and Construction*. Oxford: Blackwell.

Stich, S. P. and T. A. Warfield (eds) 1994: *Mental Representation*. Oxford: Blackwell.

Thompson, J. J. 1998. The Statue and the Clay. *Philosophical Perspectives*, 32, 149–73.

Tolhurst, W. 1979: On What a Text Is and How It Means. *British Journal of Aesthetics*, 19, 3–14.

Tolstoy, L. 1960: *What is Art?* Trans. A. Maude. Reprinted with an introduction by Vincent Tomas. Indianapolis: Bobbs-Merrill.

Walton, K. 1970: Categories of Art. *Philosophical Review*, 79, 334–67.

Walton, K. 1987. Style and the Products and Processes of Art. In B. Lang (ed.), *The Concept of Style,*. 2nd edn. Ithaca, NY: Cornell University Press, 72–104.

Weitz, M. 1950: *Philosophy of the Arts*. Cambridge, MA: Harvard University Press.

Weitz, M. 1956: The Role of Theory in Aesthetics. *Journal of Aesthetics and Art Criticism*, 15, 27–35.

Wiggins, D. 1980: *Sameness and Substance*. Oxford: Blackwell.

Wimsatt, W. and M. C. Beardsley 1946: The Intentional Fallacy. *Sewanee Review*, 54, 468–88.

Wolfe, T. 1976: *The Painted Word*. New York: Bantam.

Wölfflin, H. 1950: *Principles of Art History*. New York: Dover.

Wollheim, R. 1968: Minimal Art. In G. Battcock (ed.), *Minimal Art: A Critical Anthology,*. New York: Dutton, 387–99.

Wollheim, R. 1980: *Art and its Objects*. 2nd edn. Cambridge: Cambridge University Press.

Wolterstorff, N. 1975: Toward an Ontology of Artworks. *Nous,* 9. Reprinted in J. W. Bender and H. G. Blocker (eds) 1993: *Contemporary Philosophy of Art*. Englewood Cliffs, NJ: Prentice Hall, 322–38.

Wolterstorff, N. 1980: *Works and Worlds of Art*. Oxford: Clarendon Press.

Wolterstorff, N. 1991: Review of Currie 1989. *Journal of Aesthetics and Art Criticism*, 49 (1), 79–81.

Young, J. O. 1988: The Concept of Authentic Performance. *British Journal of Aesthetics*, 28 (3), 228–38.

Ziff, P. 1972: What Is Said. In D. Davidson and G. Harman (eds), *Semantics of Natural Language,*. Dordrecht: Reidel, 709–21.

Index

incomplete works, 109–11
indicated structure theory, 117, 147, 177, 237
  and the charge of metaphysical obscurity, 122, 181–5
  on the creatability of artworks, 44n, 185–6, 264
  on the modal properties of artworks, 106–7, 113, 122
  outlined, 77, 105–7, 210
  and the revisionism objection, 180–6
individuating conditions, 104–5, 121–2
institutional theory of art
  as defended by Dickie, 190, 242–9
  and the fine structure of the focus of appreciation, 245–7
intentional fallacy, 84
intentionalist models of interpretation
  actual intentionalism, 85–7
  "broad" and "narrow" construals of the contents of intentions, 163–7
  hypothetical intentionalism, 87–8
  interpretive intentionalism, 89
interpretive intentionalism, *see* intentionalist models of interpretation
Iseminger, G., 85, 88, 91n, 94–5

James, W., 40
Jarrett, K., *Koln Concerts*, 209, 219, 222, 228
Joyce, J., 157
Juhl, P. D., 91

Kant, I., 255
Kieran, M., 8n, 255–7, 261n
Kim, J., 168
Kivy, P., 43, 136n
Knapp, S., 91
Kosuth, J., 11
Kounellis, J., 9n, 69
Kripke, S., 105, 108n, 123–4, 216
Kuhn, T., 20n, 133n

Lakatos, I., 133, 135n
Latham, J., 10n
Laudan, L., 2n
Lessing, A., 14–16, 29n, 35, 206, 220, 260
Levinson, J.

  on the action-type hypothesis, 127n, 142n
  on aesthetic empiricism, 41–2
  on "art" defined historically, 241–2, 244–5
  on art-historical context, 64–5
  on artistic value, 254–7, 260–1
  on being a work-performance, 216–17
  on hypothetical intentionalism, 87–8
  on medium in art, 56–7, 58n
  on the pragmatic constraint, 18
  on structuralist ontologies of art, 42, 46–9, 54, 75, 83, 91n, 117, 138, 139, 219
  on works as indicated structures, 44n, 77–8, 105–7, 113, 117, 122, 147, 177, 180–6, 210, 237, 263–4, *see also* indicated structure theory
LeWitt, S., 9n, 35n, 208, 229–33
  Wall Drawing No. 623, 231
Lichtenstein, R., 65, 199
Linker, K., 197–8
Lippard, L., 2, 9, 136n, 192, 195, 208n
Liszt, F., 41
Livingston, P., 94, 109
Louis, M., 8, 70, 82, 259–61
Lucie-Smith, E., 4, 70, 82, 259

MacKay, A., 85n
Malade imaginaire, Le (Molière), 143, 144, 178
Mandelbaum, M., 242–3
Margolis, J.
  on medium in art, 56–7, 59–60
  on works as culturally emergent entities, 77, 180, 192
Marinetti, F. T., 61n, 261
Matheson, C., 226n
medium
  "artistic" and "vehicular" mediums distinguished, 56–62
  knowledge of provenance as bearing on the appreciation of, 64–74
  see also artistic medium; vehicular medium
Mendelssohn, F., 41
Michael, W. B., 91
Mingus, C., 226, 226n

modality principle
  defense of, 120–6
  defined, 104–5
  see also work-relativity of modality
modernism
  as a challenge to the common-sense
    view of art, 8–13, 189–90
  and contextualism, 191–8
  and the performance theory, 198–200
Monk, T., 226
Moore, H., 8
Morris, R., 5, 9
Mozart, W. A., 111, 140
Mueck, R., 9

Nathan, D., 87–8
Naumann, B., 209, 229, 232–3
Newman, B., 5, 8, 189
Nyman, M., 111, 140

Oldenberg, C., 192–3
Orwell, G., 111

Perec, G., 71, 108n, 199
performance arts, 207–35
  defined, 207
  the focus of appreciation in, 210–15
  improvisation in, 225–9
  relation between performed works and
    work-performances, 210–19
  work-performances as performance-
    works, 219–25
performance theory
  argument for, from the bearing of
    artistic intentions on artistic
    appreciation, 84–102
  argument for, from the work-relativity of
    modality, 107–20
  on artworks as "doings" rather than
    action-tokens strictu sensu, 167–76
  on artworks as specifications of focuses
    of appreciation, 148–51
  characterized, 80
  on the contents of artistic intentions
    taken to be work-constitutive, 163–7
  contrasted with the action-type
    hypothesis, 147–55, 175–6
  and forgeries, 202–5
  on the individuation of artworks, 151–8

and modernism, 198–200, 229–35
  and the performance arts, 207–25
  on provenance-based properties of the
    work-focus, 159–63
  and the revisionism objection, 141–5,
    178–80, 186–9
performance-works
  defined, 219
  improvisation in, 225–9
  work-performances as, 219–25
performed works
  defined, 210
  relation to work-performances, 210–19
Picasso, P., 5, 31
  Demoiselles d'Avignon, Les, 32, 34, 83,
    101, 103, 111–12, 114–15, 140, 155
  Guernica, 31, 32, 34, 50–1, 59, 66,
    72–3, 111
Piero della Francesca, *The Baptism of
  Christ*, 51–2, 66–7, 164–7, 222n
Pietroski, P., 212n
Pollock, J., 2–4, 8, 9, 199
pragmatic constraint on the ontology of
  art, 21n, 43, 45, 46, 48, 62, 75, 78,
  96, 103, 129–30, 140–1, 143, 188,
  237
  defined and defended, 18–22
  place in epistemological arguments,
    22–3
Putnam, H., 164n, 165n, 216

Rainer, Y., 17
Rawls, J., 20n
Rembrandt, 5
Ridley, A., 35n
Rivera, D., 4
Readymades, philosophical significance of,
  11–13, 11n, 12n, 41, 59, 136, 150,
  189–92, 194, 196, 243–4
revisionism objection to process ontologies
  of art
  and contextualism, 180–6
  and Currie's action-type hypothesis,
    141–5
  and the performance theory, 178–80,
    186–9
rigid designators, names of works as, 105,
  123–4
Rodin, A., 8